Theory and Practice of Curriculum Studies

Denis Lawton,
Peter Gordon,
Maggie Ing,
Bill Gibby,
Richard Pring and Terry Moore

Routledge & Kegan Paul
London, Boston and Henley

First published in 1978
by Routledge & Kegan Paul Ltd
39 Store Street,
London WC1E 7DD,
Broadway House,
Newtown Road,
Henley-on-Thames,
Oxon RG9 1EN and
9 Park Street,
Boston, Mass. 02108, USA
Reprinted in 1980 (twice)
Set in IBM Press Roman by
Hope Services, Abingdon,
and printed in Great Britain by
Lowe & Brydone Printers Ltd,
Thetford, Norfolk

British Library Cataloguing in Publication Data

Theory and practice of curriculum studies. —
   (Routledge education books).
   1. Education — Curricula
   375'.0001   LB1570   78-40522

   ISBN 0 7100 0028 6
   ISBN 0 7100 0029 4 Pbk

Contents

Part Three Philosophical and Social Issues

Part Four Evaluation and Assessment

Part Five The Teacher, Accountability and Control

Preface

This book was originally written as a series of lectures for the Theory and Practice of Education Course in the Diploma of Education, University of London Institute of Education. When we decided to cease giving the lectures and to rewrite them instead as weekly course reading material, we also decided to use them as a first draft of this book. Our thanks are therefore due to the students on the course who evaluated the chapters in their unrevised form.

All the contributors to the book are members of the Curriculum Studies Department at the Institute of Education except Terry Moore, who is senior lecturer in the Philosophy of Education Department, and Richard Pring, who left in January 1978 to become Professor of Education at Exeter University.

Acknowledgments

The authors and publishers are grateful to the following for permission to quote from the works cited:
The Schools Council and Macdonald Educational Ltd for *Science 5-13 With Objectives in Mind* (1972);
R.M. Gagné and the Dryden Press, Holt Rinehart & Winston for *Essentials of Learning for Instructions* (1974).

Introduction

Why Curriculum Studies?

Denis Lawton

Schools, and teachers, are under attack from a variety of directions: Black Paper writers, and others, complain about lowering of standards; employers complain that school leavers are ill-prepared for the world of work; at the other extreme Illich (1971) and the de-schoolers suggest that schools do more harm than good. Many others might feel that schools should not be attacked but should be subject to close public scrutiny. The idea of 'accountability' in education has been under discussion since the early 1970s but was probably given a boost by such events as the William Tyndale inquiry of 1975–6 (see Auld, 1976). The Assessment of Performance Unit (APU) recently established by the Department of Education and Science is another expression of this concern about standards and accountability.

Teachers in England are often said to be much more 'free' than teachers in other parts of the world, particularly in their freedom to decide what to teach. There is no centrally imposed curriculum for schools. Clearly this kind of freedom carries with it great responsibilities: if teachers do their own curriculum planning, perhaps the public has a right to know how they make their decisions? But another interesting characteristic of teachers in England is that they appear to dislike 'theory' – they often claim to be down-to-earth classroom practitioners rather than theorists. There may be all kinds of explanations for this lack of theory (at least one writer has suggested that it is because most educational theory is bad theory!), but at times of crisis – financial or

1

ideological – teachers are likely to be asked to justify what they do in the classroom and it is difficult to see how this can be done without taking up a position involving some kind of educational theory. Everything that a teacher does in a classroom involves values, sets of assumptions, views about the nature of children and of knowledge – all of which are the basis of educational theory. It might be suggested that the average teacher's 'theory' is half-baked or naive, or oversimplified, or self-contradictory, but some kind of theory there must be. One purpose of this book is to help practising teachers to clarify their own theory and practice; it is not to impose on you the contributors' view of what education should be.

One difficulty with educational theory in the past has been the tendency to try to explain a very complex process of educational practice by means of oversimplified theoretical positions. In curriculum there are at least three popular theories or sets of assumptions held by teachers, sometimes referred to as the child-centred view of education, the subject-centred or knowledge-centred view, and the society-centred view, i.e. education justified in terms of the supposed needs of society. Many primary schools tend to be influenced by child-centred theories of various kinds; the grammar school curriculum has been said to be subject-centred rather than child-centred (one of the most common educational clichés is that whereas primary teachers teach children, secondary school teachers teach subjects; but it is difficult to see how anyone can teach without teaching something and someone). Secondary modern schools have in their turn sometimes been praised or blamed for being society-centred. One of the sources of confusion in comprehensive schools may be that teachers are not clear about whether their curriculum is subject-centred in the grammar school tradition, or society-centred in the secondary modern school tradition. Secondary teachers are only rarely accused of being child-centred.

However, none of these three 'theories' can on its own be a complete justification for a curriculum. If we try to justify a completely child-centred curriculum, we find ourselves in a very difficult situation. If teachers claim to plan a curriculum in terms of children's needs and interests it is difficult to see why teachers are necessary at all. Unless teachers are there to

2

stimulate interest, and create needs which the child is not aware of himself, then it is difficult to see why we should have teachers or schools. The teacher who has nothing to offer the child by way of knowledge or interesting experiences is not justifying his existence. Perhaps the best way to think of the role of the teacher during the primary or middle years is to think of the teacher as someone who makes demands on children that they would not make on themselves if the teacher were not there. In some senses, of course, we are all child-centred nowadays: we have moved away from the kind of situation where schools ignored children's interests, and simply imposed on them a rigid routine, but that is very different from suggesting that the whole of an educational programme can be based on allowing children to follow their own interests without any guidance at all. The child-centred view was a much-needed reaction against nineteenth-century inhumanity and authoritarianism in schools, but in some cases it has been mistakenly seen as a complete theory of education and curriculum. (This issue will be pursued further in chapter 2 by Richard Pring.)

The knowledge-centred curriculum also has something to offer but is not a complete answer. Whatever else education may be about, it is certainly concerned with the transmission of knowledge from one generation to the next. But few would now suggest that that is the only concern of education, and few would suggest that the existing subject-dominated structure of many secondary schools is the right one. Philosophical discussions about the structure of knowledge may help to plan a curriculum in some respects, but to suggest that children must learn certain kinds of knowledge because they exist as separate and distinct forms is rather like saying we must climb Everest because it is there. Some people do not want to climb Everest, and some children seem to be unattracted by certain kinds of knowledge. If schools want to persuade pupils to embark on certain kinds of studies they must employ arguments about worthwhileness.

Finally there is the 'needs of society' or 'society-centred' kind of curriculum. Arguments here tend to suggest that the curriculum must be planned according to the changing nature of our society. The argument may be at a very naive level and suggest that because we have entered the Common Market children should spend more of their time learning foreign languages (a very doubtful proposition); more sophisticated versions of this argument talk about the need for society to have more scientists and technologists and therefore that schools should concentrate more attention on science and mathematics. This argument, however, also breaks down under scrutiny if it is employed as the only justification for the curriculum. The two main arguments against it are, first, that we may not wish to educate individuals for society: we may be more interested in getting them to change society or at least modify certain aspects of it; there is an almost totalitarian flavour about an education system which unwittingly prepares individuals for society in much the same way as factories process raw materials into manufactured goods. The second argument against this kind of justification is that it begs the whole question about the nature of society. Society is a collection of the individual members of society, so we may ask 'who says that society needs more technicians and technologists?' The idea of society 'needing' something over and above the 'needs' of individual members is a very odd one.

Thus a comprehensive theory of curriculum planning would recognize the individual nature of the pupils, and also recognize the value of education in its own right. But if we are to plan a programme of compulsory activities we will have to take into consideration the three kinds of view expressed above, i.e. the child-centred, the knowledge-centred and the society-centred. Whilst each one of them is incomplete on its own, each one may have something to contribute to planning a curriculum as a whole. One way of looking at this kind of comprehensive curriculum planning has been described as the situation-centred curriculum, which is based on the idea that schools should be concerned with preparing the young for the world as it will be when they leave school, i.e. preparing them to cope with the kind of situations which they will encounter as adults. This does not, of course, cut out the value of some kinds of experiences in their own right, nor does it mean that children are simply processed to conform to an adult world − quite the opposite; this view of education usually assumes that children should be prepared to exert some influence over their environment rather than be dominated by it. It suggests that one of the purposes of education is to develop a child's autonomy: he must learn to cope with the variety of situations which face him in society. In order to do this he must acquire different kinds of knowledge. Knowledge is in this context used in a very general sense, but it is quite clear that without knowledge a child cannot become autonomous but must remain dominated by other people and other things.

Thus neither philosophy, nor sociology, nor psychology, can on its own justify a curriculum or be used as the sole basis for curriculum planning. Figure 1, although still over-simplified, illustrates the complexity of the task.

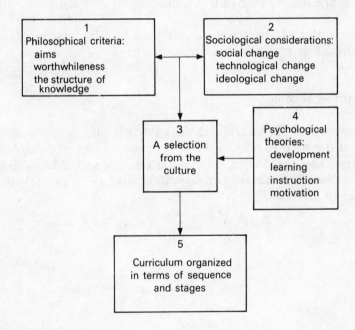

Figure 1

1 Philosophical criteria: all teachers have ideas about what is worthwhile, or the structure of knowledge, but most would benefit from rethinking these ideas systematically.

2 Teachers will also need to examine the relationship between the more permanent questions in box 1 and our society

now (box 2): in particular the fact that we are theoretically committed to the ideology of equality of opportunity in education.

3 The interplay between box 1 and box 2 will enable us to make some kind of ideal selection from the culture, e.g. that everyone should have some knowledge of mathematics, science, the humanities, etc.

4 At this stage we can consider the ideal solution in the light of psychological theories and practicalities. Piaget's stages of development could hardly be ignored; Bruner's spiral curriculum will help us to work out structure, sequence, etc.

5 We are now at the stage of organizing a curriculum in the practical terms of a time-table.

Each of these five stages involves many issues and problems which will be considered later in the book.

Further reading

Lawton (1973, chapter 1) discusses the idea of curriculum and the need to remove the gap between theory and practice. Also, Lawton (1973, pp. 153–5) examines R. S. Peters' views on 'Worthwhileness' which should also be read in Peters (1966, chapter 5).

Part One

Approaches Through the Disciplines

Chapter 1

The Nature of Educational Theory

Terry Moore

Educational theory has seldom been a popular topic of study. Student teachers, however interested they may be in the practice of education, have rarely been much enlivened by its theory. Educational theory has often been thought of as boring and in some hands it can be. It is sometimes thought of as vague, and sometimes unrealistic and irrelevant, which again it may be. It is often regarded as unnecessary, in that it is possible to be a good teacher without knowing anything about educational theory. And, it has sometimes been declared to be a non-subject; to have no substantial claim to be theory at all.

This chapter tries to put in a good word for educational theory, and to show its relevance to educational practice. To the charge that it is boring and vague we may retort by saying that it need not be, and that any such criticism should be levelled against those who teach it rather than against educational theory as such. To say that it is unrealistic or irrelevant is to fail to distinguish between good theories of education and bad ones. The charges that it is unnecessary or that educational theory doesn't amount to theory at all, are more substantial and need to be met in more detail.

We may take the second point first, and note to begin with the word 'theory' which can be understood in more than one way. Its most common meaning comes from its connection with science. Scientific theories are what most people have in mind when they think about theory at all. This is part of the trouble with educational theory. Many students, especially

9

those trained in the sciences, get exasperated with educational theory simply because it does not square with their notion of what a theory ought to be like, that is, a scientific theory. Now, a scientific theory, although its details may be complicated, is basically a simple matter. Scientific theories are *descriptive, explanatory* and *predictive* in function. They set out to tell us what the empirical world is like and what we may expect from it in the future − that gases will expand when heated, that unsupported objects will fall, and so on. An important characteristic of such theories is that they stand or fall simply by the way the empirical world happens to be. Scientists can *test* their theories, by seeing whether or not the world turns out according to their predictions. If it does, then their theories are confirmed; if not, then the theory in question has to be amended or perhaps rejected altogether. Scientists are always examining, observing, measuring the physical world, since their theories depend on this for their validation.

One of the objections to educational theory, and especially to the important educational theories of the past, is that they don't operate like scientific theories. The great historical educational theorists, Plato, Rousseau, Froebel, for example, didn't go about their work in the way that scientists go about theirs. They did little in the way of educational research; they carried out no systematic collection of evidence, and, moreover, their theories don't seem to be testable, or accountable, or disprovable in the way that scientific theories may be. So, it has been suggested, educational theory is a spurious sort of theory, one in which great thinkers can say more or less what they please and not be subject to the rigorous kind of checking-up that scientific theories have to undergo. Hence the view that, except for the bits of psychology and sociology contained in them, which may be subjected to scrutiny, educational theory doesn't amount to theory at all. At best it is admitted as theory only by a kind of intellectual courtesy. This charge needs to be looked at.

In doing so we must recognize that educational theory is somewhat different from theories in science. Scientific theory is primarily explanatory, descriptive and predictive in function. Educational theory, by contrast, belongs to another category, to what are called 'practical' theories.

Practical theories do not set out primarily to *describe* the world or to predict its future, but to tell us what we ought to be doing in it. They give recommendations for practice. Some moral and political theories come into this category, as do most general educational theories. Now, since there is this difference in function it is not surprising that the two kinds should operate in different ways, and that the methods of validating them should be different. A practical theory can't be validated in exactly the same way as a scientific theory, because it is a different kind of theory. But it doesn't follow from this that a practical theory, an educational theory for example, can't be tested or validated at all, or that an educational theorist may say more or less what he likes. An educational theory is, logically, more complicated than a scientific theory, and consequently it needs to be assessed and validated in different, more complicated ways.

We may think of 'education' as a group of activities which takes place at different logical levels. At the basic, ground-floor level there are activities like teaching, persuading, motivating, learning, examining, which go on generally in schools and colleges. Arising out of this is educational theory, which may be regarded as a body of prescriptions, designed to realize certain ends, and directed towards what goes on at the lower logical level. Educational theory tries to give counsel, advice, recommendations for practice, to those who are employed in the concrete day-to-day business of education.

Any such theory involves a certain structure. There are some initial assumptions:

1 that some end is desirable, that some educational end be achieved with the resources at hand;
2 that, in the given circumstances, certain means are best calculated to achieve that end. These assumptions are followed by:
3 detailed recommendations that these means should be employed to realize the desired ends.

An educational theory involves different sorts of assumptions, about desirable ends, or aims, about the raw material to be worked on, i.e. pupils, about the nature of knowledge and the effectiveness of methods. Granted those assumptions, the detailed recommendations for practice follow.

Assumptions and recommendations taken together comprise the theory.

We can now look at these various assumptions in turn. First, the assumption about an end to be achieved. In general terms this will be an 'educated man'. Plainly, what counts as an 'educated man' will depend largely upon the society one has in mind. The interpretation of 'educated man' will be culture-bound, or ideological in character. Differences in interpretation will account for differences in educational theories widely separated in time and place. Secondly, there will be assumptions about those to be educated, and these too will vary according to the philosophical, religious, psychological and sociological notions held about the nature of man. Here again, different assumptions will lead to different educational theories. Finally, there will be assumptions about the nature of knowledge and about the effectiveness of methods. Differences in conviction about the nature of knowledge, that knowledge is basically mathematical in character, or basically scientific, or religious, will result in different educational theories, with different emphases on the methods recommended for practice. By way of brief illustration we may take two examples of past educational theories.

Plato's dialogue, *The Republic*, contains within it an influential educational theory, the structure of which follows the outline given above. His aim is that 'educated man' is a man capable of ruling the state, a politically wise and morally developed man. Plato's assumptions about pupils, the raw material of education, is that they are bodies informed by souls, and of these two elements the soul is the more important, needing to be trained and nurtured in wisdom and virtue. Plato considers knowledge to be a grasp of a nonsensuous reality, the Forms which can be understood as one understands mathematical truths, by a kind of intuitive grasp. This led to certain assumptions about methods, viz. an emphasis on formal studies, mathematics and logic, which would enable selected pupils to grasp intellectually the truth and reality which lies behind appearances and give them the knowledge required to live well as men and as rulers of the state. These assumptions underlie the various detailed recommendations made by Plato for the education of the ruling élite.

A celebrated educational theory of the eighteenth century is given by Rousseau in his book *Emile* (1762). Here, the 'educated man' is free, independent, self-reliant, virtuous, unspoiled by society, yet capable of living well in it, corrupt as it may be. Rousseau often calls such a man the 'natural man'. His assumption about children is that they are 'growing', 'developing' creatures originally good, and capable of improvement by means of an 'education according to nature'. Knowledge, an indispensable part of a 'natural' education, involved associations of ideas gained so far as possible by direct contact with reality, and Rousseau assumes, and recommends as valuable, methods which involve first-hand, 'discovery' activity by the child, leading to knowledge appropriate to his various stages as a developing individual. Here again, the structure of the theory follows the model set out above. In both examples the form of the theory is the same, assumptions leading to practical recommendations. What differs in each is a function of time, place and social outlook. Different sets of assumptions lead to different educational theories.

The question now is: Can general educational theories of this kind be subjected to the sort of scrutiny that would put them to a real test, as scientific theories are put to the test? It has been suggested that they cannot. Educational theories, it is said, make assumptions which are neither checkable nor accountable, as scientific assumptions must be. This may be disputed. It is possible to check an educational theory but there is no methodologically simple way of doing this as in science. We have to scrutinize an educational theory at the various logical levels it presents, questioning each kind of assumption in turn and applying the kind of checking appropriate at each level. We could, for example, question assumptions about aims, and argue that, in respect of a given theory the end proposed ran counter to certain moral principles we hold. An educational theory which had for its aim the production of a white ruling élite in a multi-racial community might be shown to be unacceptable in this way. We could, at another level, criticize the assumptions made about the nature of children, on the grounds that they are false. The eighteenth-century view that children are simply small versions of adults, is objectionable because it is false. Rousseau's optimistic view that children are all born 'good' is no less so because it is strictly unverifiable, as would be the Calvinistic view that they are all born more or less bad. A theory might also be contested on the grounds that the view of knowledge assumed in it was mistaken, as for example, Plato's view that knowledge is fundamentally mathematics, or Spencer's contention that it is basically scientific, or Froebel's view that it is basically religious. Again, it could be criticized by showing that its assumptions about methods were false, or perhaps untestable. In ways like this an educational theory could be put to the test, and if necessary be rejected as inadequate. What we would not be well advised to do, and need not do, would be to treat it as a scientific theory and try it out in practice as a way of testing it. If, for example, anyone offered a theory which aimed at producing a superman of the Nazi type, out of human material assumed superior because Aryan, and by means of indoctrination, we could reject it from the beginning, without running a pilot scheme to see what happened.

A general educational theory then is open to criticism and possible rejection. But, if a theory can in principle be criticized, put to test and rejected, it is possible that one could pass the test, and be acceptable in practice. A valid educational theory would be one that made morally acceptable assumptions about aims, correct and checkable assumptions about children, philosophically respectable assumptions about knowledge and verified assumptions about the effectiveness of methods. Of course, not all educational theories would survive criticism. Many of the assumptions made by theorists in the past would not do so entirely, but this doesn't stop them from being genuine theories. They are not in all respects like scientific theories, since they contain assumptions of value, about ends and methods. They are mixed theories, involving matters of fact and matters of value and to test them we need to treat each of their components separately. They are genuine theories none the less.

The logical complexity of a general educational theory indicates what needs to be done to make an up-to-date, ongoing theory, relevant to the present needs of teachers. Any such theory must make assumptions about aims, which involve matters of value. These will depend on the kind of individual needed and the society he is to be fitted for. The scrutiny of value judgments is the job of the moral philosopher. It is not the philosopher's job to set the educational aims of society, but he can show the various ways in which value judgments may be supported and what the ultimate basis of value assumptions may be. The assumptions made about children will be primarily the province of science, i.e. child study, child psychology, sociology. These sciences provide descriptive theories about children, about how they grow, develop, about the effects on them of their familial, neighbourhood and linguistic environments. There is great need for detailed work here. The trouble with many of the historical theorists of education was that they tended to adopt unargued, unresearched assumptions about children, often dubious, sometimes false. For a contemporary theory we need the work of specialists like Piaget, Freud, Kohlberg and Bernstein, to give accurate up-to-date knowledge about what children are really like. Questions about the nature of knowledge, whether it is all one, or consists of distinct areas, again, lie within the province of the philosopher, whilst questions about the organization of such knowledge for pedagogical ends fall to the curriculum planner. For correct assumptions about the effectiveness of methods we need help from psychologists, learning theories like those of Skinner and Bruner, as well as from those with practical experience in the classroom.

Educational theory, then, is logically complex and multidisciplinary in character. It is not an intellectual no-man's-land, where pundits may say as they please. It is rather a field in which all the main disciplines of educational study may be used to support practical recommendations, and its validation will depend on work of a critical kind, at various logical levels. So much for the charge that educational theory is a non-subject, theory only by courtesy.

The charge that educational theory is unnecessary will not do either. No doubt actual practice precedes theory in point of time, in education as elsewhere. But logically, all good practice presupposes a theory. Intelligent practice just is practice according to a sound theory. It is logically impossible to engage in an *activity* without having *some* end in mind and without making *some* assumptions about present circumstances, materials and methods. The question is not:

15

Do I need a theory to teach well? but: What theory is it that I follow, consciously or not, in what I do? Teachers are in the grip of some educational theory whether they recognize it or not. The important thing is that their practice should be supported by good theories rather than by bad. It is not proposed to write in the details of an adequate theory here. Some criteria for adequacy have been briefly sketched in above, viz. that the various assumptions made within the theory should be open to scrutiny of the appropriate kind at each logical level.

In British educational thought and practice we discern two major traditions, resting on different assumptions and giving two distinct models or general theories of education. On the one hand there is the model generally called the 'traditional'. Its assumptions, in outline, are these: The educated man is the knowledgeable man, one who has taken in the wealth of human culture which is seen as primarily important. This model emphasizes the role of knowledge as something worth having, necessary indeed for the good life. Knowledge has to be won by effort, by determination. The teacher is the full man, the repository of knowledge, whose task it is to hand out to children the knowledge and skills which they lack. The assumption about children is that they are empty vessels, needing to be filled up, and it is often assumed that they are, on the whole, disinclined towards work and learning, and so need to be directed and often coerced. Knowledge involves the joining together of experiences, by methods of repetition and attention to the task. With this notion of application and concentration, goes the belief that in this way character is developed as well as the intellect. This model has had a long history in practice. We find theoretical support for it in Plato, and both theoretical and practical support for it in James Mill. The work of Skinner in psychology is perhaps more sympathetic to this model than to any other.

Set against this is what is generally known as the 'progressive' view. Its assumptions are rather different. For the progressivist the 'educated man' is not so much a knowledgeable man as a 'well-developed personality' a 'self-realized man'. The emphasis here is on the individual as a growing, developing, experiencing organism, and knowledge is regarded as important mainly as a means to this development. In this context we hear more about 'interests' and 'creativity' than about effort and application. The pupil is viewed not so much as an empty vessel as an unrealized personality. Personality rather than character tends to be stressed. The teacher functions not so much as a transmitter of knowledge as a helper and organizer of the pupil's environment, a contriver of situations in which the child's self-development can be furthered. This child-centred approach gets its theoretical support from the work of Rousseau and from Pestalozzi, Froebel and Dewey, and its translation into practice is a commonplace in primary and middle schools today.

These two general theories and the practice derived from them may be thought to be mutually incompatible alternatives, such that if teaching is formal or traditional it can't be child-centred, and vice versa. There has been in schools and in public mind an opposition between these two sorts of educational styles. It can be argued that this opposition is not necessary, either in theory or practice. It is not the case that teaching must be either traditional *or* progressive; indeed as research carried out by Bennett at Lancaster University seems to indicate, there is much of value to be derived from both styles in practice and there is no good reason why the two should not be combined in the classroom, giving a concern both for the personality of the pupil and for the stringency demanded by the need to master knowledge and skills. At the theoretical level a reconciliation of the two approaches might be brought about by suggesting that instead of regarding them as recommending opposite and alternative practices we might see each of them as performing a different function, that of drawing attention to aspects of education which are important and ought not to be overlooked, yet which each side may overlook if not corrected.

The traditional approach takes its stand on the importance of knowledge and the need for standards. Knowledge is necessary for the good life, and knowledge isn't simply a matter of whim or impulse, but involves standards, which have to be achieved by application, by understanding, by respect for truth and evidence. Plato and Mill may be seen as making this point and teachers who are mindful of it in their teaching are giving practical application to an important truth. On the other hand, education is to do with children or pupils, and the educator must take account of their nature as children, their development, their needs, interests and impulses, if he is to be successful. The child-centred theorists from Rousseau onwards make this point, and this too needs to be emphasized. An adequate educational approach would be one which recognized both sorts of consideration, advocating methods which combine both a respect for the traditional virtues of knowledge and understanding and respect for the nature of children. The great aducational theories of the past, however lacking they may have been in scientific stringency, have something to contribute to present practice to the extent to which they can draw our attention to these important truths.

Further reading

The contents of this chapter are worked out in more detail in Moore (1974). A bibliography and suggestions for further reading are given at the end of the book. A point of view critical of educational theory in its traditional sense is given in O'Connor (1957).

For a fairly technical discussion of the nature of educational theory see the articles by Hirst (1972) and O'Connor (1972).

Chapter 2

Philosophical Issues

Richard Pring

Introduction

Education is concerned with the improvement of the mind. Central to the development of the mind is the growth of knowledge, and central to this is the development of concepts through which experience is organized. Hence, at the very centre of educational issues are philosophical problems about:

1 the nature of knowledge and the validity of particular knowledge claims (epistemology);

2 what knowledge is of most worth (ethics); and

3 the nature of mental activities (philosophy of mind).

I intend briefly to introduce each of these in turn, but what I say here will be developed further in chapters 13 and 14.

Knowing how and knowing that

Although the development of knowledge is central to the improvement of mind, knowledge must not be understood simply as facts to be learnt or theories to be understood. Practical knowledge or knowing *how* to do things is equally important. An important distinction to make then is between 'knowledge that' (what can be stated in propositions) and 'knowledge how' (abilities to do things well or correctly). For example, John knows *how* to ride a bicycle but does not know *that* the laws of balance are such and such. Very often

19

we know *how* to do things long before we know the theory (the knowledge *that*) that explains this practical knowledge. Indeed, theoretical knowledge has very often arisen from systematic reflection upon practical knowledge. Schools, therefore, in their concern for the development of knowledge, should be equally concerned about practical know-how, and about the connection between theory and practical knowledge. For example, a child needs to know *how* to speak grammatically before he comes to know *that* the rules of grammar are such and such; he might better reflect on the principles of democracy if he has learnt how to participate democratically in school activities; he will have a basis for moral theorizing if he has learnt how to act morally.

The differentiation of knowledge

Not only might we usefully distinguish between 'knowing how' and 'knowing that' but also we should distinguish between kinds of 'knowledge that'. To say that someone (Peter) knows that something is the case, e.g. that force F is equal to the product of mass M and acceleration A, is to say:

1 Peter believes that $F = MA$
2 It is true that $F = MA$
3 Peter has good grounds for believing that $F = MA$.

However, there are different ways in which condition 3 might be satisfied — in which one might justify as well as express one's beliefs. Hence it is argued by philosophers that there are different kinds of knowledge. And these different kinds of knowledge (mathematical, sociological, biological, moral, etc.) become the resources (the subject matter) upon which the curriculum draws.

This is crucially important, and therefore needs to be expanded. Over the centuries, man has engaged in different sorts of inquiries, asked different kinds of questions. Such inquiries and questions have become more systematic and disciplined, each generation benefiting from the discovered facts, the conceptual innovations, the acquired skills and methodologies of the previous one. Such disciplined modes of inquiry can be characterized by certain features:

1 The concepts that organize our experience and thoughts in a certain way — for example, concepts like 'molecule' in chemistry, 'duty' in morals, 'God' in religion, 'role' in social science;

2 the way in which a statement is thought to be true or false — for example, scientific statements are true because of certain observable facts; mathematical statements, on the other hand, are true by reason of the axioms and rules of the system;

3 the techniques and methods of setting about an inquiry — for example, historians have certain skills and procedures for sifting evidence, scientists have developed ways of setting up experiments, social scientists control their investigations in certain well-tried ways;

4 the range of problems tackled — for example, social scientists, whatever the theoretical differences between them, are united in the sort of problems which concern them, e.g. an understanding of social groups and their institutions.

To illustrate all this: physicists have their own departments in schools and universities, are trained in a particular set of methods, have mastered and apply a closely knit set of concepts (e.g. atom, electron, molecule), insist upon certain very stringent tests for the truth or adequacy of proposed solutions to problems. The subject-based curriculum might be seen as an attempt to introduce the pupils to a range of such logically distinct ways of thinking.

The characterization of different ways. of inquiring or of disciplined ways of asking questions in terms of 'structure' owes much to the work of Jerome Bruner. Bruner (1960) argues that by introducing pupils to various structures of thinking you introduce him to the 'basic ideas that lie at the heart of all science and mathematics and the basic themes that give form to life and literature' and that these are 'as simple as they are powerful'. Furthermore 'to be in command of these basic ideas, to use them effectively, requires a continual deepening of one's understanding of them that comes from learning to use them in progressively more complex forms'. Here we have the essence of Bruner's 'spiral curriculum' — the continual introduction of pupils to the more powerful ideas that discipline our various inquiries.

However, it should be remembered that, when a discipline is not characterized by basic organizing ideas (e.g. philosophy), it cannot be 'spiralled' in this way. (Bruner's ideas are introduced more fully in chapters 3 and 10.)

On this view, then, it is the job of the teacher to know the basic structuring ideas and procedures in the various established disciplines and to ensure that (at different levels, depending on his capacity) they are grasped by the pupil. It would, therefore, be an important teaching task to decide what are the structured modes of thinking that pupils, at different ages, should be introduced to, and what the essential features are of those modes of thinking. Such reflective and analytical thinking is essentially philosophical.

Worthwhile knowledge

'Education' is an evaluative term. To say someone is an educated man is to compliment him – he possesses certain worthwhile qualities. And an educational process would be one that produced such valuable qualities in people. Hence, at the centre of education are questions about value: firstly, general questions why we should value the development of knowledge and understanding at all; secondly, more specific questions why we should value some knowledge more than others.

This, of course, means that educational questions take on the most intractable problems of ethics. What is the objective basis for saying that some activities or some qualities are more worthwhile than others? On what grounds, for instance, can we say that a classical is better or worse than a scientific culture, that some newspapers are better quality than others, or that we should introduce the pupil to certain literature (the 'great tradition') rather than to others?

Two different kinds of answer (there are of course, others) illustrate the role of philosophical thinking here.

1 *Utilitarian.* The utilitarians argued that since pleasure or happiness is what is universally valued, then the best thing to do is to promote the greatest amount of happiness for the greatest number. On such a view the measure of a

school's worth would be the extent to which it promoted the happiness either of the pupils (reluctant though they may be) or of society at large.

The utilitarian argument can be pursued so far. Don't mathematicians get pleasure from their achievements, and isn't there intellectual satisfaction to be had from history and science? Moreover, such learning, though for many not pleasurable in itself, is a means to other things that give 'pleasure' – better jobs or a more efficient economy. None the less, it would be difficult to make the promotion of happiness the main justification for a lot of the curriculum activities we intuitively feel desirable – compulsory mathematics rather than compulsory fishing, for example. The point is, as Mill (1861, chapter 2) argued, there are qualitatively different pleasures, and qualitative differences between pleasures cannot be explained in terms of their respective quantities of pleasure.

2 *Cognitive concern.* Such qualitative differences might partly be explained in terms of the greater discrimination, awareness, understanding that are contained within certain activities – in extending the powers of the mind. It would be argued that pleasure is certainly valuable, but not the only kind of value, and that the pursuit of truth and understanding is also valuable – even when such a pursuit leads to unhappiness. Better Socrates dissatisfied than a fool satisfied.

The defence of this position would need to show that somehow the truth mattered, irrespective of the pleasure or displeasure that its revelation produced, and hence that the ways of getting at the truth were worth acquiring. What extended the powers of the mind or gave greater insight into human affairs would be seen to be superior to those activities that did not. Peters (1966, chapter 5, section 4) argues that the significance of theoretical activities (science, philosophy, history, etc.) is their transforming quality – they affect at root the very ways in which we conceive and appraise what we are doing. Hence, a person who seriously asks questions about the value of an activity must be more committed to those sorts of activity 'which have this special sort of cognitive concern and content built into them'. Anyone seriously asking the question 'why?', must value those cognitive pursuits which help provide an answer. Put crudely, the argument is that, as thinking, reflecting, questioning, curious beings, we necessarily value those activities which help us to pursue our thinking and reflecting further, to answer our questions, and to satisfy our curiosity. And such activities are precisely what scientific, historical, aesthetic inquiries (at their best) are doing.

I have, in this section, no more than shown the relevance of ethics to educational issues. The issues are pursued further in chapter 13.

The child-centred view

A way of organizing the curriculum that reflects some disagreement with the analysis of knowledge above, and at the same time heeds the ethical argument in the last section, would be to focus it upon the active interests of the pupils. This would of course meet with considerable practical limitations with so few resources in any one school. But it is often argued that there should be more concentration upon the child's active reconstruction of experience as he pursues some interest than upon the adult's way of conceiving experience as it is enshrined within particular subjects. Hence, especially in primary schools, 'interest areas' are sometimes set aside, the fairly undirected 'exploration' of the environment encouraged. Of such an 'integrated day', Brown and Precious (1968, p. 19) say 'subjects and interests soon became integrated quite naturally as children worked out their individual ideas, the school day was gradually being determined by the interests and need of the children.'

Two kinds of argument (that reflect the philosophical concerns referred to above) are put forward to justify a curriculum centred upon what the children are interested in rather than upon what the adult thinks they ought to be interested in.

Argument 1. There is no basis for saying one activity is more valuable than another, other than that people value it. A distinction is made therefore between what is judged by society to be useful for the child and what the child intrinsically values for its own sake. The job of the school is twofold: to train the child in socially useful knowledge and to help the child develop satisfactory (intrinsically worthwhile to him) interests. To develop the latter the school should organize at least part of the curriculum around what it diagnoses to be the potentially satisfying interests of each child.

Argument 2. All subject matter is ultimately rooted in some original attempt to solve problems that people find puzzling and in the solutions which they value. At certain stages of schooling, the process of inquiry (learning how to articulate the problem, how to formulate a hypothesis, how to find evidence, etc.) is more important than the product, and furthermore is roughly the same in all cases. The logical ordering of subject matter that the teacher is familiar with is the result of the unitary process of inquiry. It is not to be presented as such to the pupil, but is to be treated as a useful resource and guideline in helping the pupil with his inquiry into his problem — the inquiry that *he* finds of value.

If you agree that at least part of the curriculum should focus upon the interests of the pupils, you would not be able to prepare the content of the curriculum too much in advance. What is required is a close observation of the child and a constant analysis of what is really interesting him or her. The teacher would need to be very flexible indeed, and gradually build up a set of resources that would meet varying interests.

Mental qualities

So far I have illustrated how two areas of philosophical thinking — viz. the theory of knowledge and ethics — contribute to educational thinking. Finally I wish briefly to demonstrate how questions in the philosophy of mind are equally relevant to educational studies.

The philosophy of mind is principally concerned with finding an adequate way of talking about mental activities (such as 'thinking', 'trying', 'believing', 'wanting') and of relating these to the material world which we perceive and which such activities somehow 'reside in'. What is the relation between mind (and its many activities) and the body? Are, for instance, the naughty boy's mischievous pranks 'caused' in the same way that pulling a switch 'causes' the light to go on? If so, then how can he be held responsible for what he does? We are constantly blaming and praising people, ascribing responsibility, urging them to do better, criticizing for lack of effort, and so on. But to do all these things presupposes that students are not just material bodies. It would be absurd to stand blaming and punishing a stone for falling on my toe, or to urge the trees to grow faster, or to criticize my tomato plants for lack of effort. But it is not absurd to blame, praise, or criticize one's students. What then is it to have a mind, to be something different from being just a material object, to be a person?

Behind some psychological theories of learning there are certain assumptions about the nature of mind which I would find philosophically questionable. For instance, behaviourism (see chapter 7) as a theory of learning is prepared to take account only of what can be observed. It endeavours to be as scientific as physics or chemistry. In order to do this, it needs to abstract from any private world of consciousness and from what can be felt (by me) but not observed by others. Behavioural symptoms of my inner reality become the reality itself.

Now this begs many questions about the existence of 'mind'. Is it or is it not in some way different from a mere collection of observable behaviours? One's position on this matter affects profoundly the value one attaches to a lot of psychology of learning – especially the experimental psychology that based much of its conclusions upon a study of the behaviour of animals.

Again, as teachers, we are very much concerned with the motivation of children. Psychologists have developed theoretical accounts of motivation (see chapter 8). But there is an important philosophical job to do to map out the language of motives – it is much more complex than a lot of psychological theorizing would have us believe. See, for example, Peters' (1958) critique of various psychological theories. The theoretical world of the psychologist, that might try to dispense with the unscientific world of 'wants', 'wishes', and 'intentions' (see Atkinson, 1964), has none the less to be linked logically to that common-sense world, because it is in the context of wanting, wishing, intending that teachers raise questions about motivation and that theoretical explanation must apply. (See Pring (1977), where I develop this point at some length.)

Hence, the philosophy of mind – what it is to be a person, to learn, to develop, to have feelings and thoughts – is at the centre of educational questions. In particular it is basic to understanding and criticizing the theoretical assumptions of psychology.

Further reading

In Pring (1976, chapters 1 and 2) I tried to cover these issues. For a detailed analysis of 'education' and its connection with 'knowledge' read Peters (1966, chapters 1 and 2) or (a more recent account in which he meets the arguments of his critics) Peters (1977, chapter 1). A useful introduction to the philosophy of knowledge is Scheffler (1965).

The distinction between 'knowing that' and 'knowing how' is made in Peters (1966), Scheffler (1965) and Pring (1976) but for a detailed analysis see Ryle (1949, chapter 2). Bruner (1966) distinguishes between different ways in which we 'represent' experience – through practical activity, as well as through imaginings and symbols.

The differentiation of knowledge into different kinds is argued by Hirst (1965), and also in Hirst and Peters (1970, chapter 4). A similar argument is put forward by Phenix (1964) and it is worked out into the detail of particular subjects. For the interconnected notions of 'structure' and 'spiral curriculum' see Bruner (1960). A very useful contribution is Schwab (1964).

A classic text on the justification of activities, especially from a utilitarian point of view is Mill (1861, chapter 2). Peters (1966, chapter 5), argues for the intrinsic value of those activities that are concerned with the development of knowledge and understanding. But his more recent papers (Peters, 1977, chapters 1 and 5) develop the ideas in response to critics. The *British Journal of Educational Studies* (1967) has an interesting argument between Wilson ('In defence of Bingo', 1967) and Peters ('In defence of Bingo: a rejoinder', 1967) about the basis for justifying curriculum activities.

For the philosophical background to this kind of 'child-centred' curriculum, read Dewey (1916); Dewey (1933, pp. 106–7); Kilpatrick (1934). A recent defence is Wilson (1971, especially chapter 2). An interesting critique is Archambault (1956).

Peters (1958) is an excellent philosophical critique of prevailing psychological accounts of motivation. Ryle (1949) explores the problems and possibilities of a behaviourist theory of mind. An excellent introduction to philosophy of mind is White (1967).

Chapter 3

Psychological Issues

Maggie Ing

Introduction

The contribution of psychology to curriculum studies is twofold; it provides, firstly, conceptual models and information which can assist educational planning, and, secondly, it contains methodologies which can be adapted for educational inquiry. In the present state of development of the discipline, the models and methodologies are embarrassingly diverse, and the information often incomplete and contradictory. There is no one psychological theory, but a range of studies and theories of differing levels of sophistication. None the less, some fields have been sufficiently developed to offer guidelines to the teacher and curriculum planner.

Kerr (1968) defines the curriculum as 'all the learning which is planned and guided by the school, whether it is carried out in groups or individually, inside or outside the school', and goes on to divide the curriculum into four aspects: curriculum objectives; knowledge; learning experiences; and curriculum evaluation (see Figure 2). The divisions are not always clear-cut in practice, but provide a framework for discussion. The techniques of framing objectives and arriving at accurate evaluation are largely derived from psychological methodology (see chapters 12, 17 and 18), although, if we take it that objectives are drawn from the aims of our education, the desired end-product is likely to be defined by philosophical and social considerations. A knowledge of psychology can help us to be more realistic in our

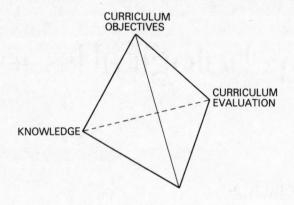

Figure 2

choice of goals, but will not determine what those goals should be.

It is in selecting appropriate learning experiences that psychology is generally recognized to be most useful. Theories of learning, theories of cognitive and emotional development, group dynamics, individual differences in ability and personality, models of attitude formation and change, understanding of motivation, all have an obvious relevance to the planning of educational experiences. Some of these theories will be discussed in chapters 7, 8, 9 and 10.

The area of knowledge, however, is not usually considered to be the province of psychology. Yet, behind studies of learning, thinking, perceiving and remembering are at least implicit views of what it is to *know*. It is axiomatic that all our knowledge is human knowledge, so the study of *how* we select, process and use information should provide not only a basis for pedagogy, but a partial contribution to discussion of what we teach.

Both Piaget and Bruner, while attempting to illuminate the processes of children's minds, offer some account of the nature of knowledge itself.

Piaget

Such, at least, was the objective of Piaget. He describes

himself as a 'genetic epistemologist', indicating the combined biological and philosophical orientation of his work. Although he is best known of teachers for his description of the growth of concepts in children, his interest is in the nature of knowledge as manifested in the processes and structures which he claims are universally observable in children (Piaget, 1971).

The problem of intelligence, and with it the central problem of the pedagogy of teaching, has thus emerged as linked with the fundamental epistemological problem of the nature of knowledge: does the latter constitute a copy of reality or, on the contrary, an assimilation of reality into a structure of transformations?

Piaget maintains that knowledge is an *active* assimilation of reality into structures, going from the simplest to the most complex and abstract. He stresses that the roots of knowledge are in action. 'To know an object is to act upon it and to transform it' (Piaget, 1971).

Most of his work emphasizes 'the spontaneous and relatively autonomous aspects of the development of children's intellectual structures', but he sees two kinds of knowledge as important in school curricula (Piaget, 1971):

there are some subjects, such as French history or spelling, whose contents have been developed, or even invented, by adults, and the transmission of which raises no problems other than those related to recognizing better or worse information techniques. There are other branches of learning, on the other hand, characterized by a mode of truth that does not depend upon more or less particular events resulting from many individual decisions, but upon a process of research and discovery during the course of which the human intelligence affirms its own existence and its properties of universality and autonomy; a mathematical truth is not dependent upon the contingencies of adult society but upon a rational construction accessible to any healthy intelligence.

In effect, Piaget sees some kinds of knowledge as socially constructed, others as transcending particular groups and possessing a universal validity, which seems to derive from the nature of mind.

The great strength of his work is in the careful mapping out of children's mental operations, which has obvious implications for both structured curricula and more open-ended educational experiences. Piaget has chosen to study the maturation of intelligence, but he does not claim that growth is independent of experience. Spontaneous processes are a necessary but not a sufficient condition for the development of intellectual capacities.

Bruner

The point is made more forcefully by Bruner, who is equally concerned with spontaneous growth, drawing heavily on the work of both Piaget and Vygotsky, and the effect upon it of experience. 'The range of man's intellect, given its power to be increased from the outside in, can never be estimated without considering the means a culture provides for empowering the mind' (Bruner, 1971).

He sees organized education as potentially the means of 'translating experience into more powerful systems of notation and ordering' (Bruner, 1960). His respect for the natural learning process of children does not lead him into a naively maturational standpoint (Bruner, 1971):

Save in the artificial setting of the school, dominated as it is by telling and a lack of guiding feedback, there is an exhilarating property of self-reward about the act of learning during growth. . . . This does not mean, of course, that what a child learns is what is most empowering of his capacities but, rather, what happens to be available. It is here that the innovation of school and teacher can be critically important.

In one sense, Bruner's view of knowledge is more conventional than radical. He tends to accept traditional subject boundaries, but he emphasizes the *how* and the *why* of knowledge, rather than the *what* (Bruner, 1966):

A body of knowledge, enshrined in a university faculty and embodied in a series of authoritative volumes, is the result of much prior intellectual activity. To instruct someone in these disciplines is not a matter of getting him to

commit results to mind. Rather, it is to teach him to participate in the process that makes possible the establishment
of knowledge. We teach a subject not to produce little
living libraries on that subject, but rather to get a student
to think mathematically for himself, to consider matters
as an historian does, to take part in the process of knowledge getting. Knowing is a process, not a product.

The curriculum implications of Bruner's view of knowledge
are twofold. First, one criterion of selecting what we are to
teach should be the power of a body of knowledge to develop mental processes. This could involve a radical reconsideration of what is 'worthwhile'. Second, the structure and
sequence of knowledge presented to children may be very
different from the coded, 'enshrined' adult version. Bruner
calls for a 'courteous translation' of the key concepts of a
body of knowledge in terms of the child's conceptualizing
ability. This is what he means by his famous statement: 'We
start with the hypothesis that any subject can be taught
effectively in some intellectually honest form to any child at
any stage of development' (Bruner, 1960).

In addition, Bruner's model of mind, of the processes of
knowing, has some bearing on how we should teach. Like
Piaget, he emphasizes the active nature of mind, though his
analysis of the actual processes is somewhat different. He
prefers to use the paradigm of three basic modes of representing reality, through action, imagery and symbol, sequential in
their development, but interacting throughout life. Knowing
involves the acquisition of increasingly good strategies for
acting upon the world. 'Cognitive mastery in a world that
generates stimuli far faster than we can sort them out
depends upon strategies for reducing the complexity and the
clutter' (Bruner, 1971).

Conclusion

It is important to remember that the theories of Piaget and
Bruner, as with most of the other psychological theories discussed in this book, are not 'true' in any absolute sense. It is
not even a sensible question to ask if they are true; we can

only ask, are they useful and, on what evidence are they based? Hypotheses about something as complex as human behaviour in different situations are unlikely to be verifiable in the same way as phenomena in the natural sciences. Interpretation of data, based as it must be on philosophical, social and political assumptions, is even less objective. In borrowing models and methods of inquiry from psychology, we must be aware of the biases and limits.

To some extent, it is up to the teacher to choose critically from the field of psychology those parts which seem useful to her. I shall try to indicate the status of the theories, concepts and findings selected for this book, together with some indication of applications that I or other writers have found helpful in structuring knowledge, planning learning experiences or evaluating outcomes and processes.

Further reading

Piaget (1971) is a collection of short essays, written between 1935 and 1965, summarizing Piaget's approach to mental growth and discussing the relationship of educational theory to practice.

Bruner (1960) is the book most often re-read by teachers in the USA. Short, readable, it contains the beginnings of Bruner's ideas on the curriculum.

Bruner (1966) is probably the most comprehensive sketch of a psychological theory applied to education that we have, even today.

Bruner (1971) is a collection of essays written between 1964 and 1970 in response to the challenges against 'establishment schooling', incorporating Bruner's earlier ideas and setting them in a wider social perspective.

Kerr (1968, chapters 1 and 4).

Chapter 4

Sociological Issues

Denis Lawton

What is sociology of education?

One of the difficulties of talking about sociology is that no
one is quite sure what it is. One possible definition of sociology is that it is a study of people in society. But even this
apparent simplicity leads to two very different schools of
thought, depending on whether you emphasize *people* or
society. The study of 'people in society' emphasizes a view of
humanity which predated sociology and was held by English
philosophers such as Hobbes in the seventeenth century.
They felt that it was essential for individuals to be kept in
order by the state, otherwise there would be chaos because
individuals are essentially greedy and selfish. For sociologists
within this tradition such as Comte and Durkheim the key
question was: Why is it that human beings who are essentially greedy and selfish manage to co-operate and live
harmoniously in a well-ordered society? This has been the
dominant tradition in sociology, including the sociology of
education of Durkheim who was much concerned with the
breakdown of values after the Industrial Revolution and the
French Revolution. For Durkheim, the key problem was
social order: a major function of education was to inculcate
some kind of moral system without which no society could
survive.

An alternative tradition in sociology – but much less
influential – has been connected with the questions asked by
some Marxists. Those who emphasize the centrality of *people*

35

Denis Lawton

rather than society tend to ask such questions as: Why is it that human beings who begin by being naturally co-operative end up by making each other suffer and exploiting each other? This view of society and of human nature stresses conflict, and invites the conclusion that there must be something wrong with society (rather than the individuals in society). For Marx the answer was that what was wrong with society was capitalism, and he felt that some action was called for in order to change that society.

Sociology of education: The English tradition

In England, much sociology owed more to social reform than the kind of sociological theory which was so important on the continent in the nineteenth and early twentieth centuries. A good deal of early British sociology was in the liberal tradition of social reform. One of the best known early social surveys was carried out by Seebohm Rowntree who was not a sociologist at all. Rowntree (1901) was concerned with the problem of poverty in York: in order to try to improve social conditions he carried out a survey (1899) of working class families, their living conditions, infant mortality rates and wages. Underlying this kind of social survey was a very important moral idea of social justice. Much of the early work in sociology of education was close to this tradition. In 1926 Kenneth Lindsay published a book *Social Progress and Educational Waste* stressing the unfairness of the system which allowed so few working-class children real educational opportunity at the secondary level. Gray and Moshinsky (1938) examined the degree of inequality of opportunity existing in the selection system for grammar schools. They used the results of IQ tests to demonstrate that 'opportunity' correlated with social class. This kind of work served to point out that children of the same level of intelligence did *not* have equal access to educational institutions and experienced quite different kinds of curriculum.

This line of sociological research played its part, along with trade union and Labour Party demands, for secondary education for all children, and eventually the 1944 Education Act.

Sociology of Education since 1944

The 1944 Education Act appeared to many people to promise not only secondary education for all but equality of educational opportunity. But the wording of the Act was ambiguous, and the most common interpretation was that the clause which stated that a child should be educated according to his 'age, aptitude and ability' should mean some kind of tripartite system of secondary education. This system involved three different kinds of schools: secondary grammar schools for the top ability or academic children (about 20 per cent); a small proportion of slightly less able but 'technically minded' children would go to secondary technical schools; and the majority of pupils would go to secondary modern schools. These schools were supposed to be different but equal – the doctrine of parity of prestige or parity of esteem. In practice most parents, and especially middle-class parents, wanted their children to go to grammar schools. The years following 1944 can be seen as an account of growing disillusion with the tripartite system, and eventually the collapse of the idea of parity of prestige (see Banks, 1955).

Sociologists played a part in this movement away from the tripartite system towards a comprehensive secondary system. In 1956, Jean Floud and her colleagues examined selection for grammar schools in two areas (south-west Hertfordshire and Middlesbrough) and found that proportionately fewer working-class children gained grammar school places. This was an expected result since a number of studies had shown that middle-class children tended to score more highly on IQ tests. The sociologists found that the average measured IQ of children with parents in social class 1 (professional and managerial) was fifteen to sixteen points higher than children with parents in social class 5 (unskilled manual). They also found that in the two areas investigated the working-class children were in fact getting their 'fair share' of places according to measured IQ, but the researchers also pointed out that measured IQ was not necessarily the same as innate ability: they examined the evidence which showed that measured intelligence was to some extent a socially acquired characteristic. In addition to the cultural bias of the IQ tests there were many other factors influencing the chances of

working-class children in grammar school selection. It was
shown that the selection process very frequently began at
age seven when children were streamed. Streaming was found
to be most frequently carried out either on the basis of personal assessment by infant school teachers or by reading
ability — both of which tended to facilitate 'over-scoring' by
children from favourable or middle-class environments.
Research also showed that middle-class children tended to go
to better primary schools. In other words, what began by
looking like equality of opportunity on closer investigation
proved to be a situation very much loaded against working-
class children.

This kind of university research was followed by a number
of official government reports. The Crowther Report (*15–18*)
in 1959 showed much the same picture but with far more
detail. It was found that there was a tremendous amount of
wasted ability among working-class children. Very large numbers of high ability children left school at the age of fifteen.
In 1963 the Robbins Report produced similar evidence.

From Access to Performance

So far the problem of inequality of opportunity in education
had been seen largely in terms of access to certain kinds of
educational institutions — especially grammar schools and
universities. Some of the research already quoted, however,
began to give indications that even when working-class children were admitted to grammar schools, the problem was not
altogether solved. There appeared to be a problem of dif-
ferential *performance at school* as well as the problem of
access to school. The Robbins Committee, taking GCE 'O'
level success as a criterion of good performance, compared
the figures contained in the early leaving report 1946 with
those for 1960–1 (Robbins Report, Appendix I, Table 14).
This showed that it was still the case that a professional
worker's child classified at the age of eleven as in the lowest
third of the grammar school ability range was still likely to
become a better 'O' level candidate than the working-class
child classified into the top third of the ability range. One
way of reading the report was that it would have been 'safer'

for a grammar school to select a middle-class marginal pupil than one of the working-class pupils in the high ability range. The fact that the school might have contributed to this under-achievement was at this stage almost completely ignored. The studies quoted above showed the following factors to be of importance:

1 the physical conditions of the pupil's home;
2 income of the parents;
3 age of parents leaving school;
4 parents' attitude to education;
5 the power of the school to assimilate working-class pupils;
6 Size of family.

With the exception of factor number 5, this picture added up to what would now be described as a deficit model of pupil performance. In other words it was assumed if certain kinds of pupil did not do well at school there was something wrong with them rather than with the school. In the 1950s and early 1960s there were various attempts of a social psychological nature to explain why working-class children had lower motivation, or came from sub-cultures which did not value education, or had other kinds of environmental influences which made them less 'educable'.

By the end of the 1960s some studies were, however, beginning to focus on the structure and organization of schools rather than the background of pupils. Some showed that the problem of working-class under-achievement was not automatically solved by establishing comprehensive schools (Ford, 1969); in *streamed* comprehensive schools the familiar pattern seemed inevitable — middle-class children were likely to be over-represented in the upper streams, working-class children were more likely to 'fail'. Other interesting 'unintended consequences' of streaming were shown in studies such as Hargreaves (1967) and Lacey (1970).

The New Wave Sociology of Education

By the 1970s there were at least two reactions against the traditional view of sociology of education in England. One of these began to turn away from the kind of demographic studies of why working-class children were not represented in certain kinds of educational institutions, and looked at the *content* of education itself. The argument here had moved on from the attacks on tripartite secondary education and had also moved on from discussion of the organization of comprehensive schools and now asked such questions as: What is the point of a common, comprehensive school if it is not transmitting some kind of common culture by means of a common curriculum? This kind of question stems partly from the writing of Raymond Williams who was primarily interested in literature and wider aspects of popular culture. Although he is not himself a sociologist, his two books *Culture and Society* (1965) and *The Long Revolution* (1961) have stimulated sociologists into looking again at the curriculum and its content.

A more dramatic reaction against the sociology of the '50s and '60s is associated in England with M. F. D. Young, whose book *Knowledge and Control* appeared in 1971. Young suggests that one of the failures of the traditional sociology of education was that it had *taken* problems rather than set about the task of *making* problems. In other words sociologists had accepted the conventional view that if a working-class child failed in school then this was either the result of bad teaching or some inadequacy on the part of the child — the deficit model. Young suggests that this should be open to question and that sociologists ought to regard all aspects of schooling including the curriculum as 'problematic'. So far so good, but unfortunately Young combines this very useful and sceptical view with other more extreme views which lead to pessimism and relativism. Young not only suggests (correctly) that the content of the curriculum is problematic, he goes on to call into question the whole of knowledge and even rationality itself. I have suggested elsewhere (Lawton, 1975) that before accepting or rejecting the whole doctrine it is necessary to distinguish between at least five levels of 'credibility'. The five levels may be summarized as follows:

Level 1 That the present structure and organization of education in our society serves to preserve the status quo in an unjust society — this level is particularly concerned with questions such as the social distribution of knowledge.

Level 2 That in particular the content of education – the selection of knowledge for transmission by schools – should be made into a problem for critical examination rather than be taken for granted; this level is concerned with what counts for knowledge in our society, and the stratification of knowledge.

Level 3 That subject barriers are arbitrary and artificial, existing largely for the convenience of those in control of education.

Level 4 That all knowledge is socially constructed.

Level 5 That not only knowledge but rationality itself is merely a convention.

Levels 1 and 2 do not present serious problems of credibility; level 3, however, begins to be less acceptable in detail and levels 4 and 5 are very difficult to accept as being consistent within any coherent logical framework.

Thus, before accepting arguments which suggest that knowledge is socially determined we have to be clear about precisely what is meant by that phrase. In the sense that knowledge is the result of interpersonal communication clearly knowledge is socially constructed, but if sociologists and others want to go further and suggest that any construction of reality is as good as any other (the extreme relativist position) then we have to ask further questions about the limits imposed by physical reality as well as ethical questions about the value of certain kinds of knowledge as compared with others. A further discussion of the problems of the sociology of knowledge will be found in chapter 15.

Further reading

For the origins of sociology and the early nineteenth century conservative reactions to modernism Robert Nisbet's book *The Sociological Tradition* (1967) is indispensable. Nisbet suggests that the dominant tradition is a conservative one and that sociology is an art form whose subject matter centres around the concepts of community, authority, status and alienation. He also suggests that romantic literature was also preoccupied with some of these problems in the nineteenth and early twentieth centuries. The view that there is not one sociology but two was put forward by Alan Dawe in a paper which is now reprinted in Thompson and Tunstall (1971). This book contains a number of useful papers on the nature of sociology.

As for the sociology of education, the social historical events leading up to 1944 can be read briefly in Lawton (1973, chapter 5), and in detail in Rubinstein and Simon's book (1969). The story since 1944 is again briefly reviewed in Lawton (1973, chapter 6). Olive Banks (1955) is a very detailed but fascinating account of the rise and fall of the tripartite system. Another book by Olive Banks (1968) gives a good general overview of the subject matter. An alternative to that is a somewhat shorter book by Peter Musgrave (1965). One very influential book during the 1960s was a collection of papers edited by Halsey, Floud and Anderson (1961). Most of the papers are still worth reading today.

For the new view of sociology of education the book by M. F. D. Young (1971) is important but very difficult to read. A balanced view of the new kind of sociology is a collection of papers edited by Flude and Ahier (1974) especially the first chapter by Bill Williamson on 'Continuities and Discontinuities in the Sociology of Education'.

Chapter 5

Language and Curriculum

Denis Lawton

Introduction

We saw in chapter 4 that much of British sociology in the early postwar stages was concerned with questions of values such as social justice. This had its origins in earlier poverty surveys which were concerned with achieving a fairer society by eliminating gross inequalities of life chances. One important aspect of injustice in our society which caught the attention of sociologists was inequality of opportunity in education. In this chapter I want to concentrate on one feature of that sociological discussion about inequality in education: the relation between social class, language and educational achievement.

The background

One of the features of educational discussion during the 1960s was the attention paid to language as a factor in educational achievement. This trend was due in part to belated recognition of the importance of such psychologists as Luria and Vygotsky, and also to the sociological theories of Bernstein. The Russian psychologists were responsible for refocusing our attention onto the relation between language and thought. Luria, Vygotsky and others of the school held a dynamic view of language – that is they maintained that language was not simply the outward manifestation of inner

43

thinking, but that it shapes, makes possible and even produces some kinds of thought. This implies that the more we know about an individual's or a group's language the more we know about their thinking. The other way in which the Russian psychologists saw language dynamically was in the 'self-regulating' function of language: as we internalize language we internalize society; Luria (1959, 1961), has shown, for example, that children internalize language in such a way as to become self-regulating systems rather than the passive responders to stimuli suggested by Skinner (1957) and the behaviourists. Language is the uniquely human attribute which enables us to learn, think creatively and change our social environment. This is very different from animals without language who are much more dominated by their instincts and their physical surroundings.

The interests of sociologists in language is closely related to the Russian psychological view that man becomes human largely by means of the self-regulating system of language. In sociological terms this means that children are socialized largely by means of language, and also that human beings acquire the capacity for rebellion, or at least change, by means of language: language not only helps us to understand why things are as they are, it also enables us to see what *might be*. An individual's view of reality is closely bound up with language: the language we have acquired has *some* influence on how we see the world, and how we use language is closely related to a position in the social structure. One of Bernstein's contributions was to illustrate the connection between social structure, language use and 'educability'. But his theory has been greatly misunderstood and misinterpreted: he was *not* suggesting that working-class language is inferior to middle-class language and that therefore working-class children are less educable; he was demonstrating that if middle-class children acquire the kind of oral expression classified as elaborated code this will give them an advantage in formal educational contexts, given the way that education is at present organized. The sociological interest in language is much wider than this, however. How people use language is related to social structure, occupation, community and group relations; how people think is related to their use of language.

Language and education

The dangers of oversimplifying the relationship between language and social class and education are enormous. It is all too easy for teachers to label working-class pupils as 'restricted code users' and therefore difficult to teach or incapable of benefiting from normal educational processes. It cannot be emphasized too strongly that there is no evidence at all to support such attitudes. The reality is much more complex. Working-class people have traditionally had little part to play in the power structure; they have not used language to any great extent in their jobs, and they have not needed to use language to persuade or coerce others. That does not mean that language is unimportant in working-class culture: simply that its uses may differ in some respects from certain kinds of middle-class communities.

On the other hand schools are in origin middle-class institutions; teachers are by background or education middle class, and the language of transmission is also largely middle class. It is therefore not surprising that pupils whose home background has already equipped them with the appropriate kind of oral facility will find less difficulty in adapting to some of the demands of teachers in schools. There are, however, a number of difficulties or problems inherent in this kind of discussion about social class, language and education which teachers should be aware of.

Bernstein's work

One of the difficulties in this area of socio-linguistic research is that some of Bernstein's early writings became very popular, especially in colleges of education, but they were frequently misunderstood or quoted out of context. Bantock (1968), for example, quoted Bernstein in support of his view that working-class children needed a different kind of non-literary education. A further difficulty is that this popularization occurred at an early stage in Bernstein's work: his later writings are much more complex and include important re-formulations of his earlier theory.

Bernstein's early work has also sometimes been interpreted

in terms of what later came to be known as 'deficit theory'. This may never have been Bernstein's intention but some of the terminology used may have encouraged this misinterpretation. This oversimplified view may be summarized as follows: there are basically two kinds of speech or linguistic codes – restricted and elaborated codes. Restricted code is used for communicating familiar ideas to people who can take a good deal of the message for granted; elaborated code is more appropriate for communicating with strangers, conveying complicated and abstract ideas, signifying doubt and uncertainty and so on. Bernstein's early work contained the hypothesis that these two codes exist and that whereas middle-class people can switch from one code to another according to the context, lower working-class speakers tend to use only restricted code. All this kind of discussion was not very far away from 'deficit theories' and notions of 'linguistic deprivation'. As we have seen some writers, but not Bernstein himself, made this oversimplified connection.

In his later writings, however, Bernstein has been careful to point out both the complexity of the relation between language class and educability and also the dangers of developing programmes for compensatory education based on overgeneralizations about working-class children. An extract from his essay 'A Critique of the Concept Compensatory Education' (Bernstein, 1967) may serve to put this part of the record straight.

> The concept 'compensatory education' serves to direct attention away from the internal organization and the educational context of the school, and focus our attention on the families and the children. The concept compensatory education implies something is lacking in the family and so in the child.

There are two points which ought to be made in connection with this. First, there is no evidence to support the view that the working-class children are in any way linguistically deprived. Second, linguistic difference is not the same as language competence. Both of these points will be taken up later.

Other problems concerning language and education

One of the reactions to the 'linguistic deprivation' version of the deficit thesis was the assertion that any language and any dialect can express anything that needs to be communicated in any particular community. This was first put forward in general terms by cultural anthropologists and linguists, and then in a particular context by American socio-linguist, Labov, who turned the theory on its head and claimed that black children from the ghetto slums actually used a richer language. That is probably an extreme over-reaction to the deficit thesis, but what is now generally accepted by linguists is, first, that every language is adequate for the particular needs of any culture, and, second, that you can say anything in any language, but that it may be more difficult to convey certain ideas in some languages; this would apply also to dialects and other linguistic varieties.

Translating all of that into the classroom situation, we have to ask what help does the research offer to the teacher with children from working-class or non-standard English backgrounds?

1 Children who speak some kinds of non-standard English are not linguistically deprived: their language is perfectly adequate for their own environment.

2 Certain kinds of classroom language expression may be less easy for some children to acquire, but this should not be exaggerated: much more important is the attitude of the teachers in signalling approval or disapproval.

3 Although much has been made of the statistically significant differences between middle-class and working-class children regarding certain linguistic measures (for example the use of passive verbs) there is no kind of usage which has ever been shown to be totally absent from working-class speech.

4 Some non-standard forms of English may present difficulties for children learning to read. If the dialect, for example West Indian Creole, is far removed from the written form then reading may be that much more difficult, but this can be overcome by a suitable teaching method: for example using the 'Breakthrough to Literacy' scheme rather than 'Janet and John' books.

5 Teachers need to change their attitudes to non-standard English and think less in terms of right and wrong and more in terms of appropriate and inappropriate for certain specific contexts. It will still be the duty of teachers to develop competence in standard English, but this should be seen as the task of learning a set of conventions, not something which is aesthetically or morally superior.

The language of the classroom

The work of Douglas Barnes and his colleagues (1969) has shown that most teachers have a good deal to learn about their own use of language in classrooms and also how to develop children's linguistic abilities. Barnes (1969, p. 55) has shown, for example, that teachers, especially in secondary schools, make inappropriate use of unfamiliar technical or abstract language:

> They were called city states because they were complete in themselves. They were governed by themselves, ruled by themselves, they supported themselves. These states were complete in themselves because the terrain between cities was so difficult that it was hard for them to communicate. Now because these people lived like this in their own cities, they tended to be intensely patriotic towards their own city. Now what's patriotic mean?

Teachers are also too much addicted to a form of question and answer style which Barnes describes as 'hunting the label' — an essentially closed form of learning. Barnes (1976) shows that much more use could be made of children's exploratory language in small group discussions without the teacher present. His book *From Communication to Curriculum* (1976) is a very stimulating volume which all teachers should read. Meanwhile, perhaps I might offer my own interpretation of some of the lessons which emerge for teachers:

1 Many teachers use language which is unnecessarily remote and difficult.

2 Some teachers rebuff children who try to get to grips with complicated ideas by expressing themselves in their own natural language.

3 Children (and adults) learn by talking: talk of the right kind helps to clarify thinking.

4 Most teachers talk too much.

Language across the curriculum

One of the ideas fostered originally by the London Institute of Education English Department and later given national publicity in the Bullock Report (1975) was that schools should develop a language policy for the whole curriculum — language across the curriculum. Another view suggests that one aspect of linguistic development is the acquisition of different kinds of language which would be appropriate for different kinds of knowledge. The language of science, for example, is different from the language of history: the conventions of writing up an experiment are different from writing a history essay. The concepts and terminology in both disciplines are also different. Certain kinds of linguistic competence may be common across the curriculum, but pupils also need to learn about some specialist uses of language — both receptive and active. Another way of expressing this idea is to say that most teachers would now agree that all pupils should be literate, but literacy for secondary pupils ought to mean much more than possessing the basic skills of reading and writing. Teachers need to be more specific about what they expect pupils to be able to read and write about. So we might talk of scientific literacy, or social, economic and political literacy. If we did, we would come to the conclusion that most children are not adequately prepared by schools for the linguistic skills they would need as responsible adults.

Summary

1 The idea of language deficit has gradually given way to the idea of language difference.

2 The concept of 'compensatory education' is of very doubtful validity and distracts attention from real educational and social problems in the schools.

3 Language is closely related to 'context of situation' and therefore to questions of school organization and grouping.

4 Language in education should be seen as an integral part of curriculum reform.

5 Teachers' attitudes to behaviour are crucial factors in pupils' linguistic behaviour and learning: teacher effectiveness can be seen largely in terms of verbal interaction.

6 Teacher education must be more concerned with language as a means of learning and also with the dynamics of classroom interaction and communication.

Further reading

There is now a large number of volumes published in the Routledge & Kegan Paul series 'Theoretical Studies Towards a Sociology of Language', edited by Professor Bernstein. Some of these are difficult and very technical, but there is no alternative for the student who wants to specialize in this field. They should start with *Class, Codes and Control*, vol. 1 (1973).

Most students will, however, be better advised to begin with a general introduction to sociology of language such as Edwards (1976). You should *not* rely on Lawton (1968) which is now badly out of date on the socio-linguistic research of Bernstein and his sociological research unit, but you may find some of the general background useful.

Barnes (1976) is essential reading for all teachers and his contribution to an earlier work is also very important: Barnes, Britton, and Rosen (1969). This contains a section on language across the curriculum which was later developed in the Bullock Report. This view of language across the curriculum is criticized in Jeanette Williams' interesting book *Learning to Write or Writing to Learn?* (1977).

Chapter 6

A Multidisciplinary Approach to Curriculum

Denis Lawton

The main purpose of this chapter will be to bring together a summary of the previous contributions and to focus on the practical problem of teachers planning a school curriculum.

Terry Moore (in chapter 1) established the need for educational theory, clarified its nature and suggested that although there are many different kinds of theories of education they must all possess three characteristics:

1 assumptions about the nature of man, and therefore of children;

2 assumptions about the educational 'ends' or 'aims', often interpreted as an idea of what kind of person should be regarded as 'educated'; and

3 assumptions about the nature of knowledge and the relative value of different kinds of knowledge.

Richard Pring (in chapter 2), however, questioned whether such activities by teachers amounted to having a theory or should be regarded as theorizing on the basis of practical experience. Views on planning an appropriate curriculum for children will therefore be based partly on these three different kinds of assumptions (or critical activities), but these assumptions or questions do not exist in a vacuum – they may be, to some extent, products of the kind of society the teacher/theorist was living in.

Richard Pring (in chapter 2) concentrated on philosophical answers to questions about two major concerns: the nature of knowledge and what knowledge is of most worth? On the first of these questions, it would appear that there are very strong epistemological arguments to support the view that there are different kinds of knowledge with different concepts, structures and validation procedures. At this point there is a clear overlap between philosophical and psychological questions since psychologists such as Bruner would suggest that if disciplines exist then the most efficient way of learning will be to work with the structures rather than against them. But at this stage we are simply concerned to establish whether it would seem wise or unwise to think of knowledge in terms of compartments such as disciplines or whether knowledge is better regarded as a seamless robe. On balance philosophical arguments such as those of Hirst, Phenix and Schwab would seem difficult to ignore. What Richard Pring did not do in his chapter was to identify the disciplines or forms of knowledge or realms of meaning. On that issue there is much less agreement among philosophers. Hirst's (1965) seven forms of knowledge would appear to be only one of several possible answers ranging from Phenix's (1964) six realms, Broudy's (1962) five, to Schwab's (1962) three kinds of discipline (investigative, appreciative and decisive). But it is important not to exaggerate these differences: mathematical knowledge is clearly quite distinct from literature, but whether you want to draw a line between, say, history and sociology seems much more a matter of choosing between a simple classification and a complex one. Some kind of classification, however, is certainly necessary.

Then Richard Pring dealt with the second major philosophical issue: what knowledge is of most worth? Two kinds of answer were examined — the utilitarian and the 'cognitive concern' argument. The nineteenth-century utilitarian philosophers attempted to relate the worthwhileness of knowledge to 'the greatest happiness of the greatest number', i.e. that education, as a rational activity, should increase happiness and diminish pain; and despite the difficulties involved in this, so long as happiness is defined more broadly than immediate gratification, then many of us would see some merit in the argument, even if it leaves us with difficulties in measuring the quality of different kinds of happiness resulting from different kinds of knowledge. The 'cognitive concern' argument of R. S. Peters is more complex and relates worthwhileness to kinds of truth (and since truth is necessarily related to different kinds of knowledge we arrive back at the view of the educated man as the truth-seeker and finding truth in a variety of 'forms'). Both the utilitarian and Peters' view of education would therefore be subject-centred at least in the sense that education must involve knowledge of the various disciplines. Richard Pring showed himself to be a little unhappy at that conclusion, however, and he chose to end his chapter with an attempted justification for a curriculum based, in part at least, on children's interests.

In chapter 4 another major difficulty was raised for consideration. The view, expressed by some sociologists that knowledge is 'socially determined'. Traditionally sociologists have seen the curriculum in terms of socializing the young into accepted forms of behaviour and transmitting to them what was regarded as the most 'valuable' knowledge. This view has been increasingly criticized by those who want to replace the 'normative' paradigm in sociology by the 'interpretive' paradigm which would question everything and take nothing for granted. This new sociology clearly has its attractions, and teachers for too long have been encouraged to accept an incomplete or distorted view of reality. But the difficulty here is to know where relativizing has to stop, i.e. if we accept that some of the traditional attitudes, for example high status and low status knowledge, were arbitrary does that necessarily mean that there is *no* basis for regarding some kinds of experience as more valuable or worthwhile than others? Even if we accept the view that a curriculum dominated by Latin and Greek served to sustain the power and privileges of the upper classes, does it automatically follow that a curriculum consisting of bingo and horseracing would be just as worthwhile as a curriculum based on science and humanities? The answer has to be *no*, and we are driven back to philosophical issues as well as purely sociological ones. The new sociology of knowledge view should certainly make us wary of accepting absolutes in education such as unchallengeable standards, fixed content and methods, but it is all too easy to go to the lunatic extreme of saying 'anything goes'. We must also actively question the limits of relativity as Richard Pring has also indicated: for example, to question the value of the traditional curriculum may be very sensible, but to question the value of rationality is self-contradictory.

Another danger of the global nature of the new sociology is that we may tend to ignore the kind of practical, more immediate social factors which influence curriculum planning. For example, whereas a philosopher needs to ask fundamental questions about the nature of knowledge and what knowledge is of most worth (at any time, in any place), sociologists (and teachers) have to ask what knowledge is of most relevance in *our* society *now* (and in the future). The kind of answers invited by those questions would presumably be that, for example, we are a highly industrialized, technological society (and therefore we *need* scientific knowledge), or that we are a society which is said to be democratic (and therefore we *need* political, economic and social knowledge – for everyone, not just the élite few). Sociologists – especially with the critical insights of some aspects of new sociology – should also enable teachers to put these ideals into practice, by laying bare some of the hidden obstacles on the road towards a worthwhile curriculum for all.

Finally the psychological aspects of knowledge and curriculum. Maggie Ing (chapter 3) reminds us that curriculum planning involves the interaction of knowledge and children's minds – it is not a simple transmission process; psychological theories of cognitive development are concerned with both the nature of knowledge and the mental processes of children. The work of Piaget is of particular relevance here, and the extract quoted by Maggie Ing incidentally throws a good deal of light on the philosophical and sociological disputes about the nature of knowledge. Piaget, as a genetic epistemologist, makes a most important distinction between 'man-made' knowledge such as spelling which is 'conventional', and knowledge such as mathematics which is a 'rational construction', in no way arbitrary, but possessing universal validity.

The importance of Piaget's work (as well as Bruner's) lies in the matching of structure of knowledge with what can be discovered about the processes of children's thinking. Bruner's attitude to knowledge might be thought to be traditional in the sense that he accepts conventional subject barriers and is prepared to work with them. But within the discipline structures Bruner emphasizes *process* rather than product, i.e. he urged teachers to stress not facts and rote learning but how to get children to think like historians and mathematicians.

One function of a well-planned curriculum is to select the kind of knowledge which is 'economic' in the sense that it is essential knowledge and the kind of knowledge which leads to easier acquisition of more knowledge. Knowledge acquisition is too important a matter to be left to random choice. A carefully planned curriculum is necessary if a child is to master all the knowledge necessary to cope with a modern, complex industrial society.

Planning a curriculum in this way is a complex and highly professional activity. To say that every teacher must be his own curriculum planner is a fine slogan but it is a rather hollow one unless teachers are equipped with the necessary knowledge and skills. Each teacher − or, more probably, each group of teachers − has to work out an acceptable view of knowledge, establish some kind of view of society which is desirable, and on that complex basis make a selection from the culture of our society always bearing in mind the psychological principles involved in learning and teaching. A tall order! But the alternative may well be to have a curriculum devised outside the teaching profession and imposed on teachers whether they like it or not. The Assessment of Performance Unit has already been mentioned as a possible step in that direction.

Teachers are right to resist the idea of a centrally *controlled* curriculum, but it would be difficult for teachers to resist the demands for *accountability*: where large sums of public money are involved it is quite reasonable for us to have to justify what we are trying to do in education without our yielding to demands for an updated version of 'payments by results'. The whole question of evaluation in education is an extremely complex one (as we shall see in later chapters). It is also true that the freedom of the teacher is much cherished in our society − a detailed national curriculum is strongly opposed by teachers' professional organizations. But we also have to be clear that teachers' professional autonomy cannot mean that any individual teacher has the right to teach just whatever he feels he would like to teach, any more than an individual doctor would have the right to treat all his patients with psychodelic drugs. The professional autonomy of a teacher must be related to the collective judgment of the professional community as a whole. A good curriculum has to be more than the expression of one teacher's personal taste. Individual teachers should be left with a good deal of discretion in teaching methods and selecting content, but it would seem to be unrealistic to demand that teachers should have unbridled, individual freedom to flout publicly accepted standards. However, one of the present difficulties is precisely the lack of publicly accepted standards for even a basic curriculum structure. Thus teachers not only have the job of working out a suitable curriculum for a particular group of pupils, they have to do this without the security of an accepted and acceptable national pattern or structure.

Part of the difficulty of arriving at a rational curriculum is, however, the uneasiness felt by decision-makers operating in a pluralistic society. Where there is no total consensus about certain issues or values it is easier to avoid taking decisions – or at least to pretend not to take decisions. For example, Terry Moore mentioned (in chapter 1) that educational theorizing is likely to involve making assumptions about 'human nature' and particularly the nature of children. This is a question likely to split teachers, theorists and the general public into two camps. There are those who tend to see children as 'naturally' lazy, evil creatures who have to be forced to work, and at the other extreme there are those who believe that children are (or would be) naturally good, curious about their environment and eager to acquire knowledge if only they were not perverted by various aspects of our imperfect society. How could teachers holding such opposed views possibly reach agreement on a common curriculum? This is certainly a difficulty, and whilst agreeing with Terry Moore that this is an important factor in *educational* theorizing I would suggest that it is much less crucial in *curriculum* planning. I suggest that these fundamental differences in viewing human nature are much more likely to affect teaching method than the *content* of the curriculum. Whether we believe that children are naturally idle or curious we might still reach a good deal of agreement about the kind of knowledge and experiences they need to have in a given society, even if we continue to differ about the best way of ensuring that children get these experiences. On that point the contributors to this series are clearly divided – perhaps as divided as the average staffroom – but that need not prevent us reaching a reasonable amount of agreement on what knowledge is necessary and what experiences are desirable. We could plan a basic curriculum but differ considerably on teaching methods and the range of optional extras to be provided.

Further reading

Spark, M. (1969), *The Prime of Miss Jean Brodie*, Penguin: a novelist's version of the problem of 'teacher autonomy' in curriculum planning.

Golby, Greenwald and West (1975, Part 2, especially the sections by P. H. Hirst and J. P. White).

Part Two

Psychological Issues

Chapter 7

Learning Theories

Maggie Ing

To plan a curriculum, it is necessary to have some 'theory' of how learning takes place and which conditions make for the most efficient learning. Psychological theories of learning may, at least, make explicit the implicit notions embedded in the actual practice of teachers. What you find in most text-books of psychology under the heading of 'learning theories', however, does not give immediate guidance for teachers. This is partly because the task of the learning theorist is not the same as the task of the teacher. In the scientific tradition, a theory seeks to explain the maximum number of phenomena with the minimum number of 'laws', a particularly difficult task in the face of the complexity of human consciousness and behaviour. As teachers, we may not be concerned with exactly what learning is, nor with the neurophysiological aspects of learning; and we are concerned with the differences among our students at least as much as with their similarities. We must expect to find in psychological theories much that does not help us directly. What we can find, I think, is a more systematic picture of learning processes and of the conditions most favourable to learning.

Behaviourism

The central tenet of behaviourism is that conditioning is the basic unit of learning. In its technical sense 'conditioning' has no sinister undertones, it simply refers to the attachment of a

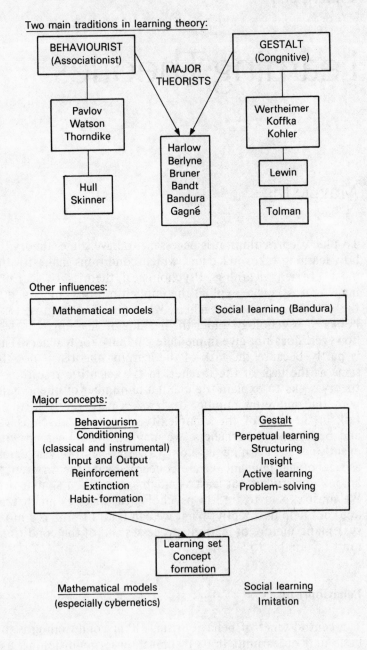

Figure 3

response to a previously neutral stimulus. In classical conditioning, as pioneered by Pavlov, the response in question was involuntary and reflexive, whereas in the work of Thorndike and later of Skinner, the responses were more complex. It is quite proper in a laboratory to try to isolate single responses and stimuli in order to study the relationship between them (although such studies are much more complicated than most elementary text-books make them appear), using organisms capable of much less than we are; but in teaching we are faced with clusters of stimuli and complex, simultaneous, often unpredictable responses. So, to think of conditioning as the basic unit of learning is of limited value to us, especially as we have to take into account the awareness of both teachers and learners, the 'meanings' both personal and social, of actions and materials. It is, however, useful to remember that emotional responses can easily be conditioned. Conditioning can help us understand why a child hates arithmetic, if not how he comes to understand it.
to understand it.

Both Hull and Skinner developed extensions of the S–R (stimulus-response) unit model. Hull was interested in what happened in the learner between the stimulus and the response, and although his almost Euclidean formulation of his learning theory seems far removed from the teacher's normal business, his concept of habit-family hierarchies fits in with structured learning programmes, skill-learning and much of common-sense experience. The process is most clearly illustrated in the learning of skills. Initially, every step in learning a skill is a separate task, like typing an individual letter. Gradually, some of the discrete bits of behaviour fuse into one, like typing the word 'the'. Eventually, smooth sequences of action are built up, with consequent economy of action. If we can identify the components of any skill or set of information that we want children to learn, and structure them into increasingly comprehensive units, learning should be improved. This is the rationale of programmed learning, in part, and of many curriculum programmes in mathematics and languages, and of course, reading. Such an approach ignores some of the quirks of individual minds; what looks like a 'unit' of learning to the teacher or curriculum planner could be several separate 'bits' to the learner, or part of a larger 'unit' he has already acquired. A child's own name, for example, is often a 'unit' to him, even if the same letters in other words are still separate 'bits'.

Gestalt tradition

The word gestalt has no exact equivalent in English. It means something like 'pattern' or 'configuration'. Originally a theory of perception, it was extended to learning, particularly to problem-solving. Its general features are that it draws attention to some of the innate, and learned, structuring processes we possess, rather than externally conditioned responses. This more active model of learning informs much of current thinking about education, including Bruner's work. As a theory, however, it is less coherent than behaviourism and more difficult to translate into practical prescriptions. To describe the moment of understanding, the 'Ah-ha' experience, as re-structuring the perceptual field is merely to couch the mystery in other terms; it gives the teacher or curriculum planner no help in ensuring that the experience will occur.

Experimental work following on Kohler's study of problem-solving in apes has confirmed that experience with materials and actions is necessary for insightful problem-solving – an important point for any curriculum plan concerned with understanding and creativity.

Wertheimer's book *Productive Thinking*, is in many ways the forerunner of Bruner and Dienes' work on the teaching of mathematics. He points out that if rules are learned, without an attempt to promote understanding, they may be wrongly applied in new situations. This is a truism today, but perhaps needs to be re-emphasized in the face of popular calls to return to an ill-defined 'basic' curriculum of some mythical Golden Age.

Lewin extended the gestalt approach into social and personality theory, which has some outcome in the development of gestalt therapy and other brands of 'personal growth' theory. I find Lewin's theory over-ambitious. His terminology, borrowed from topology, vector analysis, physics and chemistry, is more metaphorical than precise, but it does have the virtue of drawing attention to the life-experience and personal consciousness of our students, to which teachers should be sensitive. It is not possible for any curriculum plan or package to take into account these factors; but it is equally impossible for any teacher to adapt the curriculum for his students without bearing them in mind.

Theory-building on the grand scale is not a contemporary preoccupation of psychologists, although most work within a loose framework of assumptions, using largely behaviourist methodology. Attempts to encompass all of human learning in a parsimonious selection of 'laws' have almost been abandoned. The influence of the two traditions, behaviourist (associationist) and gestalt (cognitive) can still be seen; much contemporary educational psychology, for example that of Harlow, Berlyne, Ausubel, Bandura, Bruner and Gagné, draws on both sources.

A modern theory of learning

Gagné's (1974) information-processing theory of learning is a typical example. Its basic assumption is that learning processes are rather analogous to the workings of a computer, a model which fits reasonably well our current knowledge of neurophysiology, and its focus is on the transformations which occur between the 'input' of external stimuli and the 'output' of the learner's behaviour. It is an amalgamation of earlier associationist and cognitive models, and is more elaborated than either of them.

Figure 4 (Gagné, 1974) shows the flow of information through the structures postulated to exist in the central nervous system of the learner. Information from the *environment* affects our *receptors*, is coded, and initial perception takes place. Entering the *short-term memory* (which is very short term, a matter of seconds), the information is again coded. If it is to be remembered, it is transformed once more and enters the *long-term memory* where it is stored for later recall. Current theories hold that, short of damage to brain cells, storage in the long-term memory is permanent and 'forgetting' is a problem of retrieval. From the short- or long-term memory, information passes to a *response generator*

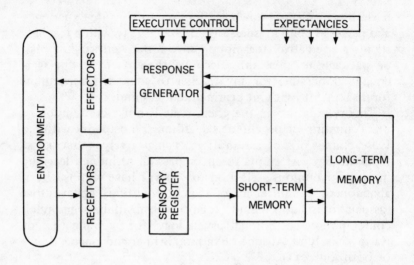

Figure 4. The basic model of learning and memory underlying modern 'information-processing' theories

which activates behaviour of some kind. The structures labelled by Gagné as '*executive control*' and '*expectancies*' activate and modify the flow of information. Differences in motivation, in the personal meanings of the input, would be examples of 'expectancies'; different cognitive strategies for coding or retrieving information would be examples of 'executive control'. Despite the technical language, these structures are not nearly so precise as the rest of the model. From this account of the process of learning, Gagné goes on to outline the events of learning; to classify the outcomes of learning; and to categorize the ways in which the teacher can influence the stages of learning. This last, instructional part of Gagné's work will be discussed in chapter 10.

The events of learning

These phases are based on the processes shown in Figure 4, with some important amplifications. Obviously, the learning sequence depends upon what is initially attended to by the learner; not all signals are, or could be, received. Our perception

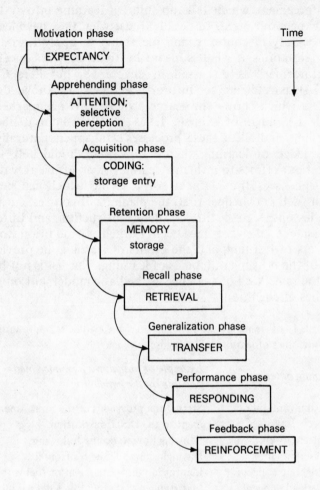

Figure 5. The phases of an act of learning, and the processes associated with them

is selective, dependent on motivation (a state of need, like hunger, makes us more likely to pick up cues related to food, but less likely to notice unrelated information) and on prior knowledge, as well as on features of the external stimuli, like intensity and suddenness. The first diagram illustrates one act of learning, the second adds the phases of transfer and reinforcement which link up 'bits' of learning into systems. We expect our pupils to be able to use what they have learned in a variety of contexts, and the ability to apply learning to new situations is what is meant by transfer. The concept of reinforcement is discussed in chapter 8, but here Gagné (1974), is referring to 'informal feedback' or knowledge of results which shows the learner whether he has reached his goal. Learning, of course, takes place without deliberate teaching, and all of these processes can happen 'naturally'. A knowledge of learning theory, however, should help us to direct our efforts to influence learning in an efficient way.

Gagné sees three aspects of teaching which can benefit from such knowledge: first, the planning of courses, curricula and lessons; second, the conduct of instruction; and third the assessment of what has been learned. In addition to the process of learning, and the events of learning, he provides a list of the possible outcomes of learning. This list is not based on the same kind of evidence as the basic model, but on prior studies of cognition.

TABLE 1   Five major categories of human capabilities, representing the outcomes of learning with examples of each

Learning outcome	Example of human performance made possible by the capability
Verbal information	Stating the provisions of the First Amendment to the U.S. Constitution
Intellectual skill	Showing how to do the following:
Discrimination	Distinguishing printed b's from d's
Concrete concept	Identifying the spatial relation 'below'
Defined concept	Classifying a 'city' by using a definition
Rule	Demonstrating that water changes state at 100° C.
Higher-order rule	Generating a rule for predicting rainfall, given conditions of location and terrain
Cognitive strategy	Originating a novel plan for disposing of fallen leaves
Attitude	Choosing swimming as a preferred exercise
Motor skill	Executing the performance of planing the edge of a board

Using outcomes of learning for planning and assessment fits an 'objectives' model of the curriculum, which pre-specifies exactly what has to be learned. The limits and uses of this model are discussed in chapter 12. But even if we do not accept entirely an objectives model, learning theory can guide us in the presentation of what is to be learned; in some aspects of our interaction with pupils, for example stimulating motivation, giving accurate and full feedback, allowing adequate time for rehearsal, facilitating transfer by posing tasks demanding generalization; and in the testing of what has been learned. Gagné (1974) goes still further:

> When teachers verify their activities against the standards of learning theory, they are accomplishing two highly desirable things. First, they are avoiding the grossly inappropriate actions which, although seemingly desirable on other grounds, nevertheless fail to promote learning in students. And second, they are adopting and maintaining attitudes which support learning as the central purpose of their activities. In the face of many potential distractions in the practice of teaching, the teacher keeps student learning as a primary focus of concern.

This statement makes assumptions about the purpose of teaching which are outside the realm of psychology. It also shows the implicit values embedded even in the most apparently 'scientific' work.

Further reading

Introductory: Lawton (1973, pp. 49ff).

Basic texts for those who have not studied much psychology: Child (1973, chapters 6 and 7), probably the best of the basic text-books. Stones (1966), a sound, basic book, but not quite so up to date as Child.

More detailed and technical reading for those with some previous knowledge of psychology, or a wish to read in more depth is Stones (1968; 1970 section 3, chapters 1, 2, 3 and 7). Mainly behaviourist in approach, using the techniques of programmed learning is Hill (1964). Lunzer and Morris (1968), are critical of the S-R approach. Roberts (1975) is a collection of short papers, excellent for browsing through; it includes humanistic and transpersonal psychology as well as more traditional views. Gagné (1974).

Chapter 8

Theories of Motivation

Maggie Ing

Motivation is an ambiguous word, referring to both an inner drive and a push from without. Children are 'motivated' or we 'motivate' children. This double meaning is reflected in theories of motivation, which can roughly be divided into those which emphasize external stimuli, and those which emphasize internal processes. This categorization is not completely clear-cut; most theories have a biological basis, and most pay some attention to the interaction of inner states and external circumstances. The differences are of emphasis and elaboration. But in their application to education, there is a real difference between the reinforcement model and the horticultural model; Skinner and Dewey make for very different classroom practice.

Central common concepts in theories of motivation are of *need*, which sets up a *drive* impelling the organism to seek *satisfaction* of the need. Upon satisfaction, the drive is reduced, and the actions leading to satisfaction are likely to be repeated. They are, in fact, learned. This simplified model fits reasonably well, though not perfectly, simple instances of animal behaviour. Human learning, however, is not so neatly explained. It is not easy to categorize even our most basic needs. There is some evidence that exploration or curiosity or stimulus-seeking is part of our nature (see Vernon, 1969), and it is a motive-force that we would hope to channel in school. But even with this addition to a list of physiological needs, some extension of the simple model is necessary to account for human behaviour. Hull postulated a system of *acquired* or *secondary* reinforcers, socially learned and often indirect means of satisfying basic needs. Money would be an example. This still does not explain why many people devote so much energy and time to acquiring money when their basic physiological needs are well-satisfied.

Peters (1958) rejects the notion of a 'motive' behind every action. He sees much of our behaviour as understandable within its social context in terms of *goals*. We need, in his view, to look for motives only when actions are inappropriate. In the classroom, we may sometimes have to ask, why did he do that? what was his motive? But this is not the sort of question we usually ask when we want to motivate children to learn. From the many existing theories of motivation, this chapter will focus on two contrasting, but possibly complementary, approaches. The first is not really a 'theory' at all, but a set of empirically tested principles; the second is an over-arching theory, largely untested and even untestable. Each has something to offer the teacher.

Principles of reinforcement

The work of Skinner, though based on behaviourist assumptions, is pragmatic rather than theoretical. He refuses to speculate about what should be reinforcing and why, but concentrates on demonstrating the effects of reinforcement on learning. Most of his work was carried out on hungry animals, but the principles seem to work for well-fed humans, too. His work derives from Thorndike who stated that actions followed by pleasant consequences were more likely to be repeated, and vice versa. By following this simple hypothesis, Skinner has been able to elicit extraordinary sequences of behaviour, like pigeons playing ping-pong with their beaks, by manipulating reinforcements. Many teachers reject his approach on moral grounds, but changing behaviour by reinforcement need not be morally offensive, if it is done with the knowledge and consent of the learner. It can even be done by the learner himself. One could claim that any curriculum is an attempt to change the behaviour (I am using the word in a very wide sense here to include thinking and attitudes as well as more easily observable actions) of students, so why should we not do it as effectively as we can? Every day, we are reinforcing and reinforced; at least a knowledge of how reinforcement works could help us to avoid reinforcing non-desired responses. One mistake often made even by the best of teachers is to reinforce by attention to a troublesome pupil, while withdrawing the reinforcement when she is doing something constructive.

Using reinforcement

1 Choose a reinforcement that works for the individual pupil. Most of us respond to praise, attention, success, but there is usually a wide range of reinforcements open to the teacher. Programmed learning is based partly on the assumption that knowledge of results (usually knowledge that you are right) is reinforcing, but knowledge of being wrong is not reinforcing to all learners, and probably to none if the information is insufficient to help better understanding.

2 Select the behaviour that needs to be changed and label it as accurately as you can. Much of the experimental work is concerned with such simple behaviours as sitting down at desks, not shouting out, slow work-rate, but in theory we could increase more cognitive kinds of behaviour if we were able to recognize instances of them. We could, for instance, deliberately reinforce original responses, or the asking of questions.

3 Establish a base-line for the frequency of the behaviour. This exercise alone can be illuminating. It is easy for any of us to have an inaccurate, impressionistic view of what is actually happening. An example quoted by Harris *et al.* (in Roberts, 1975) concerned a nursery-school child who pinched adults. Ignoring the behaviour did not work, because he pinched too hard, so the teachers tried to develop the 'substitute behaviour' of patting. The rate of patting, which was reinforced by praise, certainly increased, but the data recorded by the observer who was actually making a count of the pats and the pinches showed that, contrary to the teachers' impressions, pinching continued at its previous level.

4 Use effective reinforcement immediately after the desired behaviour. If the final behaviour is not within the

student's repertoire, use 'successive approximations'. For the student who finds writing an onerous task, you might reward him for writing a short caption in the first few sessions, gradually stepping up your criteria until he is writing paragraphs. Skinner calls this 'shaping' behaviour. Obviously all teachers try to do something like this, but what is new about his work is the precision and consistency with which he applied the common-sense principles. In the average classroom reinforcement is usually haphazard rather than methodical.

Once the behaviour has been established, it is not necessary to reinforce every manifestation. If reinforcement is completely discontinued, however, the behaviour will tend to be extinguished. Skinner found that different schedules of reinforcement produced different patterns of behaviour:

Fixed interval. Reinforcement given for the first response after a fixed period of time. This is the sort of pattern we use when students know when their work will be seen or tested. It produces a high rate of response just before the reinforcement is due, and a steep drop immediately after. For discouraging some behaviours it is useful as the response is highly resistant to extinction, for example administering a reward for each hour that a student does not interrupt others.

Fixed ratio. The piece-work pattern. This produces a high rate of response, as the faster you work, the more reinforcements you gain.

Variable interval. The timing of reinforcements is irregular, but must obviously be within reasonable limits. On this sort of schedule, a teacher might plan to see each student's work within a certain time, but vary the intervals so that any one pupil may be called on twice in succession. It is more effective to give immediate reinforcement to some pupils than delayed reinforcement to all, provided that each student has his share of reinforcement.

Variable ratio. The gambling pattern. Any response may be the lucky one. This pattern produces a very high rate of response, and is strongly resistant to extinction.

The teacher is not the only source of reinforcement in a classroom. Students can be self-reinforcing, motivated by interest, or checking out their ideas and work against information supplied in a curriculum programme. The Open University uses this strategy in its curricula. For further examples of student self-reinforcement, see Roberts (1975, pp. 159–64, 191–4).

The major application of Skinnerian principles to curriculum planning has been in programmed learning, which can be with or without machines. Essentially, the information to be learned is broken into small steps, and the learner receives constant feedback about his performance. Skinner also provides a guide to the use of *incentives* by the teacher; very often a necessary supplement or stimulus to whatever self-motivation the pupil brings into the learning situation.

Humanistic psychology

By contrast, humanistic psychology is interested in self-motivation, and stresses the powers for learning which we possess without external prods and systems of reward and punishment. The term 'humanistic' can be seen as a reaction against the mechanistic approach of behaviourism which dominated psychology until the 1960s, and against the translation of experiments with animals into statements about human beings. Psychologists like Maslow (1954), Schutz (1972) and Rogers (1969), are interested in the attributes of persons, rather than organisms, attributes like consciousness, self-awareness, will, intention. It is true that humanistic psychologists owe something to psychoanalysis, but they are more optimistic in their view of human beings, concerned with enlarging potential rather than curing neurosis.

Maslow

Abraham Maslow was one of the earliest of the 'Third Force' or humanistic psychologists, and one who has given us a more worked-out theory than the others to date. Because humanistic psychology concentrates on *being*, on present experience, it is rather short on theoretical underpinning and convincing evaluation. Maslow's hierarchy of needs accepts the 'animal' and 'human' nature of persons, bridging the two views of motivation.

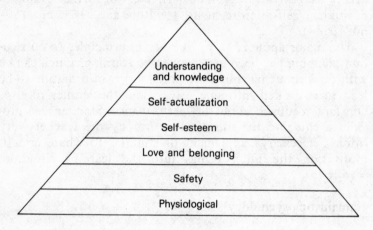

Figure 6. Hierarchy of needs

He believed that we become fully human when the inherent needs of our nature are realized. The higher orders of need do not emerge until those below are fairly well satisfied. Psychological needs, like hunger, will occupy our attention and energy until they are satisfied, then we are free to move on. The most brilliant lecture ever given is likely to be lost on the student whose bladder is bursting. There are obvious exceptions to Maslow's hierarchy, like fasting for reasons of religion or vanity, but if it, in general, represents reality, it is obviously important for us as teachers to ensure that the needs preceding the level of understanding and knowledge are satisfied, and not merely assume, as we so often do, that our concern is with the final level only.

One criticism made of humanistic psychology is that it ignores the social context in which we live, and is narrowly individualistic in its orientation; a psychology for the privileged, for whom choice is possible. Certainly, it is existential, presupposing some power of the individual to make decisions at every point. But when we consider the motivation of children in school, rather than using the crude measure of social class, it might be helpful to think in terms of the unsatisfied needs that could interfere with learning.

Significant learning

Carl Rogers (1969) defines significant learning:

> *It has a quality of personal involvement* – the whole person in both his feeling and cognitive aspects being in the learning event.
> *It is self-initiated.* Even when the impetus or stimulus comes from the outside, the sense of discovery, of reaching out, of grasping and comprehending, comes from within.
> *It is pervasive.* It makes a difference in the behaviour, the attitudes, perhaps even the personality of the learner.
> *It is evaluated by the learner.* He knows whether it is meeting his need, whether it leads toward what he *wants* to know, whether it illuminates the dark area of ignorance he is experiencing. The locus of evaluation, we might say, resides definitely in the learner, *its essence is meaning.* When such learning takes place, the element of meaning to the learner is built into the whole experience.

This has a double implication for the curriculum. First, that we should attempt to make significant for our learners what we think they ought to know; second, and more radically, that we should try to find out what is significant to them, and allow that to be the substance of the curriculum.

Carl Rogers believes that there are ways of facilitating (a term he much prefers to 'teaching') significant learning in our students. Much of his work is based on his experience as a psychotherapist, as well as a teacher. Most teachers shy away from anything that smacks of psychotherapy; British reserve makes us smile or shudder at the Californian excesses of 'personal growth'. The term 'encounter group' conjures up bizarre visions of nudity, murderous anger, destruction of defences, tears and maudlin avowals of insincere love. How different from us.

Instead of resisting, quite properly, the intrusion of medical concerns into teaching, it is possible to see psychotherapy as an educational process. What has to be learned is both wider and narrower than the usual school programme, but we as teachers can learn a lot from the descriptions of the learning processes that occur in therapy. It is not until people are emotionally involved that real learning can take place; mere

77

verbal learning has no influence on behaviour. The qualities in the facilitator which seem to foster real learning are, so Carl Rogers says, the same as those of the good teacher. The first quality is realness or genuineness: 'he is a person to his students, not a faceless embodiment of a curricular requirement nor a sterile tube through which knowledge is passed from one generation to the next'. This may cut against the role of teacher to which most of us have been socialized, but if you think back to the teachers who most influenced you, they probably brought more of themselves into the classroom than is usual. Being real means being able to express negative feelings, too. But there are ways and ways of doing this. Consider the difference between: 'I don't like the classroom to be messy. What are we going to do about clearing up?' and 'What kind of homes do you come from to make a mess like this? You are the most disgusting, sloppy class I ever met.' Being real gives more freedom to others to be real also.

The second quality cited by Carl Rogers is: 'prizing the learner, prizing his opinions, his feelings, his person. It is a caring for the learner, but a non-possessive caring. It is an acceptance of this other individual as a separate person, having worth in his own right.' Most teachers would agree; then talk in the staffroom of the 'rubbish' in their classes. But when a student of yours has flourished, how often has it been because you saw him/her as a person, to be respected, rather than as a cipher, to be graded?

The third quality is empathic understanding, the ability to see things from the student's point of view. Sometimes, an imaginative effort is called for. One teacher recently described his experience in following through an entire school day with a first-year secondary pupil, with a view to assessing the language demands made on him. He was amazed by the bewildering variety of tasks demanded of the child. Empathy is very different from the I-know-what's-wrong-with-you sort of diagnosis; it is non-evaluating, accepting.

There is a place in teaching for both views of motivation. Maslow can help us to see our day-to-day activities against a wide background; Skinner can help us to ensure efficient learning of a particular task. A structured course of learning will sometimes be appropriate; at others, a more open-ended exploration of possibilities based on what the learner *wants* to know will provide the best learning. The art of teaching is to know when to encourage, when to exert pressure, and when to leave alone.

Further reading

For a summary of theories of motivation see Child (1973, chapter 3). A more detailed account is in Vernon (1969). For an account of feelings in learning, and how they can be used, see Jones (1972). Essential reading in humanistic psychology is Maslow (1943, 1954, 1968), Rogers (1961, 1969) and Lyon (1971).

Chapter 9

Theories of Cognitive and Moral Development

Maggie Ing

The study of the mental development, and to a lesser extent of the emotional and social development, of children has had a profound influence on curriculum. Both *what* and *how* we teach has been reconsidered in the light of new theories of children's capabilities and thought processes. Two of the most significant theorists for curriculum studies are Piaget and Bruner.

Piaget

Every teacher knows of Piaget, but few have read much of his own work. It is difficult, in considering his work, to arrive at a level between oversimplification and great complexity. Two main strands run through his books:

1 the phenomena he demonstrates, which are striking, easily grasped and full of apparent relevance for teaching;

2 the conceptual system he evolves, which is difficult, complex and subtle.

His concern is the study of knowledge as it is revealed in the cognitive growth of children, with the emphasis on the development of logico-mathematical thought. In the conceptual system he evolves three themes:

1 **Logic**, which has a central role. If logic is inherent in the mind, in biological processes and in the laws governing the physical world, it must be the key to man's understanding.

2 **Relativity**. The conceptual judgments of a person are always relative to the position of the observer making those judgments. 'Reality' always involves some subjective element – it is always, at least in part, a projection or externalization of thought or action. This concept permeates Piaget's thinking about the *construction*, rather than the acquisition, of knowledge.

3 **Dialectics**. Piaget sees the dynamics of mental growth as a dialectic process. We constantly test hypotheses about the world. Mental growth is determined by maturation, physical experience and social experience. To these, Piaget adds *equilibration*, which determines the interaction of the other three. At each level of development, there are two poles of activity: changes in the structure of the organism in response to environmental intrusion (accommodation) and changes in the intruding stimuli in contact with existing structures (assimilation). An equilibrated system is never static, but always mobile and open.

The importance of Piaget for the curriculum

Piaget's stages of conceptual development have been very influential. The Nuffield Mathematics Project, for example, is based on an acceptance of their validity. Some summarized version of his work has been taught to student teachers for many years so it is likely that his influence, however diluted, is widespread. For a brief summary of the stages, see Lawton (1973, pp. 50–1). Those of most concern to teachers are:

Pre-operational: Intuitive (mental age approximately four to seven years). At the beginning of this stage, the child is very dependent upon superficial perceptions of his environment. He appears to be unable to hold in mind more than one aspect of what he sees at any one time. Hence, in the well-known experiments where children are asked if water poured into a different container is the same as or different from what it was before, they may respond that there is more (or less) according to the shape of the vessel. A child may respond to the water level, but fail to take into account the width of the container. Clay moulded into different shapes evoked the same results — a ball rolled into a sausage will be seen as 'more' because it is longer, or occasionally 'less' because it is narrower. It seems that children at this stage cannot mentally reverse the operation they have just seen. Piaget's interpretations have been challenged. Peter Bryant (1974) suggests that what the child cannot do is recall what he has seen; strategies for remembering rather than illogical thinking may account for failures of conservation.

Concrete Operations (mental age approximately seven to eleven years). Conservation is essential for reasoning at the concrete stage of operations. A child would, for example, have to be aware that $3 + 4 + 1$ is the same as $1 + 4 + 3$, or any other sequence of the numbers. According to Piaget, conservation of different properties emerges at different times during this stage; conservation of substance is acquired early, then conservation of weight, while conservation of volume appears at the end of this stage. The child becomes increasingly able to take into account several features of what he sees. Consistent classifications are formed, but the child's reasoning is still tied to objects and experiences.

Formal Operations (mental age approximately twelve to fifteen years). At this final stage, the child can reason hypothetically, without being in the presence of material evidence. The form of an argument can be grasped, independently of its content. Hypotheses can be set up mentally, rather than in the trial and error method of earlier stages, and inconsistencies perceived.

W. Kenneth Richmond (1971) in 'The School Curriculum' is rather critical of Piaget's view of developing mental powers. He comments:

> Eventually this detachment from the senses becomes total and he (the child) attains the symbolic level where he is at last free to enjoy the combinatorial power of rational thought, to inhabit a stratosphere where all baser passions have been left behind, and where all his subjective hunches are transcended by his mastery of problem-solving.

Experience certainly shows us that not everyone over the age of fifteen applies strict rationality to every area of life, and the use of formal operations does not seem to be uniformly attained. But the postulation of a hierarchical unfolding of conceptual skills is of obvious importance in curriculum planning and implementation. Lawton (1973) suggests that Piaget is useful in a negative way – he can inform us about what we should not attempt with children at different stages. Much of the research generated by Piaget's work has concentrated on the conditions which can accelerate transition from stage to stage; instruction, as Bruner showed, is an important variable, as is experience, which Peter Bryant's (1974) work demonstrates. Individuals are not always at the same stage in every aspect of school work. Most of Piaget's work has been applied to mathematics and science; more research is needed to provide us with similar maps of growing competence in other kinds of knowledge. None the less, Piaget has highlighted the need for us to move from practical work to more abstract thinking; his notion of the construction of reality suggests an active, exploratory approach to learning; and he has made us aware of the qualitative difference between the thinking of children and the thinking of adults, even if we do not accept his account of those differences in totality.

Bruner

Piaget's work provided the starting point for Bruner, who takes up a more flexible view of the development of thinking, involving three *modes* rather than stages of thought. The three modes of thinking he outlines are:

1 the enactive – which corresponds to Piaget's sensori-motor stage;
2 the iconic – in which imagery is dominant;
3 the symbolic – which grows with language.

Bruner says that these modes of representing reality develop in that order, but that they all remain with us in adult life. The dominance of any mode will depend partly on maturation, partly on personality, partly on the task in hand and partly on cultural influences. In this, he differs significantly from Piaget. In his cross-cultural studies (Bruner, 1965; 1971, chapter 2) he shows that schooling makes a great deal of difference to the dominance of the symbolic mode.

Bruner sees cognitive growth as the process of internalizing the ways of acting, imagining and symbolizing that exist in the culture. Three major issues emerge in his work.

1 *The growth of equivalence.* Western children go from initial reliance on surface sensory properties to reliance on common uses to which things can be put, then to common linguistic classification. The logical structures in a child's language are more advanced than the logical structures of behaviour. For example, category and hierarchy are present in the language even of a two-year-old, but he cannot group blocks of different size and colour using these principles.

2 *The development of 'efficient' information seeking.* The child's mode of search for information changes in a regular way with growth. Initially, he/she deals with a single feature of a problem, then deals with more than one feature, and finally analyses information largely through the use of language.

3 *The establishment of invariance as a tool of thinking.* When the child has to *do* something rather than *tell* the answer, he/she is capable of actions that are rooted in conservation, i.e. the concept that although appearances may have changed, substances can still be the same.

On these, the notion of the spiral curriculum is based. Bruner sees the basic structure of concepts existing in the enactive mode of thought, so that it should be possible to introduce a child to concepts in a form appropriate to his way of thinking, then to return to re-present the concepts in different ways as he becomes capable of handling them in more advanced forms.

Influence of Bruner on the curriculum

The idea of translating the key concepts of knowledge into materials that can be grasped by children has exciting implications for the curriculum. Bruner first worked out this hypothesis with mathematics, then applied it to the social sciences in his 'Man: a Course of Study' (MACOS) curriculum.

His aim was not to 'get across' a particular content, but to develop the powers of the learners. 'The more "elementary" a course and the younger its students, the more serious must be its pedagogical aim of forming the intellectual powers of those whom it serves' (Bruner, 1972, p. 57). The three basic questions which shaped the course were: What is human about human beings? How did they get that way? How can they be made more so? The content chosen to stimulate the asking and answering of these questions was a series of films, slides, tapes and written presentations concerning tool-making, language, social organization, the management of man's prolonged childhood, and man's urge to explain. Its aims were fivefold:

1 To give the pupils respect for and confidence in the powers of their own minds.

2 To give them respect for the powers of thought concerning the human condition, man's plight, and his social life.

3 To provide them with a set of workable models that make it simpler to analyse the nature of the social world in which they live and the condition in which man finds himself.

4 To impart a sense of respect for the capacities and plight of man as a species, for his origins, for his potential, for his humanity.

5 To leave the student with a sense of the unfinished business of man's evolution.

It is obvious that, despite their excellence, the particular materials chosen to develop these aims are only a few of the many possible choices. For Bruner, the aims of fostering cognitive growth precede selection of content. This is a very different approach from one which would specify the content of a curriculum that children should be expected to learn by a given age or stage. He is more concerned with skills, processes and attitudes than with facts. Not that facts are not important; skills cannot be learned in the absence of experiences and materials; but *which* facts and experiences should be selected depends on their power to develop cognitive growth. The same results could be achieved by many different selections from all the possibilities. If schooling is concerned with the development of the three modes of representing reality, and their integration, it follows that we should provide opportunities for manipulating the environment, for perceiving and imagining, and for symbolic representation to their fullest extent. To focus on one mode only is to constrict the growth of understanding. Bruner's famous statement that any subject can be taught in some intellectually honest form to any child shows the need for us to understand how a child is structuring his knowledge at present, so that we can amplify his power.

Bruner has been criticized on several grounds (apart from the apparent assumption in MACOS that we live in a uni-sexual world). One pressing practical question is, given that it is possible to teach anything to any child, can it be done by any teacher? A spiral curriculum would ideally need a team of experts, including teachers. If we all have to be experts on every subject, are impossibly heavy demands being placed on teachers, especially teachers of young children? And is the alternative of a teacher-proof curriculum without problems? Richard M. Jones (1972) criticizes Bruner for overconcentrating on cognitive development at the expense of emotional development. But since Bruner is openly dealing with cognitive growth, this may be a misplaced, if useful, criticism.

Piaget offers a more definite pattern of intellectual development, but Bruner's more flexible scheme, and his active interest in the effects of teaching and experience, could make his work more relevant for teachers.

Moral development

Whatever else we would include in a school curriculum, moral education is of urgent concern to most teachers. An increasingly secular and pluralistic society has not lessened this concern, but impelled teachers to seek out more varied and more appropriate ways of bringing children to act, think and feel in morally responsible ways. The last few years have seen the development of several projects in moral education, like

'Lifeline', the Schools Council Project for Secondary Schools; the Farmington Trust has produced several studies, though not curriculum materials, relevant to moral education; and new curriculum projects in religious education, like the Schools Council Religious Education in Primary Schools Project currently being developed at Lancaster University, are remarkably like moral education projects in many of their concepts and suggested activities.

Moral education is a complex concept, involving emotion, reason and action. R. S. Peters, in *Reason and Compassion* (1973), argues against what he calls 'a view of the relationship between reason and passion which is both widespread and wrong-headed'. He maintains 'that the use of reason is a passionate business and that the emotional life can be more or less reasonable'. One might expect psychology to enlighten us about all three aspects of moral life, but the distinction between reason and passion is as widespread in psychology as in the rest of Western thought. Information and theory about the ways in which we come to think and feel in moral ways tends to come from different sources, so the teacher or curriculum planner has to draw on a range of sources. Most of the work on passion, or emotion, is derived from clinical studies of people judged by their societies to be malfunctioning; and most of the work on reason, or cognitive functioning, excludes consideration of feeling.

As early as 1908, William McDougall wrote, 'the fundamental problem of social psychology is the moralization of the individual by society'. Different psychological schools have offered their own explanations of how we become moral. Freud saw 'conscience' as derived from the child's internalizations of parental standards, with the consequent distortion and irrationality of the anxiety that children can feel. The super-ego he saw as part of the unconscious, driving us to unrealistic aspiration and guilt, unless the rational, conscious ego is strongly developed. The behaviourists see moral behaviour as the product of externally controlled rewards and punishments. Social-learning theorists like Bandura stress the importance of modelling and imitation. All of these observations are important when we consider moral education, but each offers only a partial view of what it takes for us to become morally responsible people.

Theories of moral development also offer a partial view, because they have been concerned with the growth of moral judgment, a necessary but not a sufficient condition for moral development. Within these limits, however, the theories of Piaget and Kohlberg have considerable implications for all teachers.

Piaget

The Moral Judgement of the Child (1932) presents a view of moral development very much in line with Piaget's theory of the development of the child's reasoning on a wider front. The first part of the book is concerned with the child's use and understanding of rules, for which Piaget chose the game of marbles, familiar to the children of four to thirteen (all of them boys) with whom he worked. The experimenter asked individual children how the game is played. From the children's responses, Piaget formulated four stages in the mastery of the 'jurisprudence' of the game.

Stage 1. The motor stage. At the earliest level, children were not aware of the rules, though their movements were not random.

Stage 2. The egocentric stage. The child begins to imitate others, but when a number of children at this stage play together, there is no attempt to use a unified set of rules. Each plays his own game.

Stage 3. The stage of incipient co-operation. At this stage, children act in accordance with a unified set of rules, and truly play together, though when questioned later they are not always able to formulate the rules.

Stage 4. The stage of codification. This stage does not emerge until the child is eleven to twelve; he knows the rules which are fixed in detail and known to the children's society as a whole.

In the second part of the investigation, children were asked to talk about rules in fairly free interviews. They were asked to invent a rule, then probing questions were asked, such as: 'Is it a real rule?' 'Is it a fair rule?' 'Do you think your father followed that rule when he was a little boy?' The youngest children had an egocentric concept of rules, which for them had no binding power. From above seven, at what Piaget called the transcendental stage, rules were seen to have come from adults and to be 'sacred and untouchable for ever'. Finally, the children became more autonomous, and saw rules as arising from mutual consent, therefore changeable by mutual consent.

In the third part of the book, Piaget explores children's concepts of justice and fairness. They listened to short stories involving intention and the consequences of actions, and were asked about the punishments that should follow. One story was of two boys who smashed cups — one boy, with good intentions, smashed a dozen cups on a tray behind the door; the other deliberately smashed one. Younger children thought that magnitude of punishment should depend on magnitude of damage; they could not include intention in their judgments. Only later could subjective responsibility be taken into account. In the same way, younger children thought that telling lies to adults was 'worse' than telling lies to children. 'Fairness' at first meant equal shares; but later, children took account of the needs of individuals.

Piaget sees two kinds of morality operating in children's lives; authoritarian, adult-imposed rules and the democratically evolved rules of the peer-group. He does not think that the second, and implicitly better, morality derives from the first. He says: 'it requires nothing more for its development than the mutual respect and solidarity which holds amongst children themselves'. He goes even further:

> It is . . . absurd and even immoral to wish to impose upon children a fully-worked-out system of discipline when the social life of children among themselves is sufficiently developed to give rise to a discipline infinitely nearer that inner submission which is the hallmark of adult morality.

This seems to imply a Rousseauesque view of the superiority of the uncorrupted child; later in the same passage, Piaget recommends Dewey for providing the sort of school in which children can develop their own morality. But it is likely to be greeted cynically by teachers faced with bullying and extortion rackets, not uncommon even amongst junior school children, and the rest of the unacceptable face of peer-group morality. He has not really solved the paradox of moral education, that children somehow must move from habit to reason, from acting out of fear or expediency to acting out of principles based on understanding and caring, by relegating the development of reciprocity to the social life of children. He can tell us what to expect, and what not to expect, by way of reasoning in children at different stages of development, and remind us of some of the ways in which schools can help to foster morality based on co-operation.

Traditional schools, whose ideal has gradually come to be the preparation for competitive examinations rather than for life, have found themselves obliged to shut the child up in work that is strictly individual: the class listens in common, but the pupils do their homework separately. This procedure, which helps more than all the family situations put together to reinforce the child's spontaneous egocentrism, seems to be contrary to the most obvious requirements of intellectual and moral development.

It is useful, if at times disheartening, to reflect on the 'hidden curriculum' and its messages for moral life; and it is useful to know the kinds of reasoning on moral matters that children are likely to be using. But, although Piaget does say that 'it would be unwise to rely upon biological "nature" alone to ensure the dual progress of conscience and intelligence', he does not suggest many positive strategies for accelerating or ensuring the development of rational morality in the usual school situation.

Kohlberg

The work of Lawrence Kohlberg (1963, 1964), in the USA, holds out more promise for the teacher. For twelve years, he and his colleagues at Harvard studied the same group of seventy-five boys (it is, incidentally, interesting that these studies of moral thinking should have included boys only; it could be simply that what boys do is regarded as typical of the rest of humankind; not an uncommon assumption in psychological research — studies with girls and women tend to be separately regarded, but studies with boys and men are used to make generalizations about both sexes) interviewing them at three year intervals. The boys were aged between ten and sixteen at the beginning of the study; twenty-two to twenty-eight at the end. In addition, Kohlberg has explored moral development in other cultures – in Britain, Canada, Taiwan, Mexico and Turkey. His technique was to present moral problems for discussion; the answers were taped and then analysed. Over the years of his study, Kohlberg elaborated a typological scheme describing general structures of moral thought.

Kohlberg's stages of moral thought. There are three distinct levels of moral thinking, and within each stage, two related levels, which may be considered as separate moral philosophies.

(a) *Pre-moral level*
Stage 1 The child is oriented to punishment and obedience. At this level, the only constraints are those imposed by potential punishments.
Stage 2 'Naive instrumental hedonism' – rewards are also important. The child conforms to rewards. The likely learning process is conditioning and moral considerations do not enter into the child's thinking.

(b) *Level of conventional rule conformity*
Stage 3 Good-boy, good-girl orientation. Good behaviour is that which is approved by others. There is much conformity to stereotyped images of what is majority or 'natural' behaviour. For the first time, intention becomes an important consideration. Kohlberg puts Charlie Brown of the Peanuts cartoons at this level. The child (or adult – one of the advantages of Kohlberg's scheme is that his stages are not strictly linked to ages) seeks approval by being 'nice'.
Stage 4 Orientation towards authority, fixed rules, and the maintenance of the social order. Correct behaviour consists of doing one's duty, showing respect for authority, and maintaining the given social order for its own sake.

(c) *Level of morality of self-accepted moral principles* (post-conventional level)
Stage 5 The morality of contract. Right action tends to be

> defined in terms of general rights, and standards that have been examined and agreed upon by the whole of society. The resulting point of view is somewhat 'legalistic', but laws are seen as changeable rather than frozen, as in stage 4.
> **Stage 6** The morality of individual principles of conscience.
> At this level, principles are abstract and ethical, not concrete moral rules like the Ten Commandments.

Kohlberg is not sure whether all people at stage 6 go through stage 5, or whether these are two alternative mature orientations. But he is certain that the preceding stages represent an invariant sequence of development. It is possible for someone to stop at a given stage, but not to skip any.

One of his moral dilemmas 'Should the doctor mercy-kill a fatally ill woman requesting death because of her pain?' elicited these responses from the same boy at different stages of his development:

> Maybe it would be good to put her out of her pain, she'd be better off that way. But the husband wouldn't want it, it's not like an animal. If a pet dies you can get along without it – it isn't something you really need. Well, you can get a new wife, but it's not really the same.

(Age thirteen, stage 2; the value of the woman's life is partly contingent on its hedonistic value to the woman herself, but even more on its instrumental value to the husband.)

At the age of sixteen, he had moved to stage 3.

> It might be best for her, but her husband – it's a human life – not like an animal; it just doesn't have the same relationship that a human being has to family. You can become attached to a dog, but nothing like a human, you know.

(The value of the woman's life is no longer seen in instrumental terms, but is based on the husband's love. A stage 4 response would see life as sacred in terms of its place in a categorical moral or religious order.)

Kohlberg found the same structures, but different content, in cross-cultural studies. In one village in Taiwan, he asked boys of ten to thirteen what should a man do if his wife is starving, but he has no money and the shopkeeper won't give him any food. Many of the boys said that he should steal the food, 'because if she dies, he will have to pay for her funeral'. The response from Mexican boys tended to be that he should steal the food because he needs his wife to cook for him (all stage 2 responses).

In planning moral education, Kohlberg's scheme is more flexible and more informative than Piaget's. Typically, Kohlberg found, a child will make 50 per cent of his responses clearly at one stage, while the other 50 per cent tend to be spread in the stages immediately above and below. This is where teaching could make a difference. Each step of development is a better cognitive organization than the last; it takes account of everything present in the previous stage, but makes new distinctions and organizes them into a more comprehensive structure. In experimental discussion classes, Kohlberg discovered that:

1 children and adolescents comprehend all stages up to their own, but not more than one beyond;

2 they preferred the next stage;

3 a child at an earlier stage tends to move forward when confronted with the views of a child one stage ahead, but a child at a more advanced stage does not accept, though he understands, the arguments of the earlier stage.

This points out the usefulness of discussion amongst children, a way of harnessing the possibilities of peer-group learning.

Research following on Piaget (e.g. Simon and Ward, 1973) has found a positive correlation between moral judgment and measured intelligence. But, as Kohlberg says, 'You have to be cognitively mature to reason morally but you can be smart and never reason morally.' He connects moral growth with *social* development, especially the amount of opportunity for role-taking. The everyday social life of school and classroom provides many opportunities for moral learning, especially if the teacher deliberately or intuitively is sensitive to the possibilities. A more structured programme should involve discussion and problem-solving. Turiel (1974) tested out, and confirmed, two of Kohlberg's hypotheses, that the sequence of stages is invariant, and that each stage represents a reorganization and displacement of preceding stages. He postulated that cognitive conflict is the central condition for reorganization.

The strategies and rationale that served earlier become insufficient in the light of new experiences and new problems. Although Kohlberg, like Piaget, maintains that adult intervention is not essential for this process, it should be possible for a teacher to create or use problems, thus facilitating the transition from stage to stage, provided she does not try to move the child more than one stage from his current position. This demands close knowledge of individual children; Kohlberg found that not all children of the same age were equally developed in their moral reasoning, and that some children with high measured intelligence were 'slow developers' in moral matters. It is only by inviting children to talk, and by *listening* to what they say — not such a common practice in schools — that we could find out the kind of thinking used by our pupils. Piaget and Kohlberg chose to confine their investigations to moral judgment, but as teachers we cannot ignore the importance of feeling and motivation. No one has yet given us a clearly defined set of stages in emotional development. But moral education must develop the capacity to empathize and to care. R. S. Peters (1973) asks: 'Is not the capacity to love, as well as the capacity to reason, important in the form of morality?'

Further reading

Cognitive development

Introductory: Lawton (1973, pp. 49–57).

Slightly more detailed basic reading: Child (1973, chapter 5).

More advanced reading: Stones (1970, section 2, chapter 7). Halford (1972), a useful summary of research stemming from Piaget's work. Turner (1975, chapters 1, 2 and 4), up-to-date and inexpensive, if rather tightly packed, overview of theories and experiments. Bryant (1974), an alternative, based on experimental work, to Piaget's theory; particularly recommended to those interested in primary and middle school children, or those with a strong interest in Piaget's theories. Beard (1969). Boyle (1969), a fairly simple introduction. Flavell (1963), difficult, but probably the next best thing to reading Piaget himself. Piaget and Inhelder (1958). Bruner (1965, chapters 1 and 2), the most comprehensive statement of his modes of thinking; difficult. Bruner (1972, chapter 2), a short, relatively easy account of how a school curriculum should develop children's minds.

Moral development

Introductory: Wilson, Williams, Sugarman (1967, chapters 5 and 6).

Basic source books: Piaget (1932). Kohlberg (1963 and 1964, pp. 383–431). Peters (1973, especially chapters 1 and 2).

Research on Piaget and Kohlberg: Simon and Ward (1973) and Costanzo (1973) on Piaget. Turiel (1974) and Kohlberg (1976) on Kohlberg. Duska and Whelan (1977), a guide to Piaget and Kohlberg.

Chapter 10

Two Theories of Instruction: Bruner and Gagné

Maggie Ing

What is a theory of instruction?

Theories of learning, of development, of motivation, or of any other aspects of human behaviour relevant to the teacher, are not in themselves sufficient to provide a guide to practice. To apply their findings, concepts and models, we need an intermediate theory, setting out principles for action.

Bruner

Bruner (1966) sketches the essential features of a theory of instruction. It should certainly draw on theories of learning and development, but while psychological theories are *descriptive*, attempts to classify and explain a vast range of phenomena, a theory of instruction should be *prescriptive*. Piaget may tell us that the concept of conservation is not reached until the stage of concrete operations; a theory of instruction should set out the best ways of promoting under-standing of conservation. This involves not only psychological theory, but a sophisticated understanding of what is to be learned, of the structures of knowledge. In addition, a theory of instruction should be normative, its principles of a high degree of generality which can be adapted to a variety of learning situation.

Bruner envisages four major parts:

1 *Predispositions.* A theory of instruction should specify the experiences and conditions which make a person receptive to learning. He gives the example of pre-school experience, but it is possible that the factors governing predispositions in older students could be rather different. Information of a sociological kind could be useful here.

2 *Structure.* A theory of instruction should specify the 'optimal structure' of a body of knowledge so that it can be most easily learned by the individual. Such a structure would be relative to the learner's age, ability and experience. There would not be any one 'optimal structure', but a number of ways suitable to different students. By structure, Bruner means something more than mere content; he is referring to the power of systems in knowledge to simplify information, to generate new propositions and to increase the manipulability of what has been learned. The processes of learning, cognitive development and a grasp of the knowledge itself would be necessary.

3 *Sequence.* A theory of instruction should specify the most effective sequences in which to present what is to be learned. Again, sequence is relative to the learner. Younger or less experienced learners may do better with a sequence progressing from enactive through iconic to symbolic representation, while older or more knowledgeable learners may by-pass the first two stages. Optimal sequences are relative, too, to the criteria by which learning will be judged. Bruner cites speed of learning, resistance to forgetting, transferability, form of representation in which learning is going to be expressed, economy in terms of cognitive strain imposed, and power to generate new learning as some criteria which will not necessarily have equal weight in every task.

4 *Reinforcement.* A theory of instruction should specify the nature and pacing of reinforcements in the process of teaching and learning. Bruner thinks that the use of extrinsic incentives should be replaced by more intrinsic rewards, but when, and how? We need to know when to give knowledge of results in a way that makes it possible for the learner to use it. As Bruner says: 'If information is to be used effectively, it must be translated into the learner's way of attempting to solve a problem.'

The behaviourist studies of reinforcement, useful though they may be in establishing the order necessary for learning to take place and in helping the teacher to use extrinsic rewards when necessary, are narrower than Bruner's notion of reinforcement. To offer the right corrective information at the right time in the right way demands a knowledge of cognitive processes, cognitive development and an imaginative understanding of the individual. We need to know how to enable our pupils to become self-reinforcing. 'Instruction is a provisional state that has its object to make the learner or problem-solver self-sufficient' (Bruner, 1966).

As the title indicates, *Towards a Theory of Instruction* is a sketch and not a blue-print. Substantial information and conceptual models do exist, but we do not yet have answers to all the questions twelve years after Bruner posed them. The implications for the curriculum of his idea of what a theory of instruction should be are of four kinds. Firstly, it would be essential for a curriculum to be prepared jointly by experts in the subject-matter, teachers and psychologists. This would be feasible only for large-scale curriculum projects, and the results to date of such projects, like Science 5–13, have been somewhat disappointing (see Schools Council Research Studies, 1973). It may be possible that individual teachers working together with their individual pupils can achieve learning of a kind at least as good as that resulting from the well-planned, carefully researched curriculum package. It may be that the highly structured curriculum is more suitable for some learners and some teachers and some tasks. We simply do not know enough as yet about the kinds and conditions of learning to be sure.

It is true, second, that Bruner does mention the importance of individual differences, which argues for pluralism and 'enlightened opportunism in the materials and methods of instruction'. He agrees that no single ideal sequence exists for any group of children, but refuses to draw the conclusion that it is impossible to put together a curriculum which would satisfy a cross-section of children. The curriculum, rather, must be flexible enough to contain different ways of activating children, different ways of sequencing knowledge, different opportunities to 'skip' parts, or work on additional parts. I find it hard to imagine how a highly structured curriculum could contain all this possibility for diversity. Would there be, as in the Humanities Curriculum Project (HCP), a range of different back-up materials, which may be used or not as the teacher chooses? (But the HCP is hardly a planned sequence of instruction -- see Schools Council Research Studies, 1973.) Or would there be programmed information with several branches and loops? Bruner concludes his summary reference to individual differences, 'A curriculum, in short, must contain many tracks leading to the same goal.' It is a conclusion that seems at variance with the rest of his argument.

The third implication drawn out by Bruner is that ongoing evaluation of the curriculum is essential. However, he sees this evaluation taking place when the curriculum is being constructed, prior to dissemination, rather than while it is being used in schools. Expert observation and experimental method should perfect the curriculum in its developmental stages, after which it can safely be sent out. This view of curriculum is more likely to be embraced in a country which has more central control over the curriculum than we have been used to. A contrasted approach is explored in chapter 23.

Finally, we look at the theme which runs throughout much of Bruner's work, that the curriculum should be concerned with the business of *knowing*, not just with knowledge. Whatever we teach should increase the power of learning. We should be concerned with the process, rather than the product. Knowing, however, involves knowing *something*, and it is possible that Bruner underestimates the importance of what we should teach. It was commonplace in the sixties to point to the rapid obsolescence of knowledge and maintain that we needed to educate for flexibility, creativity, adjustment to change. The present climate seems to remind us that there are, after all, particular skills and kinds of information that all children need.

Gagné

Gagné's theory of instruction is more narrowly concerned

with pedagogy than is Bruner's. He has little to say about knowledge, except to categorize it in terms of learning outcomes (see chapter 7), and he tends to take for granted the content of the curriculum. His main interest is to show how and where teachers can intervene in the learning process, in order to facilitate it. He, too, concentrates on the importance of developing powerful learning, of a kind which leads to further learning and the transference of principles and skills from one situation to another. Table 2 shows the ways in which instruction can influence learning.

TABLE 2   Processes of learning and the influence of external events

Learning phase	Process	Influencing external events
Motivation	Expectancy	1 Communicating the goal to be achieved; or 2 Prior confirmation of expectancy through successful experience
Apprehending	Attention; selective perception	1 Change in stimulation to activate attention; 2 Prior perceptual learning, or 3 Added differential cues for perception
Acquisition	Coding; storage entry	Suggested schemes for coding
Retention recall	Storage retrieval	Not known 1 Suggested schemes for retrieval; 2 Cues for retrieval
Generalization	Transfer	Variety of contexts for retrieval cueing
Performance	Responding	Instances of the performance ('examples')
Feedback	Reinforcement	Informational feedback providing verification or comparison with a standard

Table 2 describes the *general* characteristics of an act of learning; more particular interventions are shown in Table 3.

TABLE 3   A summary of external conditions which can critically influence the processes of learning

Class of learning objective	Critical learning conditions
Verbal information	1 Activating attention by variations in print or speech 2 Presenting a meaningful context (including imagery) for effective coding
Intellectual skill	1 Stimulating the retrieval of previously learned component skills 2 Presenting verbal cues to the ordering of the combination of component skills 3 Scheduling occasions for spaced reviews 4 Using a variety of contexts to promote transfer
Cognitive strategy	1 Verbal description of strategy 2 Providing a frequent variety of occasions for the exercise of strategies, by posing novel problems to be solved
Attitude	1 Reminding learner of success experiences following choice of particular action; alternatively, insuring identification with an admired 'human model' 2 Performing the chosen action; or observing its performance by the human model 3 Giving feedback for successful performance; or observing feedback in the human model
Motor skill	1 Presenting verbal or other guidance to cue the learning of the executive sub-routine 2 Arranging repeated practice 3 Furnishing feedback with immediacy and accuracy

As Gagné himself points out, a course or lesson is usually concerned with more than one learning outcome. He suggests a checking procedure to ensure that all the desired outcomes have been covered in the planning of instruction, and a series of 'outcome questions' which are really behavioural objectives. For example, in a course in health education concerned

TABLE 4   Comparison of instructional events for three modes of instruction: group, tutorial, and individual learning

Instructional event	Group instruction	Tutorial instruction	Individual learning
Activating motivation	Teacher establishes common motivation	Tutor discovers individual motivation	Student supplies own motivation
Informing learner of objective	Teacher communicates objective to group	Tutor communicates objective to student	Student confirms or selects objective
Directing attention	Teacher stimulates attention of group members	Tutor adapts stimulation to student attention	Student adopts attentional set
Stimulating recall	Teachers asks for recall by group members	Tutor checks recall of essential items	Student retrieves essential items
Guiding learning	Teacher provides hints or prompts to group	Tutor provides guidance only when needed	Student supplies own strategies
Enhancing retention	Teacher provides retrieval cues to group	Tutor encourages student to use his own cues for retrieval	Student supplies own retrieval cues
Promoting transfer	Teacher sets transfer tasks for all members	Tutor sets transfer tasks adapted to student capabilities	Student thinks out generalizations
Eliciting performance	Teacher uses a test to assess performances of group members	Tutor asks for performance when student is ready	Student verifies his own performance
Providing feedback	Teacher provides feedback to students, varying in immediacy and precision	Tutor provides accurate and immediate feedback	Student provides own feedback

with drugs, one would wish for certain information to be understood and remembered, and for attitudes unfavourable to the abuse of drugs to be acquired. It would not be enough for the student to be able to state the required information and to originate new problems and their solutions; he would have to *choose* the intended personal action for the course to have been successful. In the area of attitudes, tests are of little use. Many educational outcomes are in the form of attitudes, and there is no way of testing real attitude change. Verbal reports of what one might do in particular situations are notoriously unreliable. Even within Gagné's apparently precise framework, faith and hope play a part.

Instruction is the deliberate intervention in or channelling of the learning process. It is not the same as 'education', but could form a legitimate part of education. The proportion of 'instruction' in the teacher's role varies from culture to culture and time to time, but it is difficult to see how teachers could avoid it altogether. The last table from Gagné, comparing group instruction, tutorial instruction and individual learning, sums up many of the debated questions of curriculum.

The third column, Individual learning, could be from Carl Rogers (see Chapter 8). We do not know when the learner is able to take responsibility for his own learning. 'Romantic' theories of education place the will to learn firmly in the child from his earliest years; 'classical' theories entrust the teacher. Practical experience suggests that most of us can sometimes be our own teachers, and at other times be in need of instruction. What we lack is guidance as to which of our pupils at which times can, and should, be allowed to conduct their own learning. It may be, as Gagné suggests, that there should be different theories of instruction for different age groups, and that theories suitable for children are being applied to the learning of adolescents and adults.

Summary

The scope of Bruner's and Gagné's theories of instruction is rather different. Both depend on theories of learning; Gagné specifically on an information-processing model of learning,

Bruner on a more eclectic but also cognitive model. There are differences in emphasis and elaboration of their assumptions about learning, but no real contradictions. Bruner pays much more attention to cognitive development; Gagné includes it as one of the factors in 'expectancies' and 'executive' control, but does not set it out in detail. Gagné offers specific strategies for teacher intervention and influence in the classroom; Bruner is concerned with curriculum planning at a more general level. The major difference between them is that, while Gagné assumes that decisions about what is to be taught will already have been made before the individual teacher puts into practice his instructional principles, Bruner is as much concerned with the nature of knowledge as with the nature of learning, and the nature of the learner. The usefulness of the two theories would seem to depend on how far the teacher is in a position to select what is to be taught as well as how to teach it to his pupils.

Further reading

Bruner (1966); Gagné (1970, 1974); Schools Council (1973).

Chapter 11

Creativity and Intelligence

Bill Gibby

In what ways have ideas about intelligence changed?

Many educationists have claimed that there is a relationship between 'intelligence' and 'creativity'. In 1904, Spearman (see Wiseman, 1973) had suggested that there was a universal intellectual ability 'g' which he claimed played a part in any person's intellectual activity, whilst, later, Thurstone (see Wiseman, 1973) presented a multi-factor view. Eventually, Spearman himself came to agree that there are general intellectual abilities more limited than his 'g'.

For many years most intelligence tests required single, correct responses, but Piaget's approach to the development of intelligence testing with children was different. He wanted to discover the kind of thought processes used by a child in responding to a question. He was interested in what actual answer a child gave, not whether it was right or wrong, and also he was concerned about the ways in which children's answers to the same question varied as they became older. During the past twenty-five years or so, research workers looking at the development of creativity have also been concerned with the actual way in which children think rather than with the precision of such thinking, and some of these workers have encouraged a relaxed atmosphere when questions were given.

Ways in which ideas on intelligence were changing can be seen from a study of the works of Burt and Hebb (Wiseman, 1973), and also in Vernon's extensions of Hebb's ideas, leading to suggestions that there were probably three different kinds of intelligence: A, B and C. Intelligence A was regarded as an inborn potentiality which we cannot measure precisely; intelligence B was claimed to be associated with the kind of all-round mental efficiency that people actually display in everyday life, at work or at school; and intelligence C was defined in terms of a 'score' on a recognized standardized intelligence test.

By 1959, Guilford (Wiseman, 1973) had provided empirical evidence against Spearman's 'g' and from that point the multi-factor theory of intelligence began to make rapid head-way. In the 1970s, some psychologists have suggested that there are many unique intellectual abilities that collectively can be regarded as composing intelligence. As a result of his experimental work on intelligence testing in the late 1950s, Guilford (Wiseman, 1973) developed a comprehensive theoretical system or model including all the known intellectual factors and predicting new ones not previously established. Guilford called this model 'A Structure of Intellect Model' and we will take a brief look at this later.

The apparent precision of Guilford's views on intelligence are perhaps in sharp contrast to the doubts raised by cross-cultural studies carried out by Jenson, Vernon and others (Wiseman, 1973), as are some of the issues raised by Hunt (Wiseman, 1973) in his attempts to see the wider implications of relating 'intelligence' and 'experience', in which he stresses more the importance of environmental conditions for developing intelligence rather than overstressing the acknowledged influence of individual genetic differences between children, but he does emphasize the importance, in this context, of considering the interaction between heredity and environment.

What circumstances led to the present stress on creativity? What is creativity?

Many writers (as, for example, in Wiseman, 1973) have suggested that current intelligence tests do tend to favour a conformist mentality in the sense that they favour those who are good at recalling facts, who accept implicitly what teachers say and who think along conventional lines. Nevertheless, the kinds of thinking which lead to high scores on conventional intelligence tests (i.e. the traditional verbal and non-verbal reasoning versions of these tests) do tend to be fairly closely related to success in school work, so that these kinds of intelligence tests do still have some use. But the usefulness of these tests is confined to obtaining information about the kind of thinking which requires single, correct answers. The thinking involved in such items is called, by Guilford (Vernon, 1970), 'convergent thinking'. Thinking which involves mainly the giving of many and varied responses is regarded by Guilford as 'divergent thinking'. It is now being claimed that intellect may manifest itself in at least two different modes, one which corresponds with what conventional intelligence tests attempt to measure through convergent thinking, with the other mode, divergent thinking, receiving less consideration.

Vernon (1970) and others remind us not only how difficult a term 'creativity' is to define but point out that the term does tend to be used very differently by different people. For example, some definitions are related to one, or more, of: personality, product, process and environmental conditions. When personality is emphasized, as by Cattell and Butcher (Vernon, 1970), a consideration of the traits that discriminate a so-called creative person from one who is not determines the factors which help to define creativity. With this kind of emphasis it could be suggested that a creative person should possess most of a defined list of traits, such as: intelligence, awareness, originality, persistence, fluency, humour and nonconformity. But a difficulty here is with the initial assumption that a person is either creative or not and with the meanings given to the listed traits, the extent to which each trait is present in a person and the doubtful assumption that the existence of such traits can be reliably and validly established. The above-mentioned general traits taken together do not seem to provide adequate grounds to separate the individual who it is claimed to be an analytically oriented person (i.e. the 'convergent' type of pupil to use Guilford's term) from the individual who it is claimed to be a creatively oriented person (i.e. Guilford's 'divergent' type). But the difference between an analytical and a creative person is probably of degree rather than of kind. Some studies, based on a detailed examination of personality traits, have looked closely at the background of people generally acknowledged to be highly creative, such as Shakespeare and Einstein, as revealed in biographical or autobiographical accounts. Such studies try to identify the qualities that such people have in common.

Then there are those who define creativity in terms of producing something new. To most of these, creative thinking means the production of something new to its creator. On the other hand there are those who insist that for a 'product' to be creative it must make a significant contribution to the culture and that it must be a considerable achievement in its own right, but most of us, as teachers, would tend not to accept this narrow use of the word 'creative'.

Others, such as Guilford (Vernon, 1970), see creativity as a mental process and part of a wider and broader concept of intelligence itself. But there are some who see creative thinking as both a process and product, i.e. who do not wish to separate the way a thing is produced from the end-product itself. But creativity can also be examined in terms of environmental conditions and Torrance (Vernon, 1970) refers to this kind of creativity when he calls upon teachers to recognize their pupils' creative talents and to provide the right kind of environment and conditions to help individuals to understand and develop their own divergence. But even before Torrance's work in this field had begun, Rogers (Vernon, 1970) had set out a tentative theory of creativity in which he considers the nature of a 'creative act', the conditions under which it occurs and the manner in which it may constructively be fostered.

Both Torrance (Vernon, 1970) and Rogers (Vernon, 1970) show considerable interest in the practical implications of any meaning that we might give to the term 'creativity' and, from their discussions, it seems clear that it is essential for any individual teacher to decide what creativity means to him personally and to make sure that he works out the best kind of conditions likely to promote and encourage his pupils' creativity in a variety of ways. But the difficulties of doing this have been emphasized by such writers as Williams (1965). For example, Williams shows that for a positive meaning to be given to words related to 'creativity' there is a need to discuss such words within an historical perspective, to relate the meanings produced to different cultures, as well as considering creative work in present-day arts and science.

An interesting analysis of what is involved in any creative process has been given by Wallas (Vernon, 1970). He suggests that such a process can be divided into four stages, which he designates as:

1 Preparation: the problem undertaken is investigated from all directions.
2 Incubation: the individual is not consciously thinking about the problem.
3 Illumination: this stage is not confined merely to a 'flash of insight' but also it includes the psychological events that precede and accompany its appearance.
4 Verification: the validity of the concepts being formed is tested and the ideas resulting are reduced to an exact form.

This classification calls for comment. All four stages are involved before a final product is created but the stages are not of equal importance and it is doubtful whether there are such discrete stages in a creative process, although (if such stages do exist at all) there may be, throughout any creative process, some kind of oscillation between stages, with the whole process gradually moving forward towards the production of an end-product.

A helpful discussion of the various meanings that have been given to 'creativity' has been offered by Jones, T.P. (1972). He discusses a number of issues, which he sees as pertinent in trying to formulate a definition of 'creativity' and these include a consideration of:

1 Einstein's assertion that the formulation of a problem is often more important than its solution.
2 Vernon's contention that without a high degree of intelligence no one is likely to produce creative results that are worthwhile.
3 Hudson's view that *both* convergent and divergent thinking could result in a creative product and his statement that the parallel between divergent thinking and creativity has been too lightly assumed. (Jones argues that the great

majority of people are both divergent and convergent thinkers according to the situation, the type of problem and the extent of the immediate and long-term motivation.)
4 Bruner's discussion of the importance of 'effective surprise', as, for example, the effect that some art has on observers. (Bruner, like Einstein, regards the creative process as more important than the product created. Bruner believes that creative quality can reside in almost any kind of human activity and that almost all people are capable of producing some creative work.) (In his discussion of Bruner's regard for 'effective surprise' and a 'shock of recognition' Jones reminds us of Hudson's belief that creativity 'if not born of unhappiness is born certainly of unease'.)

Jones concludes his own exploration of what others have to say about creativity by stressing its complex nature, and he acknowledges the impossibility of providing a universally acceptable definition.

What are the current trends in intelligence and creativity tests?

It was mentioned earlier that some writers have pointed out the one-sidedness of conventional intelligence tests, with an emphasis on so-called convergent thinking. More recently, tests have been produced which claim to concentrate more on so-called divergent thinking. These tests have often been labelled 'creativity' tests. In spite of the attempts by people like Torrance (Vernon, 1970) and Rogers (Vernon, 1970), no one is really sure yet just what the precise defining properties of creativity are, and the ability of creativity tests to predict later levels of creativeness has not yet been clearly established. The trouble with trying to measure what we feel to be creativity is that, by the very nature of its uniqueness, to produce a creativity score or quotient sounds as foolish and unacceptable as would a coefficient of humour, a kindness index or a love factor.

The really earnest work in this new testing field was pioneered by Guilford and some of this is described in his papers in Vernon (1970) and Wiseman (1973). But Guilford's experiments concerning the nature of creativity were only part of an attempt to build a general theory of intelligence. Guilford's view on intelligence testing means that he would regard both the more conventional type of intelligence tests and the newer creativity tests each as an essential component of a battery of intelligence tests. So it is in this way that Guilford has broadened the concept of intelligence to include creativity as one of its component parts.

Guilford claims that each mental ability has three aspects: content, process and product. For him, there was a need for a structure of intellect model. It is in the form of a solid rectangular block 5 units long, 4 units wide and 6 units high – giving 120 cubic units in his block. (Guilford discusses this model in his papers in Vernon (1970) and Wiseman (1973).) On this model each unit cube is claimed to be a unique combination of kinds of operation, content and product and so in this way Guilford is able to postulate 120 factors with a high proportion of them operationally defined.

Test items which tend to arise in testing the extent of convergent and divergent thinking exhibited in certain circumstances have been categorized into such sections as: 'uses of objects', 'pattern meaning', 'instances', and 'originality in plot titles'. Examples of the kinds of items set are:

1 Give some ideas for uses you could make of a brick.
(Convergent answers: build a wall; build a house.
Divergent answers: make a door stop; make a paper-weight; drown a cat.)

2 Look at the drawing below. Describe what you think it is.

(Convergent answers: letter O on a line; tangent to a circle.
Divergent answers: A bald man standing against a wall (as seen from above); a hedgehog having fun; a football balanced on a crossbar.)

3 Name all the things you can think of that move on wheels.

(Here a child's 'creativity' is measured by a combination of the total number of responses given and the uniqueness of these responses.)

4 Below is a short story. Give it a suitable title.

A missionary is captured by cannibals. The princess of the tribe wins a promise for his release if he will marry her. The missionary has a choice: death or the princess. He refuses marriage and is boiled alive.

(Convergent answers: Defeat of a princess; boiled by savages.

Divergent answers: Stewed parson; a mate worse than death; he left a dish for a pot.)

Naturally, there have been many criticisms of test items like the above and you are left to produce your own 'convergent' and 'divergent' criticisms!

In spite of being faced with much criticism, Guilford (Vernon, 1970; Wiseman, 1973) has emphasized the need for measures of both convergent and divergent thinking. He claims that convergent thinking is characterized by its dependence on the reproduction of the already learned and of fitting old responses to new situations and he feels that this kind of thinking is relatively easy to measure. He claims for divergent thinking that it involves fluency, flexibility and originality and is essentially concerned with a large number of unusual ideas and he admits that this kind of thinking is more difficult to measure.

Recently, 'creativity' test items have been included in some large-scale research projects in Britain. For example, the NFER, in their project on 'Streaming in the Primary School' (Barker Lunn, 1970), made use of such items in their experimental design and subsequently they claimed that they obtained 'useful' findings from this type of item as well as from the more conventional type of test items used.

How can teachers apply their knowledge of creativity to classroom experience and how do they react to creative children?

For most teachers, the main point in studying 'creativity' is to explore children's modes of thinking in such a way that the results will aid them in so organizing their pupils' environment that learning becomes exciting, productive and worthwhile.

Getzels and Jackson (Vernon, 1970) have offered illustrations in support of their hypothesis that, at a relatively high level of intelligence, we can distinguish between someone who scores highly on a conventional 'intelligence' test and who scores highly on a 'creativity' test. They distinguish between what they call a highly intelligent pupil and a highly creative one in terms that they regard the former as mainly a conventional person and the latter as mainly an original one. However, it is necessary to stress that they did not include in their experimental groups pupils who scored highly in both conventional intelligence tests and creativity tests and so we have no evidence here of 'pupil behaviour' from those pupils who show a great deal of originality in some situations but are quite conventional in others. Getzels and Jackson (Vernon, 1970) refer to those who score very highly on the creativity test, but not so highly on the conventional intelligence tests, as 'creative thinkers'. They claim, for this kind of thinker, compared with more conventional thinkers, that they are:

1 less concerned with scholastic success;
2 less favoured by teachers;
3 less apt to accept the teacher as a model to be copied;
4 interested in a much wider range of subjects;
5 richer in their sense of humour.

Torrance, Hudson and others (Vernon, 1970) have tended to emphasize that creativity adds to achievement by building up on to conventional intelligence and there appears to be some evidence that a minimal level of IQ is probably necessary for high levels of achievement, but that, beyond this level, the presence or absence of creativity is determined by other factors such as personality and the creation of the right kind of stimulation by good teachers. There is also some evidence to show that divergent thinking and convergent thinking interact in achievement.

Some of us, as teachers, do not always enjoy having so-called creative people in our classes and most of us do perhaps tend to favour the more orthodox, easily understandable people of high conventional intelligence but relatively low creativity. In Vernon (1970), particularly in the papers by Getzels and Jackson and by Torrance, we see evidence illustrating how creative children can be a nuisance in a traditional setting. However, it is perhaps for some of us sometimes quite difficult to distinguish between true independence of thought and high-spirited tomfoolery. Perhaps there are some dangers here for even the most capable and patient of teachers.

Some ways in which teachers can nurture the creativity of their pupils do emerge from many of the papers in Vernon (1970), from Lytton (1971), from Hudson (1972) and from Jones, T.P. (1972). Many of these writers on creativity seem to be discussing the extent to which statements like the following are applicable and workable at various stages of schooling:

1 Teachers should value creative thinking both in themselves and in their pupils.

2 Teachers should develop a tolerance of unusual ideas.

3 Pupils should be taught to value their own creative thinking.

4 Teachers should create the right kind of environment, and make available suitable resources, for the working out of pupils' unusual ideas.

5 Teachers should develop skills of constructive criticism amongst their pupils.

What criticisms have been made of creativity tests?

You will want to produce your own criticisms, but some comment on this question seems appropriate at this stage. Many people express doubts concerning creativity tests. Hudson has criticized the identification of 'divergent thinking' with 'creativity' and the assumption that tests of 'divergent thinking' are also tests of 'creativity'. Many writers decry any attempt to measure what they regard to be immeasurable.

But what doubt arises from the actual experimental evidence on available test results? It is clear from such evidence that no one has yet established that creativity tests are capable of being used to make successful long-range predictions that certain people are likely to do highly creative work.

Many criticisms have referred to creativity test items as somewhat superficial and trivial. It has been acknowledged that there may be some sort of 'intellectual fun' in attempting some of these items, but it is the claim that answers to such items measure anything of worth that really worries most critics. But, even if one admits to there being some worth in the 'scoring' of such items, would not different 'markers' of the test items tend to disagree on the convergent or divergent nature of some responses? Apart from doubting the reliability of any 'scores' given to answers of this kind, it is possible to challenge the validity of such scores as having little indication of a person's creative ability by reference to the evidence given by Wallach and Kogan (Vernon, 1970) who offer a constructive criticism of creativity tests. An appraisal of such criticisms seems to suggest that predictive values concerning the development of the creative abilities of any individual, if they can be obtained at all, can only really arise from longitudinal studies of the type suggested by Terman (Vernon, 1970).

Wallach and Kogan (Vernon, 1970) give clear evidence of the low reliabilities and doubtful validity of almost all existing creativity tests, and other papers in Vernon (1970) tend to show how much notions of what is meant by words like 'creative' and 'conventional' vary, not only from person to person, but also from culture to culture.

What are the implications for teachers of recent work on creativity?

From the work suggested for study in this chapter it is possible to ask to what extent we agree with the following types of statements posed by Torrance and others (Vernon, 1970):

1 Pupils should learn in creative ways *as well as* by authority.

2 Teachers should invite original responses *as well as* expected ones.

3 Teachers should emphasize creative, imaginative thinking *as well as* correctness in form, grammar and spelling.

4 Each one of us should learn to trust his own perceptions, ideas and judgments *as well as* being open to the ideas of others.

A great deal of imaginative and creative thinking will be needed to translate the implications of what has been considered here into something productive and worthwhile for the children or adults we teach. Blind, uncritical acceptance of some of the existing discussions and findings may well lead to classroom chaos. In some cases perhaps it already has.

Convincing evidence can only really come from a continuous evaluation of what is being done, linked subsequently with full-scale longitudinal studies of the type suggested by Terman (Vernon, 1970).

Further reading

Ways which ideas on intelligence have changed:

Wiseman (1973) edits a selection of papers illustrating how notions of intelligence have fluctuated somewhat between extremes:

Pioneer work:	Spearman's 'g'.
Structure of mind theories:	Vernon, Burt, Guilford.
Nature v. Nurture:	Hebb, Burt.
Cross-cultural studies:	Jensen, Vernon.
Wider implications:	Hunt.

The meaning of creativity; 'measuring' and stimulating it:

Vernon (1970) edits a selection of papers illustrating the complexity of this topic as a field of study:

Longitudinal studies:	Terman.
Theoretical contributions:	Wallas, Rogers.
Psychometric approaches:	Guilford, Getzels and Jackson, Hudson, Wallach and Kogan.

Personality studies: Cattell and Butcher.

Stimulating creativity: Torrance, Haddon and Lytton.

Williams (1965b), in chapter 1, examines the significance of the 'creative' idea.

Jones, T.P. (1972) discusses the meaning and possible measurement of 'creativity' and considers its relevance to educators, as well as providing some useful suggestions for nurturing 'creativity' in the curriculum.

Hudson (1972) considers the scientific 'converger' and the artistic imaginative 'diverger'.

Lytton (1971) analyses the creative process, discusses the relationship between 'intelligence' and 'creativity', considers what creative people are like, explores ways of nurturing creativity and gives examples of test items used for testing 'creative thinking'.

Part Three

Philosophical and Social Issues

Chapter 12

Tradition and Change in the Curriculum

Peter Gordon

The two traditions in English education

Any attempt to account for the curriculum offered in most schools today must be seen in terms of its historical background. It will then be possible to discern why some of the traditional views of the nature of the curriculum have persisted and to account for those factors which have made for change.

From the early nineteenth century we can broadly delineate the emergence of the two 'traditions' in English education. Robert Lowe (1867, p. 32), a leading Liberal statesman and in the 1860s the Vice-President of the Committee of Council on Education, summed up the situation as follows:

> The lower classes ought to be educated to discharge the duties cast upon them. They should also be educated that they may appreciate and defer to a higher cultivation when they meet it: and the higher classes ought to be educated in a very different manner, in order that they may exhibit to the lower classes that higher education to which, if it were shown to them, would bow and defer.

This dichotomy between the so-called elementary and grammar school traditions was reflected in the curriculum of the different schools.

Elementary education was equated with mass education using methods calling for mechanical obedience which were appropriate for future workers in factories. Joseph Lancaster's monitorial system, introduced shortly after the beginning of the nineteenth century, employed the principle of division of labour. It claimed that large numbers of children could receive instruction from one master only: that one book would serve a whole school instead of one for each child. Cheapness was combined with efficiency. The curriculum was necessarily a limited one. Most of the early schools were established and financed by religious bodies; one of the main objects of providing such education was to propagate the ability to read the Bible. Writing was at first discouraged but computation was considered useful. When the state began to take an interest in education from the 1830s, this narrow approach to the curriculum was continued. One inspector (in the *Minutes of the Committee of Council on Education 1840*, p. 168) suggested that it should comprise

> The 3 Rs, grammar and use of language; training in objects — use of clothes, money, clock, flowers, seeds, distance, etc; cottage economy — how to buy food cheaply, also clothes and fuels. How to keep out of hands of pawn-broker. On need for temperance. Savings banks and provident societies, on how to look after their health by training in adequate dieting, cleanliness and exercise. (How to survive in cellars); taught history, political economy, why laws should be obeyed, knowledge of the institutions of the country, rights of property; singing, art and music, knitting and sewing for girls.

The introduction of payment by results in 1862 made it essential for elementary schools to concentrate on the 3 Rs together with plain needlework for girls to the exclusion of 'non-paying' subjects. Accountability in the form of examination of individual children was established. Although the regulations were relaxed by the 1890s, the predominance of the 3 Rs in the curriculum did not disappear until well into the present century.

The other tradition was enshrined in the *secondary* or grammar school curriculum. This stemmed largely from the medieval grammar school which laid emphasis on ancient languages and the humanities. With the availability of a good transport system in the nineteenth century, public schools flourished. These schools aimed at producing gentlemen of character with a view to later public leadership. The continuity of the public school ethos is seen, for example, in a book, *The English Tradition of Education*, written in 1929 by the then headmaster of Harrow, Cyril Norwood. In a section entitled 'Ideals' there are three chapters on religion and one each on discipline, culture, athletics and service. The curriculum for those preparing to enter the Indian Civil Service in the late 1880s was suggested by one writer as

> Fairly good instruction in Latin and Greek, something more than in Porson and Elmsley's criticisms and a facility for composing verses; and a thorough acquaintance with French and German. I should require, were it possible, that the young men selected should have the manners and self-respect of well-bred English gentlemen; a good training in horsemanship; and I should go so far as to welcome as an adjunct a course of veterinary study.

The Taunton Commission investigated the state of 'secondary' schools. In 1868 it recommended the liberalizing of the traditional curriculum by introducing mathematics, one spoken language, two natural sciences, history, geography, drawing and music. Reforms were slow in taking place for two main reasons. Latin and Greek were considered the hallmarks of a first-class education and therefore retained their supremacy. Perhaps of greater importance was that there was no real effective central control over the secondary curriculum until the beginning of the present century. Even here the Board of Education Regulations (1904) steered it away from a scientific/technical bias which had been growing.

Little attempt was made to bridge the gap between the two types of curricula during the period under review. Indeed, where attempts were made by elementary schools to introduce 'advanced' subjects, as in the higher grade schools in the 1880s, these were countered with an expression of the 'over-education' of the board school pupil. This culminated in a test case being brought by the district auditor of the School Board for London against the authority in 1899 which established that it was illegal for certain subjects to be taught in elementary schools (*Cockerton* v *London School Board*).

So far, we have been considering the nature of the curriculum as practised in schools over time. There are, as can be seen, a number of important factors which will govern the direction given to changes whilst at the same time encouraging the persistence of existing practices.

Some important variables

The two traditions illustrate one of the crucial factors – the existing *ideologies* underlying the various types of curriculum. Raymond Williams (1961) has identified a number of different ideologies stemming from the nineteenth century, which determined the sort of curriculum which was adopted. Elite education, demanded by the landed gentry, was less concerned, as we have seen, with utilitarian aspects of the curriculum and stressed the importance of classics. An alternative ideology which received wide support was that the curriculum should aim at preparing pupils for their future occupations, mainly in the form of industrial, i.e. practical, training. Here the stress was on instruction rather than education. A third view was that a liberal education for all would be the most desirable; this view depended on a fairly narrow interpretation of what constituted culture. A redefinition of this last ideology is to be found in the attempts to achieve the full development of each child's potentiality by deliberate action by, for example, the proposition of a common curriculum. All three ideologies are to be found today to a greater or lesser degree, in discussions on the nature of the curriculum which should be offered.

A second influence on the curriculum was the rise of *bureaucratic procedures* over the past hundred years. This refers to the formal organization of institutions which are increasingly characterized by impersonal rules and an authority structure with rational procedures. A good example of this is the growth of the examination system, which will be dealt with in a later section. Reforms in the Civil Service, the armed forces and the professions led to selection by merit rather than by patronage, and schools responded to these changes in their examination procedures. It would be wrong, however, to link the existence of examinations with post-industrial society. Rupert Wilkinson (1964) shows that in Confucian China examinations had also held a central place.

Imperial servants were chosen by this method; the system combined élitism with democracy, as in present-day Western society.

The state of *school technology* governs to a large extent the range of curricular activities which can be undertaken. In the nineteenth century furniture was designed to eliminate unnecessary movement. It was recommended by the newly formed Committee of Council on Education in 1839 that schoolrooms should be arranged in the following manner:

> The desks of the writing classes are arranged next after those of the first or second class; they are to be four inches higher than the latter. . . . At the right-hand extremity of all the desks a board is fixed perpendicularly in the ground, and nailed against the further side of the desks. This board is of the same breadth as the desk, and rises one foot and a half above it; upon this the dictating lessons and class-marks are to be hung.

Resources come under the same heading. Text-books were not generally provided free until 1891 which would help to explain the teaching methods employed. Science and cookery, to take two subjects, were taught by demonstration; the pupils were not expected to participate in the work themselves.

Linked with this is the appearance (or non-appearance) of *'new' subjects* in the curriculum. Subjects in this context may simply be new to a type of school. Algebra and geometry up to the 1830s were considered necessary for the training of the higher faculties in public schools rather than arithmetic, which was more suitable for future shopkeepers. Explanations of why some subjects successfully established themselves in the curriculum are often more complex than it would seem at first sight. The introduction of domestic economy by the Board of Education Code of 1882 was seemingly aimed at making girls more aware of nutritional and hygienic aspects of home-making. At the same time, there was a growing volume of contemporary literature which condemned the wastefulness by servants in the preparation of food.

Passing on to the effects of *war*, we can observe that, from the time of Napoleon, educational reform has occurred in post-war eras. (See, for example, some of the major Education Acts of the present century, 1902 and 1944.) War has also had a startling effect in displaying shortcomings of knowledge in industrial and technical skills. The South African War which required an army ten times the size of the Boers to succeed, exposed the poor state of science teaching in schools. It also showed the alarming proportion of young men who were unfit for military service; this led to a re-appraisal of the aims and content of the physical training curriculum.

Technological and economic factors are responsible for curriculum change. Fears raised by continental competition in the mid nineteenth century led eventually to a wider definition of the nature of elementary education. Similarly, inter-nation rivalry in the space programmes of the 1950s was a stimulus to the proliferation of new mathematics and science projects in Britain and the USA. Musgrove (1964) has shown that the lessening importance of children as wage-earners has significant implications for schooling. In 1870, the leaving age was ten. Since the 1930s children have been born into an economy in which technological change has brought about an upgrading of occupations and an increase in the amount of skilled employment required.

A more difficult category to summarize is the effect of *educationists' views and knowledge* on the curriculum. In the eighteenth century and for part of the nineteenth, societal and educational views were virtually identical: this can be seen in the attitudes towards the provision of girls' education and the differences between boys' and girls' curricula. The writings of psychologists, philosophers and sociologists, taken together with the changing view of childhood as the incidence of infant mortality diminished, have had much influence on teaching methods and attitudes to learning. In a different way, psychological findings on the nature of intelligence, earlier this century, were taken up and misinterpreted by official government reports and translated into 'types' of child. The tripartite system of education was thus created and justification for selection and streaming was also attributed to measured intelligence.

An allied set of factors which might help explain tradition and change concerns the shift from the *religious to the secular* basis of education. This is exemplified in the moral instruction movement started in the 1870s which laid emphasis on character formation, virtue and good behaviour in a non-religious setting. This movement found expression in the Board of Education Code of 1904, which encouraged the development of team spirit; shortly afterwards, schools were provided with playing fields to make this possible. After the First World War the development of moral education took the form of citizenship and civics and from the 1930s social studies.

The next suggested category – *pressure groups* – illustrates well the theme of change and continuity; for these groups can act both to preserve a tradition or to break the mould and produce change. Some groups may be permanent – a national organization with long-term aims, such as the NUT, and subject associations. Others disband when their objective is achieved, e.g. local groups hoping to retain or change the status of a school or schools in their area.

It would, however, be unrealistic to imagine that we can account for curriculum change or stability by reference to any one or combination of the above categories alone. Many changes are brought about by chance factors which cannot be easily classified. The above list, to which many other factors could be added, is no more than a starting point.

Further reading

Curriculum change in the nineteenth century is discussed in Williams (1961, pp. 145–76). A study which brings the story up to date is Lawton (1973, pp. 79–120). Most of the standard text-books on the history of education make incidental references to curriculum but none makes this a central issue. Two of the better general books are Barnard (1971) and Lawson and Silver (1973).

For an account of teaching methods employed see Gosden (1969) and Stewart and McCann (1967, vol. 1; 1968, vol. 2).

A quick reference guide to various government reports, many of which are concerned with curriculum aspects, is Maclure (1968). On élites see Wilkinson (1970, pp. 126–42) and Bamford (1967). An historical account of the bureaucratization of schools is to be found in Musgrove (1971, pp. 88–105). Economic factors and education are discussed by the same author (1964).

Chapter 13

Problems of Justification

Richard Pring

Introduction

Most teachers (but some more than others) are in the following dilemma. They recognize that they live in a pluralist society, that is, a society that tolerates many different life-styles with different valuations of what is good and worthwhile; they may even argue that values are ultimately a matter of taste, without objective foundation; and they may conclude that they have no right to promote one set of values rather than another, one life-style in preference to another. Indeed the emphasis is often on the pupil's freedom to choose or to make up his own mind about what is worthwhile, because the teacher does not find the promotion of a particular set of values easily defensible.

On the other hand, it would seem impossible in practice not to subscribe to the superiority of certain values. Children do not come to school of their own free choice, and I imagine that those responsible for making them go, as well as those (the teachers) who help enforce it, must believe that going to school provides experiences and opportunities superior to what the children would otherwise get. They may be wrong, of course, but that in no way affects the commitment of those who make or enforce this law to the value of schooling. Furthermore, within the school, decisions are being made all the time about what is of most value — children are not allowed to play snakes and ladders all day, mathematics is almost universal on the time-table, the *Dandy* is not (officially) read, and Shakespeare remains a fairly good bet. There are gradual curriculum changes, of course, but these are frequently justified — thus, again, reinforcing the belief that some things are regarded as more worthwhile than others and that choice of what is valuable is not just a matter of taste.

Of course explanations why things are as they are or why things change might be given in terms of tradition or social forces without any reference to values. But such explanations cannot be the whole story for, whatever the constraints of tradition or social forces within which we work, there remains scope for deciding between alternative courses, for choosing particular subject matter, for subjecting children to one kind of experience rather than another. And such choosing or deciding is made in the light of values held by the school and teachers, which they believe in some sense to be superior to values which might otherwise prevail.

The problem of how values might be justified enters into our educational concerns at two levels. First, as I have indicated, schooling is a commitment to promoting certain qualities in life. Children go there reluctantly very often and the fact that so much effort is spent in persuading them and in carefully selecting experiences for them shows how the problem of justifying what we think to be worthwhile is central to any educational theory. Second, many would argue that values (moral ones, for example) ought to be promoted on the curriculum. They may be particular moral values such as that it is wrong to steal or to kick a chap when he's down or more general ones such as one ought to respect other people or be concerned about justice. How far one should promote particular moral values on the curriculum is open to argument, but it would be difficult to argue that this is no concern of the school whatsoever. Does not a great deal of literature incorporate certain moral ideals which are being taught indirectly to children in so far as the literature is taught? And don't children learn as much possibly from the 'hidden curriculum' — the beliefs, values, ideals, etc. implicit within the very organization of the school and the teaching?

The problem then of what is worthwhile is centrally important to education and yet how we set about justifying one set of values rather than another is most elusive. In what follows I will outline briefly four different theories of value

129

which are relevant to our attempts to justify what we do. There is not the opportunity here to consider the more specific problem of teaching particular values within the school. (This problem is introduced by Maggie Ing in chapter 9.)

Emotive theory of values

It is useful to start with an extreme case of a highly 'subjective' theory about values because it makes explicit what a lot of people subscribe to implicitly when they say that one man's values are just as good as another's or that one has no right to promote one set of values rather than another (or to prevent someone from having access to what you might think is corrupting). On this theory we can justifiably talk about knowledge only when there are agreed public tests for deciding about the truth or falsity of what is said. Where there are no such public tests, claims and counterclaims are just 'so much wind' or expressions of feeling. What is the point of claiming something to be true or arguing about something if there is no means for proving it is true or for deciding the argument? Such claims aren't genuine ones at all, and to express them is but a pseudo-statement — expression of taste dressing up in the wrong grammatical clothing.

On this view there are agreed public tests only in empirical and purely logical matters. Thus only in science, mathematics, and logic do we find genuine knowledge. All else — metaphysics, religion, morals, aesthetics — is no more than an expression of taste or feeling. There is certainly no justification for teaching these things as though they were bodies of knowledge for they merely reflect the feelings of the person holding them.

There are many difficulties in such an ethical position. It rests upon a rather narrow theory of meaning, and certainly it is difficult to subscribe to it in practice. As I have said, people do make decisions in the light of values they hold and these values are discussed, criticized, and transformed as a result of reflection, and certainly it would be inconsistent to say that since all values are a matter of taste one has no right to promote any one set of values, for 'right' is a moral concept and would in such a case be no more than an expression of the speaker's feelings.

Utilitarianism

One attempt to put questions of value on a more objective basis was that of the utilitarians and this I briefly introduced in chapter 2. Roughly, utilitarians argued that the one certainly good thing was pleasure, and thus that the greatest good was the promotion of the greatest happiness of the greatest number. 'Pleasure' must in no way be interpreted in a purely hedonistic sense. For some doing mathematics is pleasurable, for others reading books or painting pictures. Obviously the best life will have all kinds of pleasures. On this view, educational activities would be justifed in utilitarian terms — their value would be measured in terms of their tendency to make life more pleasurable either for the individual himself or for society generally. Thus learning science might be thought good either because it gave the student a great deal of satisfaction or because (although he was personally made miserable by it) having scientifically literate people was essential for a smooth working society.

It would, I think, be difficult to justify a lot of what goes on in school simply in terms of its promotion of happiness. Clearly a lot of children would be happier fishing or playing football and I personally would need a lot of empirical evidence to be convinced that many of them, though immediately not made happy, would be happier in the long run as a result of some of the experiences selected as worthwhile for them. And certainly the promotion of happiness has rarely been appealed to as the justification for teaching reluctant children mathematics or Greek. None the less, the utilitarian might argue that so much the worse for most schooling. Ought it not to be radically reformed so that the children's happiness and the happiness of society became the major concern?

There are difficulties in pinning too much faith in utilitarianism. The difficulties were partly spelt out in Mill (1861). Generally speaking he was meeting the argument of those critics who, amongst other things, pointed out the absurdity of calculating the merits of one pleasure against another. How, for instance, can one compare the quantity of pleasure obtained from listening to poetry with that obtained from playing pushpin? Though both roughly called pleasures, they are of a different order, and Mill conceded that some pleasures were *qualitatively* superior to others. Such a concession, however, has left the utilitarian case very weakened, for the definition of *qualitative* superiority cannot itself lie in quantity of pleasure. A new, non-pleasure principle of value has entered into the utilitarian theory.

Intuitively most of us would agree with Mill. Take, for example, the distribution of grants by the Arts Council. Many provincial theatres and orchestras are kept going by such subsidies because there is not enough public demand — if you like, not enough people get enough pleasure from them to keep them going without 'artificial' aids. At the same time bowling alleys are dying through lack of public support and lack of public subsidy. Distinctions then are made between those activities which are worth supporting and those which are not, independently of any calculation as to what would maximize pleasure. And indeed would not the value we place upon many school activities be rather analogous? We certainly believe, say, that reading literature or solving mathematical problems is pleasurable, but we would not question their superior value simply because as a matter of fact most pupils got more pleasure from playing tiddlywinks.

Intrinsically worthwhile activities

One weakness in the utilitarian position is that many people value certain activities even though they lead (and they know they lead) to unhappiness. Knowledge, especially self-knowledge, can be a painful thing. The pursuit of knowledge would seem to contain its own intrinsic value.

This was the sort of position that Professor Peters (1966) sought to explore. He pushed the utilitarian argument as far as it would go but found it wanting as a comprehensive theory of value. It would not account for the value we attribute to many educational activities. The values picked out by education are concerned with the development of mind, and central to this is the development of knowledge and understanding. The educated man is one that we value not because he amuses us or because he is virtuous (although he may be more amusing or virtuous because educated) but because of a certain breadth and depth of knowledge and understanding. To educate someone, therefore, is to introduce him to those activities and understandings that will give him that cognitive perspective.

This then is Peters' thesis but it needed to be pinned down to a much more water-tight argument. How can we demonstrate the intrinsic, as opposed to the instrumental, value of those activities which increase knowledge and understandings? Peters argues that anyone who seriously asks that question is already committed to the value of answering it – and thus, in general, to 'getting at the truth' and therefore in particular, to those specific activities and inquiries through which the truth is articulated and discovered. Put crudely, the argument is that concern for truth is as much a value as concern for happiness and that this is not just intuitively plausible but cannot be denied without absurdity. The corollary would be that once you are committed to getting at the truth you must also be committed to those activities through which in different ways the truth is made manifest.

Interests

A criticism of Peters' position is Wilson's (1967) article 'In defence of Bingo'. It is reminiscent in many ways of the issues debated in Mill's *Utilitarianism* (1861). Wilson's position is that in the absence of any satisfactory philosophical arguments for putting values on an objective basis, that alone might be considered intrinsically valuable which people find value in – what engages their interest. If bingo is what absorbs the mind and attention of a particular person, then on what ethical grounds might we dispute the value of that interest? It is clearly what *he* values. To educate *him* would be to help him advance his interest, have an even more intelligent involvement in the game. And to those who object that bingo's potential for more intelligent interest is limited, it would no doubt be replied that the number of children who have total hang-ups on bingo would itself be extremely limited. The point is that most children have a wide range of interests each of which can be more intelligibly engaged in and many of which will lead on to further activities and inquiries. To educate *him* is to develop *his* interest.

It is with the interest-based curriculum in the sense of 'educating interests' that educational philosophers such as Dewey and Kilpatrick were associated, and it is within the context of a concern for the pupils' interests that the practical developments took place in school organization, methods of teaching, and curriculum content, especially in America during the 1920s and 1930s. Thus Kilpatrick spoke of the children's interests determining curricula content and structure, and of common learnings resulting from common interests. In introducing the account of *An Experiment with a Project Curriculum* (see Collings, 1923), he denied that the aims of the school were the 'conventional knowledge of skills'. The starting point was 'the actual present life of the boys and girls themselves, with all their interests and desires, good and bad'; the first step was 'to help guide these children to choose the most interesting and fruitful parts of this life as the content of their school activity'; and the consequent aims were 'first to help the boys and girls do better than they otherwise would the precise things they had chosen, and second, by means of the experience of choosing and through the experience of the more effectual activity gradually to broaden the outlook of the boys and girls as to what they might further choose and then help them better effect these new choices'. Thus the child's interests rather than history or geography constitute the subject-matter of the curriculum. Wilson recently restated this position: 'a child's education (as opposed to schooling) can only proceed through the pursuit of his interests since it is only these which are of intrinsic value . . . (and) whatever enables him to appreciate and understand his interest more fully and to pursue it more actively and effectively is educative'.

Conclusion

Education picks out certain activities as worthy of initiating future generations into — often against their will. But this leaves us with some obligation to justify why we think certain activities rather than others have such value, and our attempts to find adequate justification soon lead us into difficult areas of ethics. We could, of course, easily retreat into a subjectivist position in which attempts to 'justify' or to declare what is of most worth or to distinguish between good and bad are declared to be simply matters of taste or the expression of emotion. That, however, is not the position of those who in practice promote certain activities and experiences in schools to the exclusion of others, and indeed could not be without considerable cynicism.

Three ethical responses have been considered then. Certainly pleasure is one factor in evaluating the worth of an activity and, if the possibility of giving pleasure and satisfaction were totally absent, I would argue that that activity or experience has no intrinsic worth. On the other hand, the pursuit and provision of pleasure cannot be the only consideration. Education is not concerned solely with making people happy (otherwise it might be cheaper and more effective simply to instal large tickling machines). There are values arising out of the fact that we have minds, ask questions, are curious about how things work, are able (and want) to understand and know more. It is difficult to deny without absurdity the value of those activities which can be shown to promote the development of mind. But this statement is still pitched at a very general level. What activities are most worthwhile in so far as they, rather than others, develop the mind? The reply of the 'child-centred' philosophers of education is that no one set of activities can be said to be of most worth − this or that book, this or that subject. Anything can be − it depends upon what the child is interested in or what he at that time is absorbed in or puzzled about. History, for such philosophers, is not valuable in itself, but valuable only in so far as it extends the mind of this child or that.

Further reading

Those who wish to see how people have tackled the problem of teaching values in a pluralist society should look at the material of two Schools Council projects: Moral Education 13–16 and 9–13 and Humanities Curriculum Project. The thinking behind the projects can be found in McPhail *et al.* (1972), and Humanities Curriculum Project (1970).

The best account of the emotive theory of ethics is to be found in Ayer (1946). But a good account of it and the difficulties in it is to be found in Warnock (1967, chapter 3).

Mill (1861), especially chapter 2, is the best, most readable account of utilitarianism — by someone who believed in it.

Peters (1966, chapter 5), sets out clearly the argument for intrinsically worthwhile activities. But read also Peters (1977, chapter 5) for development and modification of this position.

For Dewey, read Dewey (1916 and 1938). A more recent account of his child-centred position is Wilson (1971, 1974).

A recent philosophical book that puts forward a justification for certain kinds of curriculum activities is Warnock (1977, chapter 4).

Chapter 14

Curriculum Content: Principles of Selection

Richard Pring

Introduction

In chapter 2, I argued very generally that, as educators, we are centrally (but by no means exclusively) concerned with the development of knowledge and understanding. Furthermore I argued:

1 that we must never lose sight of practical knowledge, partly because it is valuable in itself and partly because practical knowledge is so often what theoretical knowledge is theorizing about;

2 that there are many different kinds of knowledge, developed into various disciplined modes of inquiry. You should look back at the third section of that chapter before continuing with this because I wish to argue that it is from these public traditions of thought and inquiry that the subject-matter of the curriculum should be drawn.

Public traditions

There are many different kinds of knowledge, characterized by particular concepts, techniques and methods of inquiry, ways of testing the truth, concern for specific problems. These have been developed over the centuries in order to meet particular problems or make intelligible various aspects of experience — hence you might, as Denis Lawton (1973) does, talk of significant aspects of our *culture*. They are not arbitrary. Their growth has been the social product of the co-operative inquiry, in which ways of formulating the problems as well as solutions to them have been subjected to criticism and examination. There are, you might say, many different traditions which themselves contain the seeds for yet further criticism and growth. A subject is ideally a distillation of what is central in such a tradition, a means of introducing the newcomer into a way of inquiring and reflecting that has been found fruitful in the past and without which the pupil would be more limited in his mental powers. For example, to be introduced to biology is to be provided with a set of concepts (for example, 'cells', 'tissues', 'organism') which organize in a powerful and fruitful way how we observe and understand living things. To be introduced to literary criticism is to be given a tool for reading with greater discrimination the literary achievements of others and doubtless to communicate more effectively one's own thoughts and feelings. To be taught religion would, on this view, be to enter into the systematic and thoughtful responses of others to certain kinds of experience, thereby extending the powers of imagination and thus the very capacity to experience.

It may be objected, of course, that, certainly at primary schools, such an approach to curriculum content is inappropriate. The very thought of 'subjects' or of a structured curriculum is anathema to some. But such an objection is not easy to maintain. Firstly, it is necessary at a very early age to extend the pupil's mastery of language and, in doing so, one is introducing him to a particular way of organizing experience and understanding the physical and social environment. He is, you might say, entering into a socially developed way of seeing things — a particular culture — which is the basis for later, more differentiated modes of inquiring. Secondly such differentiation is already there, at least embryonically, in the teacher's concern for number work, the understanding and relating of shapes, the classification of objects, the observation of living things, the exposure to certain kinds of nursery rhymes, the enjoyment of music, the acquisition of certain artistic skills. From the vast range of activities that a child could be engaged in at the infant school, certain ones are chosen to be significant. The principle of choice, I would suggest, should be that such activities introduce the pupil to skills and concepts and approaches which are basic to different traditions of thought and inquiry which later will be developed in a more differentiated way.

Hence, the teacher, at any level, is drawing material from traditions of thought and inquiry — selecting from the culture — which, in his judgment, the pupil needs to be introduced to if his powers of mind are to be extended. But this gives rise to two problems in the selection of curriculum content.

1 There are so many different kinds of inquiry, so many different subject matters — biology, cybernetics, astronomy, musical criticism, history, sociology, social psychology, physical geography, anthropology, etc. — how do we select from this vast range the particular subject matters we want the children to master?

2 How can we ensure continuity in the presentation of these selected subject matters so that the content of the primary school curriculum leads on to the content of the middle or secondary school curriculum?

Continuity

The problem of continuity presents fewer problems in theory than in practice. It should be possible, once the selection from the wide range of possible traditions or subject matters has been decided upon, to work out what the essential features of such a way of thinking are, and then to agree upon some sequence in the gradual mastery of such a way of thinking. This can be illustrated through certain curriculum projects. Science 5-13 (see Schools Council, 1972) for example, seeks to develop certain skills, concepts, and mental operation central to scientific work, and to do this in a sequential way. Two considerations enter into the sequencing. First, it is necessary to work out what is 'logically presupposed', e.g. what concepts must be acquired prior to further scientific understanding. Secondly, it is necessary to respect the mode of operating at various stages of children's thinking, e.g. children at the primary level do, generally speaking, develop mental operations through the exploration of concrete objects and materials, later they are able to handle the same sort of issues in a more abstract and hypothetical way. One might see similar concern for continuity and sequencing in Nuffield Mathematics where the development of mathematics is seen as a spiral in which the same concepts, concerned, for instance, with shape and size or with graphs, are met over and over again, but illustrated in a different way at each stage. Or, again in Bruner's 'Man: A Course of Study', certain concepts and modes of inquiry are picked out as essential to the understanding of man from the point of view of the social sciences and these are introduced in different ways at different stages of development (Jenkins, 1976).

In practice, however, such theoretical possibilities of sequence and continuity in the selection of subject matter are not easy to achieve. It requires a high level of co-operation and planning within, and between, schools. The need to achieve these is one strong argument for weakening the autonomy of schools and teachers, and for strengthening other forms of control.

Principles of selection

The major problem, however, lies in selection of particular subject matters from the vast range of possible ones. There is, after all, only a limited amount of time on the time-table.

One answer to this is given by Professor Hirst (1965). He argues that the wide range of different kinds of knowledge can, by philosophical analysis and argument, be reduced to seven fundamental forms. To be ignorant of any one form is to have a gap in one's mode of thinking — it is to be cut off from a large and significant area of experience. Hence, those subjects should feature on the curriculum which most typically represent a given form of knowledge. For example, physics would introduce people to the scientific form of knowledge better than botany.

Hirst's argument should be read in detail (Hirst, 1965). I personally am not convinced of the philosophical argument (Pring, 1976), and hence, without such philosophical reductionism, I am still left with all these different subject matters from which a selection has to be made. There need to be other principles of selection.

I believe that since philosophical argument alone fails to give us a blue-print, many different sorts of consideration might enter into our selection of subject matters. I would suggest the following as examples — they are by no means meant to be exhaustive.

1 *Social utility.* Certain subject matters such as technology (including technical drawing), the physical sciences, mathematics, should be taught because they provide a necessary basis for surviving in a complex technological society.

2 *Social responsibility.* Certain subject matters such as politics, sociology, social psychology might be argued for because of the importance of social and political awareness in any democratic society.

3 *Common culture.* In the past history has certainly been used to provide a common heritage that would serve to promote some kind of social unity. Maybe, one would want to preserve a common background of values and meaning through a shared literary tradition.

4 *Personal satisfaction.* Some subjects, especially aesthetic and sporting ones, might be defended because they introduce pupils to activities that give considerable personal satisfaction and, in that sense, increase quality of life. This, of course, harks back to the child-centred view I referred to in the section 'The child-centred view', chapter 2 (see in particular argument 2). A variation on this is White's (1973) argument in which those subjects should be compulsory which, if not understood, would curtail considerably the children's choice of alternative ways of gaining satisfaction in life.

5 *Cognitive concern.* In the second part of the section 'Worthwhile knowledge' of chapter 2, I very briefly summarized a philosophical argument for the value of truth-seeking activities. (This was pursued further in chapter 13.) One might argue that certain subjects are of particular importance, even if they may not give too much pleasure or may not be too socially relevant — for example, philosophy, archaeology.

6 *Parental and social pressure.* There is at present increased

pressure for schools to be more accountable to outside factions — especially parents. There is, in other words, more encroachment upon the autonomy of the school. If parents have some rights in what children are taught, then the subjects on the curriculum should in part reflect parental wishes.

7 *Mental powers.* It was argued in the past that certain subjects (such as Latin) were particularly good at increasing general powers of the mind — analytic or logical thinking in particular. Whatever the merits of such a specific claim, it could be argued that a range of intellectual activities could, with particular children, develop worthwhile mental powers — the ability to pursue an argument, to search out and respect evidence, to marshal and communicate ideas, to take into account objections, to sift the essential from the inessential. This, of course, would be an argument for early specialization, it not mattering what you learnt so long as it had this intellectual mileage in it.

Conclusion

Selection from public traditions of thought and inquiry and the systematic and planned introduction into what is selected, must be central to a curriculum. But the principles of selection are many and thus any curriculum must be a compromise. I have not attempted to specify in detail what such content should be. That would have to be argued in particular schools, or school systems, in the light of principles which a teacher or school or authority finds defensible. But whatever content is chosen, as the result of whatever principles are found acceptable, it should be noted that continuity and sequence will be important. And it is that which, for me, lends weight to greater outside control over the curriculum.

Further reading

For a general account see Lawton (1973) and refer back to chapters 2 and 13 of this book. In Pring (1976, especially chapter 7) I covered in much greater detail some of the arguments here and criticized (chapter 2) Hirst's reduction of knowledge to seven different forms. Bruner (1960) argues for the structure of subject matters and the 'spiralling' of teaching the essential features of such structure. Examples of such spiralling would be the Schools Council Science 5–13 Curriculum Project and Schools Council/Nuffield Mathematics 5–13 (summaries of these can be found in the Schools Council (1977)).

For more information about 'Man: A Course of Study', see Jenkins (1976). Hirst's argument for a liberal education can be found in Hirst (1965).

Chapter 15

Curriculum Content: Sociology of Knowledge

Peter Gordon

The nature of the sociology of knowledge

Perhaps the main difference between the sociologist's approach to questions concerning the nature of knowledge and that of the philosopher can be stated as follows: the latter will be concerned with asking questions about the very possibility of knowing anything at all and about logical differences between different kinds of knowledge claim, whereas the sociologist will look at the differences that can be socially explained, and of organizing this knowledge, either between our society and another, or within society. Basil Bernstein (1971) has noted that 'How a society selects, classifies, distributes, transmits and evaluates the educational knowledge it considers to be public, reflects both the distribution of power and the principles of social control.'

Marx's study of ideologies of social classes led him to an interest in the sociology of knowledge. The reality of society does not lie in its appearance as it is dominated by the bourgeois view of knowledge: our view of, for example, religion, politics and art, is governed by the prevailing view of knowledge. This view of reality as seen through the eyes of capitalism will ultimately be changed by revolution, to be replaced by Marxian socialism, which will reflect working-class consciousness.

Karl Mannheim (1936) explored the field more systematically. Writing after the First World War, he perceived the sociology of knowledge as a way of building a more stable

144

society and without the necessity of revolution. As there was difficulty in establishing the validity of beliefs or knowledge by generally agreed criteria, he saw the main hope for the future in a 'socially unattached intelligentsia', separated from family and community, an aggregation between, but not above, the classes. Mannheim distinguishes between manual and intellectual performance, making clear that the duty of the educator was to ensure the increase in numbers of the intelligentsia, who would not be encouraged to follow vocational pursuits. This was an élitist view of the educative function found, for example, in the ethos of the nineteenth-century English public school. Although Mannheim agreed with Marx on the relation between class, ideology and knowledge, the solutions adopted were very different. Education for the masses should be planned to produce personal autonomy, but the highest good of society could only be achieved by educating for a certain amount of conformity. The contradictory nature of the ultimate objectives of Mannheim's new social order and the means whereby they may be achieved is apparent throughout his writings.

Berger and Luckmann (1966) and other sociologists advance the view that the special problem of ideology is only a part of the larger problem of the sociology of knowledge and that the main concern is with everything that passes for knowledge in society. The 'knowledge' of the criminal, for example, differs from the knowledge of the criminologist. How does society become a subjective reality for individuals? What is 'real' to a Tibetan monk may not be 'real' to an American business man. It is necessary here to distinguish between two types of socialization – primary and secondary. In the first, 'significant others', e.g. parents, are mediators of reality, and learning is difficult to forget: in secondary socialization, the institutional context is paramount, e.g. teachers, schools and children, the first transmitting specific knowledge. There is less subjective inevitability of what is learned in secondary socialization. 'The child lives willy-nilly in the world as defined by his parents, but he can cheerfully leave the world of arithmetic behind him as soon as he leaves the classroom' (Berger and Luckman, 1966).

In complex societies, counter-definitions of reality may be postulated by groups with a possibility of even primary socialization itself being transformed. Although examples of this are rare, partial transformations can be achieved through such means as the individual's social mobility or occupational training. Thus the nature of knowledge — what is taught and learnt and how it should be transmitted — becomes problematical and gives rise to a questioning for instance of the nature of schooling and the curriculum offered.

This view of the sociology of knowledge relies to some extent on the recognition of the individual as a self-determining entity. The work of psychoanalysts such as Freud, who viewed human thought as distortions, and social psychologists, particularly G. H. Mead (Blumer, 1965), were responsible for new advances. Mead reversed the traditional sociological view of the individual as a product of factors — drives, needs and motives; instead, the individual could be regarded as an actor who transforms his relation to the world by interacting with himself — analysing and organizing his actions with regard to what he has perceived.

Similarly, Alfred Schutz (1972) has stressed that the world as experienced by an individual and shared by his fellow creatures is a *social* world: it is therefore necessary to formulate a theory of knowledge based on the behaviour of others and which takes into account the importance of linguistics. This phenomenological approach has been advanced in an attempt to free sociological analysis from ideological bias: at the same time, it challenges the notion of a parallel between the natural and social sciences.

Some of these views have been criticized on various grounds. Popper (1952) pointed out that sociologists of knowledge tend to disregard the grounds given by agents for their beliefs: and furthermore claim that the grounds are incapable of being tested. If this were the case, then it could be argued that the views of Marx and Mannheim reflect their own class position and do not necessarily have any wider validity. Popper's comment in *The Open Society and its Enemies* is pertinent in this context:

is it not clear that, assuming the theory of total ideologies to be correct, it would be part of every total ideology to believe that one's own group was free from bias, and was indeed that body of the elect which alone was capable of objectivity? Is it not, therefore, to be expected, always assuming the truth of this theory, that those who hold it will unconsciously deceive themselves by producing an amendment to the theory in order to establish the objectivity of their own views?

Curiously both Marx and Mannheim (1936) exempted science and mathematics from the types of knowledge which are free from ideological distortion. Mannheim's solution of a socially unattached intelligentsia would now hardly be regarded as a serious proposition.

Berger and Luckmann's (1966) notion of common-sense, every-day knowledge as the basis of a sociology of knowledge is an important one. On the other hand, it could be argued that the adoption of a purely sociological approach to knowledge ignores some of the major epistemological issues which are in the philosopher's province.

Implications for the curriculum

It is only in the last decade or so that sociologists of education have begun to explore some of the implications of the sociology of knowledge for present-day society. The contributors to M. F. D. Young's *Knowledge and Control* (1971), for example, have raised interesting questions on the nature of schooling (see Denis Lawton's chapter 4 for further details). For some sociologists this approach is characterized by a shift from the normative (or conventional) to an interpretative paradigm. The former assumes that the educative function is largely a socializing one and which will assist in supporting the *status quo*. This functional view of society led sociologists of education to investigate a number of areas such as inequality of opportunity between children (cultural deprivation) and organizing schools efficiently, with reference to social justice (comprehensive education).

The interpretative paradigm takes into account the common-sense view of knowledge and questions many of the assumptions underlying the functional approach. Educational knowledge should be treated problematically with questions being asked on why, how and what is taught and in which way. The selection of knowledge for schools raises questions relating to the status of subjects: whether it is 'given' and if there is any logical distinction between high status (mathematics and science) and low status (social studies and home economics) subjects. How curriculum knowledge is defined, evaluated and dispensed by teachers affects pupils' achievements. The selection of knowledge also relates to views on its distribution, i.e. who has access to high and low status curricula: as well as questioning the basis of organizing pupils – whether it be streaming, banding or mixed ability – and the structure and legitimation of hierarchies in schools which has given rise to the phrase 'the hidden curriculum'. The political nature of education is stressed in examining the decision-making agencies involved in curriculum development and dissemination – DES, Schools Council, local education authorities and teachers.

This reconsideration of the nature of school curriculum as a result of recent developments in the sociology of knowledge has led to a fruitful and stimulating debate. But as it draws largely from Marx, Berger and Luckmann (1966), Schutz (1972) and Mead (Blumer, 1965), it is susceptible to the same sort of criticisms which have been made by Popper (1952). To dismiss the normative paradigm without adequate consideration of, for example, the nature of intelligence and differences between the form and structure of knowledge is questionable. It is argued that subjects are human constructs and subject boundaries are artificial. The existence of subjects *per se* is not necessarily invalidated by this statement although it may have more reference to the way that they are presented: Pring (1972) mentions that there are obvious limits to the number of ways in which we can organize our experience taking into account the limiting features of the person making the discriminations. Can sequential and meaningful learning take place in a relativist approach especially if there are different views of knowledge? Lawton (1975) has pointed out that the new sociology tends to ignore anthropological and ethno-linguistic studies which shows striking similarities rather than differences between cultures in language and logic. The political nature of education, although throwing light on the relationship between how knowledge is controlled and what is learnt, does not itself indicate what

148

counts as knowledge. Finally, theories of knowledge are themselves continually changing; the sociological contribution to the debate is only one part of it and must take into account the findings of other disciplines.

Further reading

A useful general book for this chapter is Flude and Ahier (1974). Two short books on Marx are McLellan (1975) and Bottomore and Reubel (1963, part 1, section 1).

Mannheim (1936) presents a full exploration of his thinking; it also has a brief survey of the history of the sociology of knowledge. His later work (1956, pp. 91–170) contains an important contribution – 'The Problem of Intelligentsia' – a revised view on the topic. A commentary on Mannheim is to be found in Stark (1958). For a shorter appreciation of his work, see Heren (1971, pp. 1–15).

See pp. 149–82 of Berger and Luckmann (1966) for their notion of primary and secondary socialization; the introduction to the book sets out well the nature of their arguments. Mead's work is dealt with concisely in Blumer (1965, pp. 535–44) and reprinted in Cosin (1971, pp. 16–22). A more difficult book is Schutz (1972) which investigates the nature of social interaction and views of reality.

The application of the sociology of knowledge to the curriculum is discussed by Bernstein in Young (1971). Aspects of it are examined in Lawton (1975, pp. 52–69). See also the contributions in *Education for Teaching* by R. Pring and D. Gorbutt (1972) and Eggleston, 'Definitions of Knowledge and the School Curriculum' (1973) which has a good bibliography.

For an early critical analysis of the sociology of education, see Popper (1952, vol. II, especially chapter 23).

Part Four

Evaluation and Assessment

Chapter 16

Curriculum Objectives

Bill Gibby

The formulation of curriculum aims and objectives

Earlier, in chapters 3 and 7, the formulation of curriculum objectives has been discussed in the context of a curriculum model and a learning theory. From this earlier discussion it is clear that any detailed declaration of the precise intended direction and form of a curriculum would be a statement of its objectives. However, there is an important distinction between long-term objectives and short-term ones. The phrase 'long-term objectives' often refers to high level aims and tends to be related to broad reasons why particular activities are being organized or why a particular course is being done, whilst 'short-term objectives' are more directly concerned with what specifically is being attempted over a relatively short period. Broad aims, or long-term objectives, can be regarded as expressions of strategy, whilst short-term objectives are essentially tactical in character.

A curriculum project in which an 'objectives' type of approach was used

In the Science 5–13 Curriculum Project (Schools Council, 1972), a rigorous objectives type of approach was used, which was claimed to be 'essentially child-centred'. Primarily, the project planners were thinking of how they could help children to learn rather than what they should be taught, but they did stress that what the children working through this project did actually learn was indeed important. We see in this project a clear statement of broad aims followed by a precise classification of nine sets of objectives illustrated with possible examples at each of three Piagetian stages (see the appendix to this chapter for further details).

Two main types of criticism can be aimed at this project. The first is concerned with teacher participation in the planning of the project, the second with the formulation and measurement of the objectives. Some teachers felt that the approach used in the initial planning of this project was too much in the hands of the 'experts'. Such critics felt that 'experts' should only act in an advisory capacity and not control the main course of direction of the project. With regard to the formulation and measurement of objectives, there were many teachers who felt that the large number of specific objectives listed in 'With Objectives in Mind' bewildered them and that attempts to measure whether such objectives had been achieved were time consuming, costly and of doubtful validity.

A curriculum project in which the learning outcomes could not be pre-determined

The Schools Council Humanities Curriculum Project (see Stenhouse, 1975) is an example of a course in which such learning outcomes as do finally emerge cannot be pre-determined. Stenhouse, the director of this project, identifies the term 'humanities' with a programme concerned with the exploration of human issues. The project, intended for pupils of 'average' and 'below average' ability and of age fourteen to sixteen, explores nine issues, all of which are claimed to be controversial ones. For example, these issues include a study of 'relations between the sexes'. Initially, the general aim of this project was to provide a programme which would enable pupils to engage in learning experiences which would develop for them an understanding of the nature and structure of certain complex value issues of universal human concern. Such an understanding was to come mainly from the pupils' own part in such experiences and by their reading

154

of a cross-section of opinions on the issue in hand (these being provided in the form of carefully prepared 'packs') and discussing this reading freely amongst themselves, in the light of their own experiences. It was stressed that the teacher was to be 'neutral' in such discussions in the sense that he would not indicate his own opinions concerning the issue under discussion or, in any way, encourage or discourage particular points of view, either in the reading or as expressed by any pupil. Because of the type of discussion used, where pupils' opinions could not be pre-determined, the spelling out of specific objectives had no meaning in the context of this project's methodology. However, in trying out the project in schools, it was found that many teachers experienced difficulties in understanding its methodology. Almost all teachers felt that freedom to speak one's own mind was certainly good for pupils but some teachers indicated that the 'neutral' restriction imposed on them was sometimes difficult to apply. Some difficulties arose because pupils were not usually trained in discussion techniques. Many pupils found difficulties in selecting appropriate material from the available sources whilst others found difficulties in reading and understanding it.

The need to formulate instructional and expressive objectives

Eisner (1969) outlines ways in which it is possible to resolve some of the differences between those who say that normally they believe in formulating specific behavioural objectives at the beginning of a course and not modifying these at all during the course itself and those who claim that this is often harmful and, in many cases, cannot be done in any way that makes sense. Eisner distinguishes between what he calls instructional and expressive objectives. For him, both instructional and expressive objectives are needed in most courses with the proportion of each varying with the nature of the material being tackled and the circumstances in which teachers and pupils find themselves.

He regards instructional objectives as objectives which specify unambiguously the particular behaviour (item of knowledge, skill and so forth) the pupil is to acquire after having completed an activity. In an effective curriculum, using instructional objectives, the intended terminal behaviours, i.e. those things which should be done and understood by the end of an activity or course, of the pupils concerned are identified with the initial instructional objectives, i.e. the objectives are precisely pre-determined and not modified in any way.

But, Eisner (1969) claims, it is possible to have a kind of objective where the precise nature of the terminal behaviour is not pre-determined. He calls this type of objective an expressive one. For him, an expressive objective describes an educational encounter. It identifies a situation in which pupils are to work at a task but it does not specify what they are to learn from that encounter. So even in an area like mathematics which is usually associated with instructional objectives like: 'a pupil will solve correctly a simple equation', there is need for expressive objectives like: 'a pupil will produce his own set of patterns or designs in any mathematical experience of his own choice'.

Thus, with an expressive objective, what is desired is not homogeneity of response among pupils but rather diversity. However, Eisner stresses that an expressive objective does identify the general type of encounter a pupil is to have. Accordingly, Eisner suggests there is a need to formulate expressive objectives for pupils to express themselves freely.

Historically, in mathematics and science, there has been a tendency to give greater attention to instructional objectives, whilst in the visual arts the main emphasis has been on the expressive; but, clearly, both types of objectives are important over the whole curriculum, with instructional objectives emphasizing the acquisition of the known, whilst expressive objectives stress the elaboration of the known, its extension and modification, and moves on to the production of imaginative, original work.

So, from Eisner's point of view, a sensible balance of instructional and expressive objectives seems essential to meet the needs of a particular area of the curriculum, a particular situation, a particular teacher and a particular pupil. The fact that all four of these need to be considered makes the exercise of producing a so-called 'sensible balance' a difficult one.

An 'illuminative' approach to curriculum planning

Many writers, including Stenhouse (1975), have suggested that, in certain circumstances in curriculum planning, a precise allegiance to a 'traditional', or 'classical', model is in many cases undesirable, sometimes not possible and often unrealistic. Such a model might be illustrated as follows: Objectives → Means (content and method) → Evaluation. Supporters of this model claim that if the evaluation shows that the objectives have not been attained then *either* the 'means' are inefficient *or* the objectives are inappropriate. (An influential statement of this position was given by Tyler (1949) almost thirty years ago.)

Stenhouse (1975) and others have called for an approach to curriculum development which is descriptive and on-going, being related to what happens as courses develop and calling for adaptations in the light of what happens in practice. They feel there is a need for the interpretation of the form and direction of any course as it proceeds rather than a rigorous concentration on precise predictions initially, followed later by measurements aiming to determine whether these predictions have been achieved. So here the approach is an enlightened, pragmatic one, where inspiration, or 'illumination', is sought as a course develops. Thus such an approach is seen as being influenced by the various school situations in which it is applied. It aims to discern the course's most significant features. In other words, it needs to address and illuminate a series of on-going questions as the course proceeds and to relate subsequent action to the answers to these questions. It stresses more a free discussion, with all concerned, of what is happening at all stages of the course rather than considering periodic precise measures of what has been achieved and what has not. But even though this approach seems a quite sensible one its change of emphasis raises new problems which are considered in some detail by Denis Lawton in chapter 18.

Bloom's method of classifying educational objectives

Because the objectives of most schemes of work give rise to

lengthy lists it has become customary, in certain areas of knowledge, to define objectives in terms of types or classes of expected behaviour or learning outcomes. One of the earliest attempts to systematize such an approach was carried out by Bloom (1956) and his co-workers and their report of their earliest considerations on this is contained in Bloom's two handbooks in which he attempts to give two cumulative classifications of educational goals. However, Bloom did suggest three wide classifications which he calls cognitive, affective and psycho-motor domains (see pp. 161–2). The cognitive domain includes those objectives which deal with recall or recognition of knowledge and the development of intellectual abilities and skills. This domain was central to the work of much test development in America during the late 1950s and the 1960s. Also, many examining bodies in Britain, since about 1965, have adapted Bloom's cognitive classification in certain areas of the curriculum, as a blue-print for certain test specifications, the classifications established being used as 'check-lists' to ensure that balanced ranges of knowledge, skill, comprehension and abilities were being tested. Many recently produced 'objective' type tests for public examinations make use of this classification, or an adaptation of it, these being in evidence in some subjects at 'A', 'O' and 'CSE' levels and in some of the Schools Council feasibility studies into new forms of assessing the academic achievements of sixteen-year-old pupils.

Bloom's affective domain includes objectives which describe changes in interest, attitudes and values. Objectives in this domain are not stated very precisely, but Bloom has suggested that the classification used may help teachers to be clearer than they are at present about the learning experiences which are appropriate to these objectives. His third, psycho-motor domain is concerned with physical skills, but further details of some early work on this do not appear to have been developed.

Bloom subdivides his cognitive domain into six classes which he calls: knowledge, comprehension, application, analysis, synthesis and evaluation. 'Comprehension' is regarded as the lowest level of understanding with the simple decoding of communication, without relating it to other material. 'Application' involves the use of abstractions in particular situations. 'Analysis' is concerned with the breakdown of abstractions into their constituent elements. 'Synthesis' is concerned with putting together parts to form a whole pattern and structure. 'Evaluation' is concerned with judgments about the value of material. Bloom used the word 'taxonomy' for this classification because he claims that the later of his six categories include the earlier ones. Thus, all 'applications' require both 'knowledge' and 'comprehension' as well as something in addition to these two 'earlier' categories and it is in this kind of sense that he thinks of these categories as cumulative ones.

Much use has been made in Britain of Bloom's cognitive domain (mainly in the achievement testing field), but the subdivisions or categories suggested by Bloom for his affective domain rarely appear in any great detail in British national curriculum work or testing programmes.

There have been many criticisms of Bloom's classification of objectives (see below). Some of these have been answered by Scriven (1967) who acknowledges the overlap among the factors identified in Bloom's analysis and tries to reduce these; but he does defend Bloom's regard for factual recall and knowledge of terminology, stressing the need for much of this, in many subjects, as a necessary condition for adequate performances in them.

Overall, Bloom's classification of educational objectives, or adaptations of it, have tended to prove most useful in providing check-lists or guidelines for the systematic production and evaluation of curriculum objectives. In general, the use of an 'objectives' type specification has found its widest use in the production of programmed instruction and of various objective achievement, aptitude, readiness and diagnostic tests.

Criticisms which have been made of Bloom's method of classifying educational objectives

Some of the criticisms which have been offered by Lawton (1973), Kelly (1977) and others can be summarized as follows:

Bloom classified objectives into three separate domains. Such a separation is somewhat artificial as, in practice, all three are closely interrelated.

There is not always agreement on the appropriate classification for certain behaviours. For example, in using
Bloom's kind of classification of objectives for the setting of
test items for an examination, not all the setters concerned
will agree on the categories to be assigned to particular items.

The order of Bloom's cumulative classification in his cognitive domain can be questioned, particularly 'evaluation'
which should really run through the whole classification.

When using this kind of classification, there is a tendency
to overstress 'measurable behaviour' and to regard those
aspects of a pupil's work which are not 'measured' as less
important.

Bloom's type of classification is not applicable to all areas
of the curriculum and to all circumstances of learning.

Formulating objectives to match Bloom's 'higher' categories is a difficult exercise and usually requires lengthy preparation and discussion sessions carried out by teams of
teachers and others in order to produce anything of worth.

Further reading

Science 5-13 Curriculum Project:

The 'objectives' approach used in this project is explained,
with examples, in a booklet issued by the Schools Council
(1972).

Humanities Curriculum Project:

Stenhouse discusses the early development of this project
in Butcher *et al.* (1973, vol. 3). Also, Stenhouse (1975)
offers a more recent consideration of the project's development.

Instructional and expressive objectives:

In a paper 'Instructional Objectives' in Eisner *et al.* (1969, vol. 3) Eisner argues a case for the use of both instructional and expressive educational objectives.

The 'classical' and 'illuminative' approaches to curriculum planning:

Stenhouse (1975) offers an interesting discussion of an 'illuminative' approach to curriculum development, within the context of defining the curriculum problem and providing a critique of the 'classical' objectives model. Almost thirty years earlier, Tyler (1949) had provided a seminal piece of work that set out the classical model of 'rational curriculum planning'.

Bloom's taxonomy of educational objectives:

The cognitive and affective domains are discussed by Bloom (1956) and he includes copious examples illustrating his proposed types of classification. The way in which Bloom's approach to the classification of educational objectives can be used to guide examiners is considered in a paper, by Pilliner, in Butcher *et al.* (1968, vol. 1). Some suggestions for overcoming some of the criticisms that have been made of Bloom's taxonomy have been made by Scriven in a paper, 'Perspectives of Curriculum Evaluation', in Scriven *et al.* (1967, vol. 1). Lawton (1973) offers a detailed criticism of Bloom's taxonomy, whilst a more recent critical examination of the difficulties that arise when curriculum objectives are prespecified appears in Kelly (1977).

Appendix to Chapter 16

It would be useful to see examples of either specific objectives or classifications of objectives that have been suggested for curriculum planning or for pupil assessment.

Bloom's taxonomy of educational objectives

This is intended to provide for classification of the goals of one educational system in order to help teachers and others to discuss curriculum and evaluation problems with greater precision. Objectives are classified into (a) Cognitive, (b) Affective, (c) Psycho-motor. The cognitive domain is divided as follows:

1.00 Knowledge
  10 of specifics
  11 of terminology
  12 of specific facts
  20 of ways and means of dealing with specifics
  21 of conventions
  22 of trends and sequences
  23 of classification and categories
  24 of criteria
  25 of methodology
  30 of the universals and abstractions in a field
  31 of principles and generalizations
  32 of theories and structures
2.00 Comprehension
3.00 Application
4.00 Analysis   Each subdivided
5.00 Synthesis
6.00 Evaluation

'Science 5–13'

The specification of objectives played an important part in the development of this Schools Council Project. In the appendix to their publication *Science 5–13 Curriculum Project: With Objectives in Mind* (1972) they provide 'objectives for children learning science — guidelines to keep in mind'. They start with a broad aim 'Developing an enquiring mind and a scientific approach to problems'. This is subdivided into broad aims:

.10 Developing interests, attitudes and aesthetic awareness.
.20 Observing, exploring and ordering observations.
.30 Developing basic concepts and logical thinking.
.40 Posing questions and devising experiments or investigations to answer them.

.50
.60   Acquiring knowledge and learning skills.

.70   Communicating.

.80   Appreciating patterns and relationships.

.90   Interpreting findings critically.

Each of these is then subdivided into more specific objectives. Below are the objectives within the broad aims 'developing basic concepts and logical thinking' and 'observing, exploring and ordering observation'. You will notice that they are divided according to Piagetian stages of development.

Guide lines to keep in mind

Some objectives which can arise at various stages

	Developing basic concepts and logical thinking .30	Observing, exploring and ordering observations .20
Stage 1 Transition from intuition to concrete operations. Infants generally.	1.31 Awareness of the meaning of words which describe various types of quantity. 1.32 Appreciation that things which are different may have features in common.	1.21 Appreciation of the variety of living things and materials in the environment. 1.22 Awareness of changes which take place as time passes. 1.23 Recognition of common shapes — square, circle, triangle. 1.24 Recognition of regularity in patterns. 1.25 Ability to group things consistently according to chosen or given criteria.
Concrete operations. Early stage.	1.33 Ability to predict the effect of certain changes through observation of similar changes.	1.26 Awareness of the structure and form of living things. 1.27 Awareness of change of living things and non-living materials.

163

1.34 Formation of the notions of the horizontal and the vertical.

1.35 Development of concepts of conservation of length and substance.

1.36 Awareness of the meaning of speed and of its relation to distance covered.

1.28 Recognition of the action of force.

1.29 Ability to group living and non-living things by observable attributes.

1.29a Ability to distinguish regularity in events and motion.

Stage 2
Concrete operations.
Later stage.

2.31 Appreciation of measurement as division into regular parts and repeated comparison with a unit.

2.33 Development of concepts of conservation of weight, area and volume.

2.34 Appreciation of weight as a downward force.

2.35 Understanding of the speed, time, distance relation.

2.21 Awareness of internal structure in living and non-living things.

2.22 Ability to construct and use keys for identification.

2.23 Recognition of similar and congruent shapes.

2.24 Awareness of symmetry in shapes and structures.

2.25 Ability to classify living things and non-living materials in different ways.

2.26 Ability to visualize objects from different angles and the shape of cross-sections.

Stage 3
Transition to stage of abstract thinking.

3.31 Familiarity with relationships involving velocity, distance, time, acceleration.

3.32 Ability to separate, exclude or combine

3.21 Appreciation that classification criteria are arbitrary

3.22 Ability to distinguish observations which are relevant to the variables in approaching problems.

3.33 Ability to formulate hypotheses not dependent upon direct observation.

3.34 Ability to extend reasoning beyond the actual to the possible.

3.35 Ability to distinguish a logically sound proof from others less sound.

solution of a problem from those which are not.

3.23 Ability to estimate the order of magnitude of physical quantities.

Chapter 17

Curriculum Evaluation: with Reference to Some Projects.

Bill Gibby

What background information is needed for this theme?

Earlier in chapters 3, 6, 8 and 10, our discussions about school curricula and curriculum evaluation have implied that we are associating these two issues with what we regard to be worthwhile activities designed in such a way that pupils will attain certain desirable ends in a balanced fashion. Immediately anyone suggests in what ways the activities are worthwhile, or what the desirable ends are or what the form of the balanced fashion is, he is beginning to carry out an initial evaluation of the curriculum. Such initial valuing about any new curriculum will need to be done in the light of what it is thought that both teachers and their pupils will regard as desirable and relevant, but with realistic regard to the resources and facilities that are available for implementing such a curriculum. However, the whole issue of curriculum evaluation is made more complex when we attempt to determine to what extent, and by what means, the value judgments of teachers, pupils, 'curriculum experts', inspectors, advisers, parents, employers, politicians and others should all be considered in establishing whether a particular curriculum is worthwhile.

Recent curriculum development has been considered in the context of what is to be taught and learnt, why it is to be taught and learnt, how it is to be taught and learnt and with what success it has been learnt. Each of these is linked in some way with various processes of curriculum evaluation.

166

Earlier, in chapters 3 and 16, we saw how the basic elements of a curriculum are often expressed, in the context of a 'traditional' or 'classical' curriculum model, in terms of aims and objectives, content, method and evaluation. These basic elements have provided a framework for formulating some national and local curriculum projects. But there has been a much greater enthusiasm for setting up and implementing new ideas than in evaluating them. The related steps in planning and implementing the curriculum process of such projects have tended to be:

1 a situational analysis, i.e. a detailed analysis of what the whole situation is likely to be, bearing in mind the probable implications of any intended action;

2 a selection of aims and/or objectives;

3 a selection and organization of content;

4 a selection and organization of methods and related learning experiences;

5 assessment and evaluation.

In relating these steps there is a complex interaction between the various elements and a kind of constant oscillation of movement with the process as a whole gradually moving forward.

In this context, what is meant by curriculum evaluation? Any attempt to evaluate a curriculum is concerned with the extent to which we find it of value. But, in practice, it is soon evident that any process or technique of course evaluation involves more than value judgments made about whether a particular course should be introduced or not. We look for evidence of 'value' in a particular course, in terms of:

1 the initial value judgments of teachers about a course, their opinions as the course proceeds, their opinions once the course has ended, their subsequent opinions when the course is repeated;

2 the reactions and performances of those pupils who work through the course:

(a) when it is new and novel,

(b) when it is no longer a new one.

Almost all large-scale curriculum evaluation exercises in Britain have been concerned with particular areas of the curriculum. There have been some attempts to carry out a detailed evaluation of the whole curriculum in a wide range of schools, but full details of these attempts are not yet available.

What is involved in a so-called 'traditional' approach to curriculum evaluation?

In looking at a particular course, and examining case studies like those produced by the Schools Council, the traditional approach to curriculum evaluation adopted in some national projects appears to be done in the following four steps:

1 *Initial evaluation.* This is concerned with initial decisions about producing a worthwhile, realistic course.
2 *Formative evaluation.* The project is tried out in 'trial' schools. Consideration is given to what actually happens in practice as the course is being implemented. As the course proceeds, an on-going or formative evaluation is carried out, using various tests, inventories, questionnaires and observational and reporting techniques, to establish, first, how far the learning prescribed has been mastered and, second, the range of attitudes of teachers and their pupils towards the course.
3 *Summative evaluation.* At this stage, attempts are made to assess what has been achieved by pupils who have completed the course. In this end-of-course or summative evaluation, the tests used are related to what has been finally mastered and achieved as a result of the whole course. Also, the overall attitudes of teachers and pupils to the course are established.
4 *Longitudinal evaluation.* Finally, the question posed is: What happens when the course is widely tried out in a large number of schools and repeated by them several times? The method used to answer this question constitutes a long-term or longitudinal evaluation.

This four-stage type of 'traditional' curriculum evaluation is open to many objections. Probably the main one of these is that this kind of approach is really only suitable for evaluating those areas of the curriculum where objectives can be clearly stated and terminal assessments easily applied. In many attempts to evaluate a curriculum, with this kind of approach, difficulties have arisen because the criteria used for judging the worthwhile nature of particular courses have been quite different for employers, curriculum development workers, teachers and pupils.

What different forms of assessment are used in curriculum evaluation?

The techniques involved in producing evaluative evidence on which judgments about a curriculum are usually based are often associated not only with different kinds of tests and examinations but with observations, and related systematic recording of pupils' progress, made by teachers and others. But methods of assessment have changed in recent years both in the purposes for which they are used and in the range of abilities and traits being assessed and such is the complexity of this change that detailed consideration has been given to this issue in chapter 19.

Is there a need for an 'illuminative' approach to curriculum evaluation?

Earlier, in chapter 16, we discussed the reasons why some curriculum workers claimed that there was a need for a more enlightened, or 'illuminative', approach to curriculum planning. Similarly, in the present context, some of those concerned with curriculum evaluation deplore what they regard to be an over-emphasis on the measurement of progress made in traditional forms of curriculum evaluation. These critics prefer what has been called *illuminative evaluation*. This involves studying:

1 how the curriculum operates;
2 how it is influenced by the situations in which it is applied;
3 what those who apply it see as its advantages and disadvantages;
4 what the pupils' reactions are to the course concerned.

In some ways this approach seems to resemble the traditional model. But, in practice, it is more concerned with description and interpretation than with measurement and prediction. This kind of evaluation is claimed to be on-going and illuminative, changes occurring as the need arises. It highlights the need for co-operative attitudes between teachers and pupils and for flexible, adaptable approaches to on-going practice. But there are dangers in using such an 'illuminative' approach and these are considered, in some detail, in chapter 18. Some of these dangers are also discussed by Kelly (1977) in his chapter on curriculum evaluation.

Is there a need for a 'mastery' approach to learning, linked with a test reference for checking the 'standards' achieved by learners?

Amongst those who have been attempting to evaluate what is going on in schools are some (including, for example, Pidgeon and Allen, 1974) who challenge the attitude that it is claimed many teachers have to the standards that pupils can reach in their learning. Pidgeon and others suggest that there are certain kinds of learning in which the teachers should *expect* the vast majority of their pupils to achieve complete mastery of what they are doing, organizing their teaching strategies accordingly. It is argued that, in some cases, such mastery is not reached by many pupils because the teachers' expectations of their pupils' attainments are too low. Such an argument is often linked with a plea for the production of tests which could be used merely to check that mastery, at a predetermined level, has been achieved by almost all pupils in certain aspects of defined curriculum areas.

What approaches have been involved in evaluating particular British curriculum projects?

1 *The Humanities Curriculum Project* (See pp. 154–5 for an earlier discussion)

(a) The design of the project. The project team started with

the question: 'How can we handle controversial human issues in schools?' The team decided that an inquiry approach was the most appropriate one to adopt. They wished to develop an approach which would allow pupils to explore issues responsibly without being either restricted by their teacher's bias or subjected to undue pressure by other pupils. Nine controversial themes were selected for consideration including such issues as: 'war and society'; 'relations between the sexes'. Packs of material were prepared for pupils to use and subsequently discussed by them. The 'evidence' considered from the packs was not to be regarded as authoritative, it was merely material open to the scrutiny and criticism of any pupil who used it as part of his consideration of a particular topic.

(b) Discussions, with a neutral chairman. It was stressed, at all stages of this project, that pupils' discussions would be chaired by a teacher who would be neutral in the sense that he would allow his pupils to be free to discuss their own point of view and not be influenced by his.

(c) Objectives. The project did not have specific 'short-term' objectives. However, it did have a general aim: to develop an understanding of certain social situations and human relationships and to be aware of some of the controversial value issues which they raise.

(d) Difficulties. Evaluation of this project proved difficult because:

(i) the sampling methods used for selecting schools did not produce the expected range of schools;

(ii) some teachers and pupils did not feel that the topics chosen were the ones they regarded as of greatest interest to them;

(iii) some teachers and pupils found the demand on them difficult to meet; a few teachers found it difficult to be 'neutral', others were not sure of the role of a 'neutral' teacher; some pupils were at a disadvantage because they were poor readers; others found spontaneous discussion a difficult exercise.

(e) The evaluation of this project. All team members (after consulting many teachers) carried out some initial evaluation in deciding on the worthwhile nature of the content of this project and they gave some thought to the practicability of what they were attempting before the course was tried out. Initially, the project team did without a professional evaluation, but, as soon as the course had been implemented in schools, unexpected on-going problems arose and one person was then asked to look systematically and independently at the evaluation of on-going practice. Later, other evaluators joined the project team. Evaluation was carried out mainly to help the decision-makers involved in the project. Most of the evaluative techniques used were of an observational and a descriptive type. Some measurement of attainment was made and it was claimed that many pupils showed an improvement in reading skills as a result of doing this project and that many also passed from a 'concrete' stage of thinking to an 'abstract' one. Some pupils rated their own 'self-esteem' higher after doing work on this project than they did before doing such work.

(f) Further comments. In considering the learning outcomes of this project in chapter 16, we saw how many teachers recognized the advantages to pupils of speaking one's own mind but some teachers felt that the nature and intention of the 'neutral' restriction of the teacher was not altogether clear. Others, who accepted the 'neutral' idea, found it difficult to implement, particularly as the slightest gesture on the part of a teacher may well give some indication of his attitude. Many teachers claimed that most pupils had some difficulties with at least one of the following issues associated with the prepared 'packs': selecting an appropriate cross-section of available opinion; reading and understanding what was selected; contributing intelligently to group discussions.

2 *The Science 5–13 Curriculum Project* (see chapter 16 for further details)

(a) The design of the project. This project was planned by a small team of 'experts' and tried out in trial schools. Its main

aim was to relate topics or areas of science to a framework of appropriate concepts.

(b) Objectives. What was to be done was spelled out in behavioural terms.

(c) Evaluation. Evaluation was carried out at all stages of the project, a professional evaluator being appointed to carry out both formative (on-going) and summative (end-of-course) evaluations. The tests used included both cognitive items (i.e. those concerned with knowledge and its application) and affective items (i.e. those concerned with feelings, interests, opinions and attitudes). Also, some film loops were used for group testing. Teachers contributed to the evaluative procedures by answering questionnaires and providing periodic records of their pupils' progress. In addition, team members visited schools and reported to their evaluator any relevant information emerging from these visits. So, by using a variety of evaluative techniques, it was possible to identify changes in children's behaviour, and to obtain teachers' opinions about the relevance and worthwhile nature of the work and the effectiveness of its methodology.

(d) Teachers' criticisms. In spite of the care with which the objectives were specified, the established relevance of the related content and methodology and the continuous evaluative procedures used, some teachers criticized the kind of approach used because the initial planning stage of this project was not completely in the hands of the teachers. Such critics felt that 'experts' should act only when called upon to do so by the teachers and not control the initial and, as a consequence, the main course of direction of the project.

3 *The North West Regional Curriculum Development Project*

(a) The design of the project. Groups of secondary school teachers put forward suggestions for improving the curriculum in various secondary schools in the North West. The teachers themselves controlled the design of work done and they called in 'experts' when they needed advice. Planning

the discussions took place in local teachers' centres and material for this project was produced for ten subject areas of the curriculum. The teachers saw a need for a curriculum based on a sequence of learning experiences, each of which was aimed at the pursuit of clearly defined objectives.

(b) Evaluation. In this project the approach to curriculum evaluation included techniques similar to those used in validating programmed material, each pupil's demonstrated abilities and attributes were compared before and after the trial programme was given. Criterion-referenced tests were used and these gave an indication of the proportion of pupils who had mastered specified levels of knowledge and basic skills. So, in this project, formative and summative evaluations were related to predetermined standards.

(c) Further comments. Perhaps the teachers were too independent of the so-called experts. They sought advice, but perhaps not enough. Some teachers had difficulties with the formulation of objectives, with the construction and validation of test material and with the analysis and interpretation of results.

Further reading

Initial valuing of a curriculum

The need for more rigour in considering the initial value judgments involved in any curriculum evaluation is stressed by White (1971). For White, there is no single process of curriculum evaluation for all curricula.

Various approaches to curriculum evaluation

Whereas Wiseman and Pidgeon (1970) explain, clearly and simply, a traditional approach to curriculum evaluation, Stenhouse (1975) offers a critique of both the traditional and illuminative approaches to curriculum evaluation.

More recently, both Jenkins (1976) and Kelly (1977) consider the concept of curriculum evaluation and give critical appraisals of various evaluative models.

A *'mastery' approach to learning*

Pidgeon and Allen (1974) highlight the need for a 'mastery' approach to learning and suggestions are offered concerning an approach to the production of tests which would check whether such learning had taken place.

Evaluation of specific projects

A detailed discussion of the worthwhile nature of the Science 5–13 and North West curriculum projects appears in Entwistle and Nisbet (1972, chapter 14).

Most of the Schools Council Research Studies (1973) report considers the design and evaluation of twelve case studies, including the Humanities and Science 5–13 projects. In addition, in this report, there is a discussion of the role of the curriculum evaluator and some critical remarks on the way that curriculum evaluation is traditionally approached.

Chapter 18

Curriculum Evaluation: New Approaches

Denis Lawton

Evaluation for what?

The word evaluation is one of the most difficult concepts in the whole of curriculum studies. It is difficult because the word is used in a variety of ways with imprecise overlapping sets of meanings. In trying to clarify the use of 'evaluation' definitions are less useful than contextual descriptions. A number of writers have pointed out that evaluation is almost inevitably concerned with decision-making. Cronbach (1963; quoted in Stenhouse, 1975, p. 98) has discussed three types of decision where evaluation may be involved:

1 Course improvement: deciding what instructional material and methods are satisfactory and where change is needed.

2 Decisions about individuals: identifying the needs of the pupil for the sake of planning his instruction, judging pupil merit for the purposes of selection and grouping, acquainting the pupil with his own progress and deficiencies.

3 Administrative regulation: judging how good the school system is, how good individual teachers are, etc.

In this section I will be mainly concerned with course improvement, whether it is on the scale of a national project or the attempt by a teacher or a group of teachers in a school trying to improve their own teaching programme. Barry MacDonald has also discussed the purpose of evaluation in these terms. He suggests (1973, p. 88) that the major aim of evaluation is: 'To ascertain the effects of the project, document the circumstances in which they occur, and present this information in a form which will help educational decision-makers to evaluate the likely consequences of adopting the programme.'

What kind of evaluation?

In chapter 17 on curriculum evaluation a distinction was made between traditional or classical evaluation and the newer illuminative approach to evaluation. In this chapter I want to say some more about illuminative evaluation, make some criticisms of it and show some of the directions that evaluation seems to be moving in.

The classical or experimental model of evaluation is sometimes referred to as the agricultural botanical model. This might be an implicit criticism, and sometimes an explicit criticism, of the classical educational experiment which treated learning as a simple matter, and regarded evaluation as a process of 1 pre-test, 2 teaching programme, 3 post-test. Just as an agricultural experiment might test the efficiency of a new fertilizer by 1 measuring the height of a plant; 2 applying the fertilizer for a given amount of time; then 3 measuring again, comparing the growth with that of plants in a control group. Much of the reaction against applying that kind of experimental design to children's learning is that the teaching/learning situation is so much more complex. For example, human beings perform differently when under observation, cabbages do not; the unintended consequences of human interference are likely to be much more important in any situation involving human beings; in educational settings the 'process' is as important as — or more important than — the 'product'.

Parlett and Hamilton in a now famous paper 'Evaluation as Illumination' (available in Tawney, 1976) describe these difficulties, which apply not only to evaluation but to the whole of educational research. In fact much of the interest in the new evaluation is precisely that it shifts the style of educational research generally as well as curriculum evaluation in particular. Dissatisfaction with the agricultural-botanical model (also referred to as the output model, the engineering or factory or product model) was one motive for seeking a new evaluation paradigm; another was the comparative lack of success — or failure of 'take-up' — of many large and expensive curriculum projects: although project directors and evaluators might demonstrate the effectiveness of a new Schools Council or Nuffield curriculum project, teachers frequently appear to be unconvinced, or seem not to want to know. Could they be right? Could they somehow know that there is more to the story than the test results revealed? (See Marten Shipman's book (1974) on the difference between the official view of a project and how the teachers involved in the experimental schools actually saw it.)

Another aspect of the botanical model experiment which began to be criticized was the emphasis on size: large samples which showed differences which could be measured and which would be big enough to be statistically significant. Robert Stake, an American evaluator, has suggested that what we need at this stage is a panoramic view-finder rather than a microscope. This was not a criticism of empirical methods but was simply saying that perhaps we had moved towards detailed measurement too soon before acquiring a better means of describing the full picture of the evaluation situation. If evaluation was concerned with helping decision-makers then more was required than isolated test results. Much more information should be given on which decision-makers might make a rational choice. The reaction against traditional, experimental evaluation has taken a number of forms which might all be included in a term such as 'new wave' or non-traditional. Stake talks of 'responsive' evaluation, Parlett and Hamilton (1976) use 'illuminative', while MacDonald (1973) and his team of evaluators have tended to concentrate on 'case-study' evaluation. The non-traditional styles of evaluation (which have much in common but are not identical) lean towards the disciplines of sociology, social anthropology and history rather than experimental psychology and psychometrics.

When the investigator abandons the agricultural-botany paradigm his role is necessarily redefined. The use of interpretive human insight and skills, is, indeed, encouraged rather than discouraged. The illuminative evaluator thus joins a diverse group of specialists (e.g. psychiatrists, social anthropologists and historians) where this is taken for granted. In each of these fields the research worker has to weigh and sift a complex array of human evidence and draw conclusions from it. (Parlett and Hamilton in Tawney, 1976, p. 97).

The rules of non-traditional evaluation

But what are the rules for this new evaluation game? Clearly these new style evaluators need very high levels of inter-personal skills, but there is also a need to develop certain guidelines and certain criteria for an acceptable research methodology.

In 1972 there was a conference of the new-wave evaluators at the end of which a statement was made arguing the case for a new style of evaluation.

On December 20th 1972 at Churchill College, Cambridge, the following conference participants concluded a discussion of the aims and procedures of evaluating educational practices and agreed:

1 That past efforts to evaluate these practices have, on the whole, not adequately served the needs of those who require evidence of the effects of such practices because of:

(a) an under-attention to educational processes including those of the learning milieu;

(b) over-attention to psychometrically measurable changes in student behaviour (that to an extent represent the outcomes of the practice, but which are misleading oversimplification of the complex changes that occur in students); and

(c) the existence of an educational research climate that rewards accuracy of measurement and generality of theory but overlooks both mismatch between school problems and research issues and tolerates ineffective communication between researchers and those outside the

179

research community.

2 They also agreed that future efforts to evaluate these practices be designed so as to be:
   (a) responsive to the needs and perspectives of differing audiences;
   (b) illuminative of the complex organisational, teaching and learning processes at issue;
   (c) relevant to public and professional decisions forthcoming; and
   (d) reported in language which is accessible to their audiences.

3 More specifically they recommended that, increasingly,
   (a) observational data, carefully validated, be used (sometimes in substitute for data from questioning and testing);
   (b) the evaluation be designed so as to be flexible enough to allow for response to unanticipated events (progressive focusing rather than pre-ordinate design); and that
   (c) the value positions of the evaluator, whether highlighted or constrained by the design, be made evident to the sponsors and audiences of the evaluation.

4 Though without consensus on the issues themselves, it was agreed that considered attention by those who design evaluation studies should be given to such issues as the following:
   (a) the sometimes conflicting roles of the same evaluator as expert, scientist, guide, and teacher of decision-makers on the one hand, and as technical specialist, employee and servant of decision-makers on the other;
   (b) the degree to which the evaluator, his sponsors, and his subjects, should specify in advance the limits of enquiry, the circulation of findings, and such matters as may become controversial later;
   (c) the advantages and disadvantages of intervening in educational practices for the purposes of gathering data or of controlling the variability of certain features in order to increase the generalisability

of the findings;

(d) the complexity of educational decisions which, as a matter of rule, have political, social and economic implications; and the responsibility that the evaluator may or may not have for exploring these implications.

(e) the degree to which the evaluator should interpret his observations rather than leave them for different audiences to interpret.

It was acknowledged that different evaluation designs will service different purposes and that even for a single educational programme many different designs could be used. MacDonald and Parlett, 1973, pp. 79–80).

One of the obvious dangers of illuminative evaluations is that a so-called evaluation can degenerate into mere anecdotalism or a series of subjective impressions masquerading as objective reporting. The 1972 declaration does go some way towards establishing rules, but they are, as yet, too general. There is also a danger that a small in-group of evaluators will evolve who discuss esoteric methods of evaluation among themselves, and thus make curriculum evaluation even more remote from teachers than traditional educational research. Above all it is essential that evaluation should be discussed publicly – that is openly and in language that can be understood by administrators and teachers.

It is, however, a mistake to think of evaluation in terms of two clear-cut categories – 'classical' or 'experimental' and 'non-traditional' or 'qualitative'. The impression sometimes given in discussions of evaluation is that the two styles of evaluation are now miles apart and are forging ahead in quite different directions. This is clearly not the case. Non-traditional evaluation has evolved gradually out of certain dissatisfactions with the experimental model, but the overlap has always been considerable, and at the moment the two models may be converging rather than drawing further apart. When the Schools Council Research Study *Evaluation in Curriculum Development: Twelve Case Studies* was published in 1973, it was possible to label some of the twelve projects as employing traditional experimental evaluations and others as being much more non-traditional. But even then there were difficulties. The Cambridge Schools Classics Project was clearly experimental, whereas Integrated Studies was more illuminative. But the Nuffield 'A' Level Biological Science and Humanities Curriculum Project had characteristics of both, and even the Science 5 to 13 Curriculum Project evaluated by Wynne Harlen was by no means a 100 per cent experimental model. It may have started out much more dedicated to the experimental model but it rapidly moved in the other direction. By 1973 the best kind of evaluation seemed to be a mixture of the two styles. Getting the balance right was the major difficulty. There is a certain affinity between the objectives approach of the experimental model and behaviouristic psychology, whereas illuminative evaluation is closer to techniques of participant observation and anthropology, but this should not be exaggerated and it should not be assumed that the two models are incompatible. It is possible to be eclectic.

This point has also been made by Rae Munro in *Innovation, Success or Failure*, 1977. Munro spent a year attached to the London Institute of Education (1973–4) studying the aims and methods of curriculum evaluators in the UK. He began by being firmly committed to the experimental model but in the course of the year was more and more impressed by certain aspects of non-traditional evaluation. By the end of the year he was agreeing with those who advocated a mixture of methods or a balanced approach to the problem of evaluation: for example, that we should not neglect testing and measurement whenever they can give us the kind of information that decision-makers need. But above all the real world of the teacher should not be neglected in any kind of curriculum evaluation. This is related to the fact that many early curriculum projects, especially those in the USA, were based on the idea of teacher-proof materials (the idea that a project director would produce materials which would be so designed as to be incapable of being 'spoilt' by a teacher who did not really understand what the curriculum project was really about). This has now been shown to be a fatal mistake. In any curriculum development the teacher is central. Just as there is no play that is 'director-proof', there is no curriculum innovation that is either teacher-proof or student-proof. These are variables that cannot be left out and cannot be treated in an over-generalized way. Teachers do not react in a completely predictable way. Part of the problem is, therefore, to try to make generalizations but taking into account local and individual differences. This is clearly a much more difficult task than coming to conclusions based on test results of large samples of children.

The teacher as a researcher

Lawrence Stenhouse (1975) points to a way out of the difficulty by suggesting that we should move from product and process models of curriculum development towards a *research model*. Stenhouse (1975, p. 125) does not accept the distinction between evaluation and development so he finds it an advantage to cast the teacher-developer-research not

> in the role of the creator or man with a mission, but in that of the investigator. The curriculum he creates is then to be judged by whether it advances our knowledge rather than by whether it is right. It is conceived as a probe through which to explore and test hypotheses and not as a recommendation to be adopted.

Stenhouse illustrates his suggestion by reference to his own research into teaching about race relations. He suggests that the research project started from two premises:

> 1. That nobody knows how to teach about race relations;
> 2. That it is unlikely that there is *one* way of teaching about race relations which can be recommended.

He suggests, for example, that it is unlikely that the same materials and the same teaching strategy would be desirable in a multi-racial inner-urban school, in which two racial groups were strongly represented, a multi-racial school in which three racial groups are strongly represented, and a rural school in which pupils have little contact with any cultures other than their own. The concern of the teacher as researcher is not so much 'are these materials successful?' or 'will this teaching programme work for the whole country?' but 'how can I judge whether something is suitable in these particular circumstances?' 'All suggestions about curriculum are conditional suggestions and the conditions need to be spelt out.'

For Stenhouse the teacher is a professional and the particular kind of professionalism which is implied is 'research based teaching' which changes the emphasis from outside 'independent' evaluation to self-evaluation. There are of course considerable difficulties in the role of teacher as researcher. In particular he has to be both a teacher and participant observer in his own classroom. This is extremely difficult and in some schools may be impossible. There are, however, certain rules which can be laid down for teacher behaviour in this situation (these are discussed in Stenhouse, 1975, chapter 10). It may also be helpful for teachers to invite an observer into their classrooms – possibly another teacher. This has also given rise to another research project directed by John Elliott (the Ford Teaching Project, see chapter 22). One of the techniques developing is 'triangulation': a teacher's view of the situation is compared with that of his pupils and that of the independent observer. This has also proved to be of significance in developing teachers' expertise and professionalism, but here again there are considerable methodological problems involved. This kind of research is also closely connected with what has elsewhere been described as 'action research', that is the kind of research (see Halsey, 1972) where it is frankly accepted that the purpose of the research is not simply to observe and describe but to produce *change* during the course of the research programme. In Halsey's case this was an attempt to improve the learning of the children in educational priority areas; in the case of John Elliott's research it is an attempt to help teachers be aware of their own teaching methods and to narrow the gap between attempt and achievement. (See also chapter 22 for a further discussion of the teacher as researcher.)

Case Studies

One of the methods used in non-traditional, qualitative evaluation is the case-study approach. In December 1975 the 'Second Cambridge Conference' was held on 'Re-thinking

Case Study'. A report was written by Adelman, Jenkins and Kemmis (1976) which concluded in this way:

Possible Advantages of Case Study
Case studies have a number of advantageous characteristics that make them attractive to educational evaluators or researchers.

1 Case-study data, paradoxically, is 'strong in reality' but difficult to organise. In contrast, other research data is often 'weak in reality' but susceptible to ready organisation. This strength in reality is because case studies are down-to-earth and attention holding, in harmony with the reader's own experience, and thus provide a 'natural' basis for generalisation. A reader responding to a case study report is consequently able to employ the ordinary processes of judgment by which people tacitly understand life and social actions around them.

2 Case studies allow generalisations either about an instance or from an instance to a class. Their peculiar strength lies in their attention to the subtlety and complexity of the case in its own right.

3 Case studies recognise the complexity and 'embeddedness' of social truths. By carefully attending to social situations, case studies can represent something of the discrepancies or conflicts between the viewpoints held by participants. The best case studies are capable of offering some support to alternative interpretations.

4 Case studies, considered as products, may form an archive of descriptive material sufficiently rich to admit subsequent reinterpretation. Given the variety and complexity of educational purposes and environments, there is an obvious value in having a data source for researchers and users whose purposes may be different from our own.

5 Case studies are 'a step to action'. They begin in a world of action and contribute to it. Their insights may be directly interpreted and put to use; for staff or individual self-development, for within-institutional feedback; for formative evaluation; and in educational policy making.

6 Case studies present research or evaluation data in a more publicly accessible form than other kinds of research report, although this virtue is to some extent bought at

the expense of their length. The language and the form of the presentation is hopefully less esoteric and less dependent on specialised interpretation than conventional research reports. The case study is capable of serving multiple audiences. It reduces the dependence of the reader upon unstated implicit assumptions (which necessarily underlie any type of research) and makes the research process itself accessible. Case studies, therefore, may contribute towards the 'democratisation' of decision-making (and knowledge itself). At its best, they allow the reader to judge the implications of a study for himself.

Once again a major problem here is for teachers to decide on the rules for case-study evaluation. One of the lines of research currently being pursued by the Curriculum Studies Department is to try to develop methods of case study, to define more clearly what the guidelines are, what particular skills of teacher researchers are essential, and what the rules are for reporting.

It seems to us that the case study is an essential tool in curriculum evaluation but that its methodology is still in need of a good deal of research and development.

Further reading

Basic reading on curriculum evaluation has already been given at the end of chapter 17. In addition I would suggest the following: Munro (1977) for an up-to-date critical review of evaluation techniques in the UK; Tawney (1976), a collection of papers from member of the Schools Council evaluators group. Golby *et al.* (1975, section IV) has reprints of some useful papers. Parsons (1976).

Chapter 19

Methods of Assessment

Bill Gibby

In earlier chapters (7, 10, 16 and 17) we have seen the need for some understanding of assessment procedures in the context of: theories of learning and instruction, curriculum objectives and curriculum evaluation. In this chapter we look at some of the assessments being used in practice and consider the implications of such uses for teachers and pupils. Whereas the focus of attention here is mainly on educational assessment in schools, many of the principles involved are of similar importance in the context of further and higher education.

What is the difference between 'evaluation' and 'assessment'?

The terms 'evaluation' and 'assessment' are often given similar meanings in educational literature. What meaning is usually given to 'evaluation', which may be regarded as the broader of these two terms? To evaluate anything done in schools is to state its value or worth. Such an evaluation could arise in a variety of ways. In considering the introduction of a new course, certain value judgments could be made about the nature and desirability of the proposed course. In this context it would be possible to formulate an initial evaluation of the proposed course based on what it was thought it was desirable that pupils should do and how they should do it. But there would be other forms of evaluation to follow once the course was tried out in trial schools and then subsequently put into general practice. Value judgments would still be needed here but these, at least in part, would be related to assessments of what happens when the claimed value or worth of a proposed course is put to the test in practice. The extent to which such a course is workable and effective and the related criteria for establishing this are the kinds of issues, in this context, that might be associated with the various forms of assessment used. Thus it can be said that the evaluation of a course could be thought in terms of all the value judgments made about the course both before the course is put into practice and once it has been tried out. However, any evaluation process, once the course was being established, would need to include various kinds of assessment as these would be required to provide at least some of the evidence on which evaluative decisions could be made about the course's overall practical value. So, in this sense, appropriate assessments would form one component of an evaluation process. (In your own consideration of this issue you might find it helpful to study the discussions by Pidgeon in Pidgeon and Allen (1974), MacIntosh (1976) and Rowntree (1977) on why we need different forms of assessment anyway. In particular, Rowntree distinguishes between informal and formal assessments. He emphasizes that when a teacher meets a group of pupils new to each other, teacher and pupils alike all undertake informal assessments in their attempts to get to know everyone else. Rowntree considers the nature of the appraisals that take place in making informal assessments and regards these as just as important as the testing undertaken when more formal assessments are required.)

What kinds of assessments are being made by teachers and others?

It is possible to study the kinds of assessments that are made, and those that can be made, with reference to the following five categories (with some overlap between categories), in considering the uses of:

tests and examinations constructed to 'measure' cognitive development;

systematic observation and recording of pupils' progress made by teachers;

self-assessment records kept by pupils;

personality assessments and sociometric techniques carried out by teachers and others;

longitudinal studies of children's development made by research workers.

Some comments on each of these categories seems desirable.

1. *Tests and examinations*

Conventional standardized tests of intelligence (verbal and non-verbal reasoning) and standardized tests of attainment have tended to be in more common use in primary schools than in secondary schools. Some teachers would claim for intelligence tests that they do give some measure of a capacity for reasoning and accordingly of a capacity for learning and can be used partially as an indication of potential academic success. On the other hand, teachers who give a standardized attainment test to an individual do so in an attempt to assess the stage and level of performance he has reached in a particular activity relative to national or area norms. Such a test would measure an individual's achievement or proficiency in the area concerned. In using such an assessment a teacher is testing how effectively some defined curriculum area has been learnt.

Nowadays, there is a decrease in the use of standardized and attainment tests at primary level, but there is (in some areas) an increase in their use at secondary level. At this later level, the main uses of such tests are to help provide overall details of pupils with various kinds of difficulties and (when linked with evidence other than test performances) guidance for appropriate remedial measures. There are only a few standardized attainment tests with national norms which are available for general use at secondary level, partly because, for many pupils, public examinations are used for such assessments, but also because of the widely different kinds of treatment that many subjects or integrated courses receive at a later stage. But it is important to stress that many public

189

examinations at CSE, CEE, 'O' and 'A' level, are now using objective-type tests which are being constructed and 'validated' (i.e. 'tried out' before examination use and subject to both statistical and non-statistical rigorous scrutiny) in a similar manner to the approach used in producing any kind of standardized test. Also, many examining boards, examining pupils of 16+, now make use of suitable adaptations of forms of assessment formerly used for 11+ allocation purposes, some of these being particularly in evidence in some of the studies testing out the possibilities of a 'common' examination at 16+.

With an increase in the immigrant population in this country, with greater mobility of families and with a greater number of mixed ability classes, important uses are being made of diagnostic tests, tests of readiness and prognostic tests. Diagnostic tests are tests used to indicate points at which a pupil has failed to learn something; they usually diagnose difficulties which a pupil is experiencing and teachers use them to help in supplying the right kind of remedial measures. In using diagnostic tests, it seems necessary to stress that, for mixed-ability groups, there is certainly a need for groups of teachers to produce their own diagnostic tests for all ages and for all levels of ability — not just for the least able or slowest learners.

Tests of readiness and prognostic tests are predictive tests. For example, it is possible to devise special kinds of picture and pattern tests to establish, to some extent, the readiness of a pupil to read; it is possible to devise a prognostic test, usually an aptitude test, to indicate whether a pupil has the potential and ability for a future course, task or vocation. Here we see tests that are different from the more conventional achievement or attainment tests. That there is such a distinction is clear merely by comparing, for example, any one of the NFER standardized mathematics attainment tests with one of their mathematical 'insight' tests. This distinction is more important than at first sight it appears to be. Recent discussions by people like Lewis (1974), in considering information for university and college admission, have drawn a distinction between attainment items and aptitude tests mainly on the basis that a lower level of formal training in the subject concerned would be required in the aptitude items and that these would focus on requiring the pupil to think quantitatively and intelligently about basic skills and principles developed and tests containing items of this kind are really tests of developed abilities. Lewis points out that there is some evidence to suggest that the use of a scholastic aptitude test combined with performances at 'A' level may well be a better prediction of success in higher education than the use of 'A'-level grades only. It is important to mention that NFER have made use of scholastic aptitude tests at 16+ and that such tests are not only applicable to possible university entrance candidates. However, there are dangers in using *any* test, no matter how carefully it is devised, for predictive purposes. If the prediction is to cover too long a period, many other factors, such as good or bad teaching, continued good or poor motivation and unusual personal circumstances, may mean that subsequent performances do not necessarily match the initial suggested potential or lack of it.

Most teacher-made tests are, of course, unstandardized tests of achievement and until relatively recently, many of these tended to test mainly memory of factual knowledge and simple skills. But during the last ten years or so there has been a change in attitude by many teachers towards tests and examinations and a shift in emphasis in their own responsibility in these matters. (Guidance on the setting of conventional achievement tests is available in many of the Schools Council's *Examination Bulletins* (1963–77), but those who need detailed guidance on the selection of tests for younger children may find Jackson's (1973) suggestions for the use of various mental and scholastic tests helpful, particularly in relationship to readiness tests, reading tests and diagnostic tests.) Those who wish to make extensive use of standardized test material as part of a school's assessment programme will need to consult the NFER (1976 and 1977) catalogues of psychological and educational tests, seek the personal advice of the research officers at the NFER Publishing Company, Windsor, and refer to various NFER publications, such as those produced by Vincent and Cresswell (1976) and Sumner and Robertson (1977).

2. *Systematic observation and recording of pupils' progress by teachers*

Teachers in nursery, infant and first schools often keep simple personal records of pupils which give some useful details about the sort of things that individual children have been doing or have achieved. With younger children, this will include things like: ways they adapt themselves to new situations; how they behave under various circumstances; the acquiring of a new skill; various reactions to what they are doing, including things that particularly interest them. As the school situation gets more formal, records will also include attempts to assess progress in reading, simple number work, creative work and oral communication. There will be some diagnosis of difficulties experienced by individuals in various social, physical and intellectual activities matched with proposed remedial action and a subsequent report on the effectiveness of such actions. This kind of 'case-study' approach to the recording of individual progress is time consuming but many teachers of younger children seem to find such record-keeping an essential part of their work. Perhaps, where this is appropriate, such records should include some details of how a pupil handles his own unusual idea as well as details of his performances with conventional material and experiences. It is possibly a pity that the number of secondary school pupils that a teacher of older pupils encounters makes detailed 'case-study' records of this kind too numerous to cope with, but nevertheless it brings into question the meaning that can be given to the present kinds of marks and grades that many secondary teachers keep as the main (and sometimes the only) source of evidence of their pupils' so-called 'progress'.

Questions worthy of consideration appear to be: should marks and grades be given for things that pupils do? If they should, in what ways should they be made more meaningful? For what reasons and in what ways (if at all!) should comprehensive, cumulative 'case-study' reports of individual progress be kept? What specific assessment and evaluative techniques are relevant to anyone compiling such reports? (Useful guidance on keeping records of continuous assessment at secondary level is beginning to appear in recent *Examination Bulletins* of the Schools Council and the reader's critical appraisal of some of this material may be worthwhile.)

3. *Self-assessment records by pupils*

For a variety of reasons, many teachers of older children at primary level and of secondary school children ask pupils to keep their own brief records of such issues as: the work that they have covered, their reactions to the material studied and the conditions and ways in which it was learnt; their own progress as they see it themselves (relative to their own efforts and abilities rather than to those of their classmates); the difficulties that they have experienced and what they have done about these and with what success. The extent to which such records should be general practice and the form such records could take and how often they could be made, in logbook form or otherwise, seems to be an issue worthy of the reader's further consideration.

4. *Personality assessment and sociometric techniques*

Whether detailed records of children's progress at school are kept or not, all teachers experience behaviour and learning difficulties amongst their pupils which they feel need special treatment. Some of this they will cope with themselves, some of it they will refer to another teacher, but, from time to time, they may also want to use the services of an educational psychologist or counsellor. In particular, many teachers would feel that they should leave 'trained experts' (who would normally not be teachers) to deal with detailed personality assessment as some of the techniques that can be used need either special skill in themselves or comprehensive, difficult interpretations of results easily obtained. Some of the hazards involved in reliably and validly establishing ratings for defined personality traits are discussed by Schofield (1972) and, apart from pin-pointing the problems involved with rating scales, he considers the complications arising with: interest inventories; projective and similar tests, interviewing techniques; validating and using a questionnaire. From Schofield's detailed discussion it seems reasonable to deduce that such methods of assessment are best left to those trained to carry them out. The use of sociometric measurements is, perhaps, more debatable. With a need to form small groups in a variety of circumstances and ways, it may well seem useful for a teacher to make some use of the kind of sociometric measurements which Schofield describes.

5. *Longitudinal research studies of children's development*

During the last fifteen years or so there have been many attempts in Britain to follow the development of a large number of individual children over several years of their lives. Some of the studies carried out by Douglas, Moore, Kellmer Pringle, Newson and others are discussed in Pidgeon and Allen (1974). Such studies make use of many of the techniques already referred to in our first four categories and they aim to produce comprehensive, cumulative records of individual development. This longitudinal approach enables the researchers concerned to confirm certain tendencies which could be detected in the early stages of a survey but also to correct what turns out to be early misconceptions. But such studies do have some disadvantages and the reader may like to consider what these are likely to be.

Having given some consideration to five important categories relevant to any comprehensive study of educational assessment, let us now look, in more specific detail, at some of the issues already raised.

In what ways have teachers' attitudes to examinations recently changed?

For many years teachers have criticized the efficiency of public examinations. They have questioned their reliability (i.e. they have asked questions like: Is the examination trustworthy? Are markers consistent in their marking? Would pupils perform differently with the same or similar material on a different day?) and they have doubted their validity (i.e. they pose questions like: Does the examination measure well the outcomes of the kind of work covered by the pupils taking the examination?) Also, most teachers criticize the small and often unrepresentative sampling of a pupil's abilities tested by public examinations; some are irritated by the use of rigid time limits, others feel that too much is at stake to try to assess a range of abilities by only giving papers over a relatively short period of time at the end of a course. In addition, most teachers have been worried about the increase in outside pressures from parents, employers, university authorities and professional bodies for 'better' examination results. Most teachers are concerned that examinations dictate not only what is done but how it is done. Such critics deplore the fact that the impact of examinations on schools should encourage cramming, question spotting, unimaginative revision, learning by heart and so on. Some teachers claim the potentially most interesting parts of school work receive little or no attention because such material is never examined. Others claim the really worthwhile things done in school shouldn't be examined anyway.

It is not surprising then that a new pattern of assessment for some secondary school examinations has emerged over the past twelve years or so. Nowadays most secondary school teachers would probably claim that they would prefer to give careful thought to what is to be learnt by their pupils, why it is to be learnt and how it should be learnt and, only when such decisions have been made, would they wish to pose the question: How are we to assess what has been learnt? Many of these teachers want assessments which will give them reliable information about what factual knowledge their pupils have acquired, what skills they have learned, what principles and concepts they have understood, the extent to which they are able to apply these principles to familiar and unfamiliar situations, how much insight, initiative, imagination and inventiveness they have developed and so on. In addition, in this context, teachers want to know how to compile, for each pupil, an appropriate cumulative record of progress which might help others to give him future educational and vocational guidance.

In particular, teachers want public examinations at least to measure reliably and validly what they think it is desirable for their pupils to do, to know and to understand. Some teachers feel that a large-scale common set of test papers for thousands of children puts too much emphasis on what is often dull common ground and over-emphasizes individual differences. But, at CSE level, for example, a mode of examination exists whereby teachers determine first what they want their pupils to do, then how to teach it and, finally, in what ways the knowledge, skills and abilities they have acquired are to be assessed. However, where secondary school teachers are given the freedom to determine their own syllabus and to use their own forms of assessment for evaluating the work done by their pupils, a relatively small proportion of teachers tend to do so.

What types of test specification are being used in public examinations and what kinds of alternatives are now being proposed?

In the last fifteen years or so, in order to meet some of the criticisms levelled at public examinations, there have been many attempts to systematize the procedure for setting external examination papers. One of these results from adaptations of Bloom's (1956) suggestion for classifying educational objectives. If we were to follow Bloom's approach to the classification of cognitive objectives in setting papers for a public examination we would, for example, probably ensure that certain pieces of knowledge, techniques and skills were tested, but, also, that comprehension, application, inventiveness and so on had been assessed as well. But there are many critics of this kind of approach, for reasons which were considered in the discussion on curriculum objectives in chapter 16, and, undoubtedly, there are areas of the curriculum for which Bloom's approach has little or no meaning; some examiners who have no use for Bloom's classification are more interested in other types of 'examination blue-print' and some of these make use of Gagné's (1970) classification of learning types which includes concept learning, principle learning and problem solving. Classification of items and questions into such types is possible and one way in which this can be done is discussed in section 7 of Stones (1970). In the same section of this book there is a detailed criticism of existing test procedures and a switch of emphasis to a fundamental discussion on what is called 'test reference'. (Thyne, 1974, also considers this matter.) Almost all present attainment tests are built up on what is sometimes called a norm-referenced approach. Here the criterion of competence in a subject arises from a set of norms drawn from a typical population. The scores on a test are found and this enables us to arrange the pupils in rank order and then decide on our grades. Such tests are produced in such a way that each item or question supposedly clearly discriminates between the most able and the least able pupils. Stones, Thyne and others are suggesting that this approach puts the emphasis in the wrong place. They prefer what is called a criterion-referenced approach in which the main issue is to assess skills and concepts where the emphasis is on the achievement of pre-determined standards rather than on the discriminative value of each part of the test. This suggestion has been proposed in an attempt to get away from an over-emphasis on individual differences and competitive assessments.

In this context, Pidgeon (Pidgeon and Allen, 1974) and others have challenged the traditional educational forecast that curves of achievement must follow a normal distribution and they suggest that, in many kinds of learning in schools, it is possible to assume that criteria can be established which ensure that the vast majority of pupils master what it is proposed should be learnt. With most pupils being expected to achieve mastery learning by their teachers, criterion-referenced tests would be constructed merely to check that almost everyone had achieved the defined levels of learning in the tasks that were to be mastered. (A useful summary of the controversy surrounding and underlying the theory of criterion-referenced measurement is also given by Sumner and Robertson, 1977.)

What studies have influenced the forms of assessment now used in many secondary school examinations?

A consideration of Judge's discussion of examinations in his article in Pidgeon and Allen (1974), linked with some of the studies referred to in his list of further reading, pin-points some important evidence on the relatively poor reliability and validity of many school public examinations of the 1930s, '40s and '50s and the need not only for care in preparing examination papers but also the desirability of using more than one form of assessment for most examinations.

Perhaps surprisingly, one of the most influential groups of studies which have led to recent newer forms of assessment of pupils of 16+ was that undertaken in the mid-1950s by Vernon (1957) and others investigating suggested improvements in allocation procedures for pupils entering secondary schools at 11+. Vernon's report includes a discussion of experiments on difficulties related to the setting and marking of conventional papers of the essay kind of the long answer type. There are a variety of suggestions for improving the method of setting essays, the choice of suitable topics and the improvement in the reliability of marking them by, for example, allowing several markers to mark each essay independently with their assessments pooled to give an agreed composite mark, which is not necessarily the mean of the separate marks. The strengths and weaknesses of various standardized tests are explored. The use of teachers' assessments, and what is involved in them, are discussed. It is suggested in this report that the most reliable and valid type of overall assessment seems to result from the pooling of relevant details arising from various forms of assessments obtained at different age levels and from different aspects and features of a pupil's work and his ability to co-operate with others. The importance of a teacher's knowledge of his pupils is stressed and the report examines several ingenious methods of combining various types of test scores and teachers' scaled assessments. The dangers of too much dependence on objective type tests are considered, particularly in relation to the backwash effect on teaching in the schools. Even though these studies were aimed at producing methods of assessment that would improve procedures for eventual secondary school allocation, the results of many of the experiments described in Vernon's report have been far reaching as far as recent methods of assessment at secondary level are concerned. More recently, experiments have been carried out in attempts to improve forms of assessments used in CSE, 'O' and 'A' level and university entrance examinations and some of these are considered in various *Examination Bulletins* of the Schools Council (1963–77), in Eggleston and Kerr (1969) and in Lewis (1974) and some of the experiments reviewed are merely direct applications to assessments at 16+ (or later) of Vernon's earlier suggestions for the improvement of assessments made of primary school children's progress. An even more extensive use of Vernon's suggestions may well be needed if a 'common' examination emerges at 16+.

Nowadays, what aspects of assessment need to be stressed at primary level?

There certainly seems to be a need to keep detailed individual records of the 'case-study' type mentioned earlier and, when considering some of the older children at this level, some form of self-assessment record could be encouraged. But by the very nature of the work done at the majority of primary schools predictive assessments are needed less. Teachers at this level need more knowledge and understanding of the uses of criterion-referenced tests and diagnostic tests (for all ability ranges) as well as some clarification of the present place and value of other more traditional type tests. But where there is emphasis on so-called discovery methods, some difficulties can arise when trying to make meaningful assessments related to such methods, with suggestions for 'scoring' children's creative thinking often being deemed as lacking both reliability and validity.

If any attempt is made to set up a test specification to assess cognitive work done at primary level the type of approach suggested by Gagné (1970) is clearly preferable to the one given by Bloom (1956). But no one really seems to be clear about what kinds of assessments are needed at primary level. Even if suitable criterion-referenced tests and an appropriate combination of existing reasoning and attainment tests were used these would still only assess a small, if important, part of the picture. More and more will depend on teacher assessments, but teachers will need much more specific guidance on this, through in-service and other courses, than they are getting now, particularly with regard to the nature, form and content of any 'case-study' records that they may decide to keep. A similar type of approach to record-keeping may well be necessary for some areas of the curriculum at secondary level, particularly those concerned with integrated courses. An interesting kind of assessment now being used at primary level is illustrated in the use of the Nuffield check-up tests which have a special flavour of their own.

Clearly much more thought is needed on how both primary and secondary school teachers can make more reliable and valid assessments of all those aspects (not merely the 'cognitive' ones) which will enable teachers, in the light of such assessments, to provide the kind of experiences, materials, conditions and stimulation that will enable every individual to make the best all-round progress of which he is capable.

What kinds of assessment are being used in examinations at secondary level?

The greatest changes have taken place in the methods of setting and marking traditional end-of-course examination papers. However, recently, some stress has been given, in addition, to the need for some form of continuous assessment of pupils' work related to carefully kept teachers' records. At secondary school level, this form of assessment (when used) is usually combined with other more conventional forms of assessment. (A study of a variety of methods of assessment used in the late 1960s is considered by various research workers in the papers in Eggleston and Kerr (1969), and more recent work is considered in MacIntosh, 1974.)

Methods of setting and marking conventional papers, mainly of the essay or long answer type have been improving, although there are still difficulties to be resolved when a choice of questions is allowed, although the Schools Council has done some useful work on this. In this context, sectionalizing helps a little but produces other difficulties, whilst statistical treatment of question scores before adding them is open to a variety of objections which the reader is invited to suggest.

More attention is now given to analysing what is to be

tested before setting papers. Also, many proposed questions are often tried out with a large population to provide evidence of their 'suitability' as examination items or questions. Greater care is taken with multiple impression, independent marking of essays, and, for appropriate material, carefully prepared analytical marking schemes are used. Many examination papers include 'structured' questions which, to a certain extent, guide the candidate through related steps and this makes it easier to test certain skills and abilities. However, in some structured questions the form of the answers can be suggested without necessarily restricting the candidate too much. (See a selection of the *Examination Bulletins* of the Schools Council, 1963–77, Thyne (1974) and McIntosh (1976) for a much fuller discussion of this.) When structured questions are set it is usually desirable also to devise questions which test the candidate's ability to break down an answer into manageable units. Sometimes questions are set which ask a candidate to indicate the steps (or subsidiary questions) required to give a complete answer. A candidate may, or may not, be requested to give fuller answers to one or more of his suggested steps. Partial answers of this kind aim at testing specific abilities quickly and reliably.

In spite of the many difficulties that can arise when 'open-ended' essay questions are set in examinations we cannot really dismiss lightly the claims of those who assert that such questions are needed to test a candidate's overall range of abilities in handling such questions, particularly the fluent, effective use of language in a relatively long piece of continuous prose. But there does seem to be a need for other kinds of questions as well. Accordingly, more attention is now being focused on structured questions and various types of 'objective' tests where it is suggested that it is easier to assess a wide range of abilities. There are many kinds of recall, completion, ranking and choice-response items, and guidance on these can be obtained from various *Examination Bulletins* of the Schools Council (1963–77), from Thyne (1974) and from MacIntosh (1976).

In several of its *Examination Bulletins* the Schools Council has suggested that a new service of 'Item Banking' should become available to teachers and examiners. Here a bank of items is prepared and validated by trained test constructors to a defined blue-print specification and such a bank, it is claimed, would enable teachers and examiners to decide first what they want their course objectives to be and then to ask for items from the bank to meet their requirements for assessment purposes. (The reader is left to consider the advantages and disadvantages of such a proposed service and whether or not it is a desirable and practicable proposition.)

Many methods are being tried out, particularly at CSE and CEE level, in an attempt to reduce examination stress. These include: allowing pupils to bring notes into an examination; telling the topics which will be covered in the examination papers; using flexible time limits; using 'oral' tests or 'interviews' where these are likely to provide useful 'evidence' of special abilities; using internal tests and examinations and combining as many different kinds of assessment as possible from a representative sample of work done during the course as well as at the end of it. It is interesting to note that many practical 'external' examinations, at various levels, have proved so unreliable that some examiners are beginning to look at other forms of periodic and continuous assessment for a more valid overall evaluation of such work.

Any consideration of combining assessments must clearly include some reference to the use, by some examination bodies, of teachers' assessments of their pupils' abilities as part of the final examination results. These teachers' assessments can take a variety of forms, including some like the ones we considered earlier, but such assessments, formally made, are not liked by some pupils who, knowing that the assessments are part of the final examination result, feel that they are being examined all the time. Also, there is some evidence to show that some teachers are reluctant to give their own assessment as part of an examination procedure. Some of the reasons they give for this include: it is difficult to do; they do not feel competent to do it; they are not clear about what it is they are supposed to assess and weightings they should give to the various assessments they do make; it takes up a great deal of time; they are concerned that their assessments would be too subjective; they do not know what the 'standards' are outside their own school. Other teachers feel, equally strongly, that teachers' assessments are an essential part of the final examination result, mainly because the teacher has had first-hand continuous knowledge of his pupils' skills and abilities and that any 'external' assessments should be applied merely to moderate 'internal' assessments in any attempts that may be needed to relate them to some kind of national or regional standards or norms.

There appears to be a need for a much more comprehensive overall assessment of a pupil's progress and promise than exists at present. Is there, perhaps, a need for all of the following?

1. A continuous assessment of a full range of skills, abilities, interests and reactions in all normal day-to-day work done by a pupil, to include reference to the value of his contributions to general class discussions.

2. An assessment of two special pieces of work, one entirely an individual effort and the other as part of a group study, each done over a fairly long period and, in the case of the group study, some reference to the individual's adaptability and contribution to the work of the group as a whole; and, for both pieces of work, an assessment of his achievements in the way of skills and abilities and, in particular, his ability to show some originality and to persevere in the face of difficulties.

3. An assessment of a representative sample of work that would be completed in relatively short periods of time.

4. An examination set, with teacher participation, at the end of a pupil's course as a measure of final achievement, making use of relevant and useful techniques, with the results of this end-of-course examination only forming part of the pupil's overall 'examination result'.

This overall view of regarding the assessment of a pupil's progress as a continuous and growing process could lead us to review the ways in which the results of 'examinations' of the future are issued. A composite grade in a subject gives no detail about the level of the specific abilities of a pupil. A more helpful approach to this may well be to compile a profile for each pupil which shows the level he has reached in various abilities rather than to indicate his subject grades. Is there, too, a need to establish, for certain forms of knowledge and basic skills, a criterion-referenced standard that almost all pupils are expected to achieve? An interesting attempt to promote the use of profiles, in recording and reporting on a pupil's progress at secondary school level, has recently been validated in a large number of Scottish schools and a full discussion of this investigation is contained in a report by the Scottish Council for Research in Education (1977). As a result of this work, a form of record-keeping has been produced linked with: basic skills across the curriculum; performance in each area of the curriculum; certain non-cognitive aspects of development. It is hoped that subsequent recording and reporting, using a profile approach, may replace, or at least supplement, the present system of 16+ examinations in Scotland.

Do our present methods of assessment give a fair picture of pupils' progress and promise?

In the context of the Great Debate on education there has been concern expressed, in many quarters, for the standards reached by children in schools. Also, a matter for concern has been the types of assessment being used for monitoring pupils' educational progress, this being associated with related methods of recording and reporting on such progress. A summary of some of the problems underlying such issues and brief proposals of probable ways in which some of the suggested difficulties might be overcome are outlined in the recent Green Paper (1977).

Such is the concern of the Department of Education and Science with this particular question that an Assessment of Performance Unit (APU) has recently been set up in order to promote the development of methods of assessing and monitoring the achievement of children at school. Some of the possible advantages and disadvantages that may emerge by using such a unit will be an issue the reader will need to consider as the implications of the results of any testing procedures become known.

Further reading

Purposes of assessment

The reasons why we need various forms of assessment are considered, in some detail, by Pidgeon (in Pidgeon and Allen, 1974) and MacIntosh (1976). Rowntree (1977) offers a refreshing discussion of the nature of assessment. He looks at those purposes of assessment associated with selection, maintaining standards and offering feedback to teachers and students. He considers not only what to assess and how to make assessments but how to interpret them.

Guidance on the use and construction of different kinds of tests

The nature of certain standardized tests and the interpretation of the results when using them are both discussed by Jackson (1973).

Lewis (1974) considers various individual and group standardized tests, evaluates the present use of examinations and discusses scholastic aptitude tests and attitude testing.

MacIntosh (1974) provides advice on the use of various methods of assessment and proposes ways in which teachers can take a more active part in the overall assessment of their pupils' progress.

MacIntosh (1976) considers various methods of test construction; pre-testing; continuous and periodic assessment.

General, and specific, advice on assessment procedures is offered in various Schools Council (1963–77) *Examination Bulletins* and *Working Papers*. The earlier examination bulletins stress the need for a new approach to assessment; later bulletins scrutinize earlier suggestions. The bulletins also consider test construction; continuous assessment; uses made of teachers' assessments. Several *Working Papers* suggest a new pattern of examinations for those aged sixteen to nineteen.

Vincent and Cresswell (1976) provide an explanatory guide to, and an evaluation of, the wide range of tests available for school assessment of reading abilities.

NFER (1976, 1977) issue catalogues of their own standardized tests for psychological and clinical purposes and for educational guidance and assessment.

Personality tests and sociometric techniques

Schofield (1972) considers the principles underlying assessment procedures and testing and looks critically at tests of intelligence, personality and at sociometric and interviewing techniques.

Longitudinal studies

Longitudinal studies of children's development are discussed in the first chapter of Pidgeon and Allen (1974).

Test reference

Stones (1970, section 7) discusses the reliability and validity of 16+ examinations; pleads for a reappraisal of our present methods of educational assessment in schools, stressing the need for the production and use of criterion-referenced tests.

Thyne (1974) explains the distinction between norm-referenced and criterion-referenced tests and considers the principles involved in setting and marking different kinds of questions.

In Pidgeon and Allen (1974) we find a suggestion that criterion-referenced tests are needed to check the extent of 'mastery learning' achieved in certain circumstances.

More recently, Sumner and Robertson (1977) have reviewed some of the published work on criterion-referenced tests.

Experiments in assessments

A survey and discussion of various methods of assessment being used at primary level in the 1950s is contained in Vernon (1957).

Experiments, during the 1960s, validating some new forms of assessment are discussed in Eggleston and Kerr (1969).

Experiments with aptitude testing are outlined in Lewis (1974).

The Scottish Council for Research in Education (1977) has recently issued the results of an experiment into a profile approach to the recording of, and reporting on, the progress of pupils at secondary school level.

Assessment in the context of the Great Debate

The Government Green Paper *Education in Schools* (1977) discusses the issue of national educational standards in schools and offers a brief discussion of existing and possible future assessment procedures and record-keeping.

A new source of quantitative assessment is to be provided by the Assessment of Performance Unit (APU) of the Department of Education and Science, the principles behind this unit being explained in Kay (1975).

Appendix to Chapter 19

Historical Background to Examinations

Peter Gordon

Formal examinations in education have a surprisingly short history: they began in universities at the beginning of the nineteenth century and in schools from 1858. The direct relevance of the history of the development of the examination system has been pointed out by John Roach (1971) who states that 'the Victorian system of school examinations has survived in its essentials into the middle of the twentieth century'. A study of this topic also illustrates the obvious links between what is taught and how it is examined.

Universities and schools

Reforms in the curriculum and the imposition of written examinations were carried out, in the face of much internal resistance, at Cambridge University in 1780 and at Oxford twenty years later. The viva voce element, which had been the main method used, was retained but played a smaller part than before.

It was realized by both universities that standards were inevitably dependent on the quality of pupils in schools. With a view to raising standards, first Cambridge in 1858 and then Oxford established examinations in and for schools.

The model for this scheme, which was known as the 'Locals', was to be found in schools in the south-west where, in the previous year, T. D. Acland and others had offered examinations for boys intending to follow employment in 'agriculture, arts, manufacture and commerce'. Candidates for the Locals, after satisfying the examiners in elements of a 'plain English education', were allowed to choose from a wide range of subjects. However, as the universities in devising the school examinations had asked the advice of the Civil Service Commission, one of the very few bodies with examining experience, it is not surprising that there was more emphasis on the arts than the scientific or practical subjects.

At first, the schools played little part in the actual examining process. Brereton (1944, p. 74) has described how they were conducted:

> The examinations were looked upon as an extension of the university into the outer world rather than as a part of the school education system. For the first three years, the class lists were headed, 'Examination of Students not members of the University'. The contract for the examination was made by the individual student and his parent directly with the university. The school took no part in it, and the examinations were held, as often as not, in a public hall. On the first day, the Presiding Examiner, complete with cap, gown and hood, came direct from Cambridge with the question papers and took complete charge. For a week the university extended its premises to include these examination halls in different parts of the country.

These locally held examinations were concerned with individual candidates, but as single schools would often put forward many pupils, these public examinations began to take on the character of school examinations. Within four years, the character of the examining had changed to accommodate this change.

There were two interesting features in the methods of assessment used. First, they were internal examinations, especially arranged for each school. Teachers submitted a schedule of subjects taught and examinations were set based on the curricula offered; papers were marked by the school staff, an early example of the 'mode two' method. Second, an inspection of school premises accompanied the examination. Inspectors were appointed by the university, to report on the facilities, equipment and standards of teaching in the schools visited. In this way, a fuller interpretation of the results obtained could be made. 'School Certificates' were issued by the boards, but were not necessarily thought of as passports to the higher education.

On the other hand, a third body, London University, specifically introduced a matriculation examination in 1858 which carried with it the necessary qualification for entry to degree work. A restricted range of subjects was offered with a pass rate of less than a half. Furthermore, unlike the other two boards, it was an entirely external examination which inhibited the syllabuses of those schools entering candidates.

The Civil Service and school examinations

So far, little mention has been made of the pressures which were fashioning school curricula in any particular way. The changing political and social climate of the 1850s and '60s and the growth of larger and more impersonal institutions in society found expression in a widely felt desire to substitute competition for patronage in public offices. The Northcote-Trevelyan Report of 1854 had introduced the principle of competitive examinations in the Civil Service and the army. In the year when Oxford and Cambridge Locals began, the first examinations for the Indian Civil Service were held. Posts in the service were one of the most sought-after prizes for aspiring Oxbridge graduates.

Benjamin Jowett of Balliol proposed that candidates should be examined in two out of four 'schools' which practically coincided with the four schools of the recently reformed Oxford University. Out of the 6875 marks awarded for the examination, English language with literature and history accounted for a quarter of the total, Greek and Latin for another quarter, mathematics one seventh and natural sciences only one twelfth.

The response of the endowed and new public schools was to provide special courses for likely future candidates. The headmaster of Marlborough described the Indian Civil Service and army examinations as 'sitting like a blight on education, compelling a master to teach not what was good for the pupils but what would "pay" in the examinations'. Other like-minded headmasters also disliked the notion of specialization of professional examinations which were now proliferating, making the task of the school as a place for general education more difficult. One wrote at this time, 'The school now follows the examination − not the examination the school.' Many complaints were expressed about boys leaving school early to attend 'crammers', special establishments set up to cater for boys hoping to enter the Civil Service or other professions.

Towards central control

Governmental reforming zeal in the 1860s also took the form of appointing royal commissions to investigate the efficiency of schools. One, the Taunton Commission, examined over seven hundred endowed schools. It recommended three grades of school, each with its own curricula and catering for different leaving ages and occupations. The report criticized the Oxford and Cambridge Locals as being too expensive and too difficult, and for being taken only by a minority of the school population. It advocated an educational council, a central authority for examinations but which would be locally administered. Teachers were to be represented on the council and a professional register was proposed. Opposition to the council came from public school headmasters and the scheme was stillborn. The recently introduced 'payment by results' system in elementary schools was held up as a warning of the consequences of central direction in education.

The controversy over the appropriate body who should have control of examinations continued for the remainder of the century. By 1900, teachers were playing a greater part in examining. For instance, in 1898 the Oxford Delegacy decided to appoint mathematics examiners who had had school experience. The Incorporated Association of Headmasters, founded in 1890, appointed an examination sub-committee to work with the Cambridge Syndicate. Together they were instrumental in promoting new syllabuses for juniors in elementary experimental science and introducing the works of recent authors in the modern languages papers.

One other important development which must be mentioned was the creation of an examination suitable for sixth formers intending to proceed to either of the two universities; the examinations mentioned so far had been intended for a five-year course of study only. From 1874, the 'Joint Board', or more correctly, the Oxford and Cambridge School Examinations Board, administered the examinations. The Board provided machinery for universities to directly influence the education of their future undergraduates.

Central control

The implementation of the 1902 Education Act marks a further stage in the development of the school examination system. The Act had established municipal secondary schools mainly to provide recruits for lower middle-class 'white collar' jobs. To counteract the growing tendency for secondary education to be more involved in technical studies, regulations were issued by the new Board of Education which favoured the teaching of the arts and humanities. By providing much of the finance for secondary education for the first time, the Board's control of the curriculum was strengthened; the fact that the new local education authorities had little experience of responsibility at this level weakened their position. The years up to the outbreak of the First World War were a period of constant friction between the Board of Education on the one hand, and the schools, local education authorities and examining bodies on the other. Matters were not helped by the fact that the last three bodies often failed to agree amongst themselves.

One of the major concerns of the Board was the large number of institutions offering examinations in the secondary field. A Consultative Committee on Examinations in Secondary Schools (1911) found that the multiplicity of external examinations interfered with the best work of schools. The Board was not prepared to admit that examinations should influence this work, but held that they were merely to test it. A Secondary School Examination Council was subsequently established by the Board in 1917 to advise on the co-ordination of examinations. Although all parties concerned with the conduct of examinations were represented, nevertheless the Board's nomination of the chairman and a majority of members ensured that the official view would prevail. In addition, the Board reserved the right to approve school examinations and was able to withhold grants towards candidates' entry fees from schools or local education authorities.

Two new examinations were introduced by the Council in 1917 to replace the many existing ones: the School Certificate, a test of five years' grammar school education and a Higher School Certificate, to be taken after two years in the sixth form. The Board maintained a tight grip on the curriculum by prescribing three groups from which at least five subjects must be taken — English subjects, foreign languages and science and mathematics. A fourth group, consisting of practical subjects such as art, drawing, handicraft was envisaged but the first examinations in this group were not held until 1923 and candidates were initially restricted to entering for only one subject. This regulation hampered those girls' schools wishing to develop curricula different from the boys'.

Although the Board had endorsed the 1911 Committee's view that examinations were to assess competence rather than act as a means of competition, by the 1930s, grading into credits, honours and distinctions was introduced. Employers still demanded the old matriculation qualification at interviews: and five credits became the equivalent of matriculation, a level which became acceptable for entry to both universities and professional bodies.

Shortly before the Second World War, the Spens Committee on Secondary Education condemned the attempt to combine in examinations the two different objectives of selecting students for university and as an assessment of school work for the rest. The curriculum was being distorted and the aim of a broad general education was being overshadowed.

Reconstruction

Various innovatory suggestions were made to restore examinations to their subordinate role in schooling. The most farsighted came from the Council in its 1943 report, called after its chairman, Sir Cyril Norwood. Single subject examinations were to replace the existing group system. Continuous assessment, in the form of the candidate's school record which would be noted on the certificate, was recommended. Teachers were to have a larger voice in external examinations; and universities and other bodies were to have their own entrance tests at eighteen. It was envisaged that external examinations could eventually be replaced by teacher-controlled internal assessment.

These enlightened proposals became, as in previous attempts at examination reform, transformed into a different mould. The General Certificate of Education (GCE) at Ordinary level, first operated in 1951, took the place of the School Certificate: it was of a higher standard than the latter. At Advanced level, the examination was to be qualifying rather than competitive in nature. Many factors militated against its success. At Ordinary level, for instance, the fact that entry was for sixteen-year-olds initially excluded secondary modern pupils; and the examination was not a necessary stepping-stone to 'A' levels. From 1963 grades of performance, not originally part of the scheme, appeared on 'A' level certificates. Inevitably 'O' and 'A' level performance became an indicator of university acceptability. Schools took little advantage of the right to submit their own syllabuses. It was calculated in 1969 that the two largest GCE boards had approved between them a total of about twenty special syllabuses, mainly relating to history and English literature.

By the mid-1950s, many secondary modern schools were providing GCE courses for their pupils as a result of various pressures. Its unsuitability as an examination for all but a minority led to the Beloe Committee to recommend a new examination, the Certificate of Secondary Education (CSE). It was to be taken by the 20 per cent below the GCE cohort in four or more subjects, with a further 20 per cent attempting individual subjects. The three different modes of examining also gave the teacher a choice of assessment techniques: externally set and marked papers, syllabuses suggested to schools and externally set and internally set and marked. The thorny question of comparability with GCE was unsatisfactorily settled: a grade 1 result in CSE was deemed to be equivalent to an unspecified 'pass' at GCE.

Recent developments

Changes in the political and educational thinking in the last decade have resulted in a further look at the examination system. The spread of comprehensive education highlighted the problem of preparing pupils for two different examinations. It was argued that if there was a continuum of ability in children, this should be reflected within the scope of a single examination. The growth in numbers of those staying on to the sixth form with a variety of background and qualifications and the raising of school leaving age to sixteen were additional factors to be considered.

The move away from direct control, as exemplified in the Secondary Schools Examinations Council (SSEC), can be seen in the setting up of the Schools Council for the Curriculum and Examinations in 1964. The functions of the SSEC were transferred to Schools Council, which has a majority of teachers on its committees. Recent proposals have included a common examination at 16+, a Certificate of Extended Education for the seventeen-year-old and a new 18+ examination at two levels (N and F) to replace the existing Advanced level. It might be argued, however, that by extending the range of examinations to include a larger proportion of the secondary school population, there is a danger which earlier reformers wished to avoid — namely, of devising fairer examining techniques rather than improving the quality and content of the curriculum.

Further reading

The literature on this subject is extensive. Perhaps the most exhaustive study is Montgomery (1965).

Historical studies relating to secondary education which can be recommended are Roach (1971) and Brereton (1944) chapters 4 and 5.

Official publications mentioned in the chapter are: the Board of Education *Report of the Consultative Committee on Examinations in Secondary Schools, 1911; on the Education of the Adolescent* (Hadow Report, 1926), and *on Secondary Education* (Spens Report, 1938); and the *Report of the*

Peter Gordon

Secondary School Examination Council on Curricula and Examinations in Secondary Schools (Norwood Report, 1943).

More recent publications from the Schools Council include *Working Papers* no. 45 (1972) and no. 46 (1973) which deal respectively with curricula bases and examination structures for the sixteen to nineteen age group; and *Examinations at 16+: proposals for the future* (1975).

Finally two stimulating publications which raise a number of issues: Pearce (1972) and Pidgeon and Allen's *Measurement in Education* (1974), especially chapter 4.

Part Five

The Teacher, Accountability and Control

Chapter 20

Role of the Teacher

Peter Gordon

An advertisement for teachers in an educational journal in recent years ran: 'Come and teach in X and enjoy teacher participation in decision-making.' This recognition of the changing role of the teacher, which is to be explored more fully in chapter 21, is a far cry from the nineteenth century when the teacher's status was low. Then, it was considered necessary for teachers to be able to supplement their income by combining their work with that of, for example, acting as the village postmaster, organist and poor law clerk.

One of the most often quoted aspects of the teacher's role, its diffusion or lack of specificity, has its roots in the historical evolution of the school teacher. There are clashes between three traditional aspects of the role — that of instructor, socializer and classifier. Wilson (1962) mentions, for example, the difficulty in defining where the teaching responsibility ends: the affective aspect of the teacher's role has been increasing over the years, as well as the pedagogical.

It should be noted that the professional career of school teaching (see Purvis, 1973) although outside the scope of our concern, influences a teacher's performance in the classroom. He or she has to manage the often conflicting expectations of headmasters, inspectors, local authorities, parents and children; and he is judged by the outside world more in terms of career advancement than in his effectiveness as a teacher. We shall mention other constraints later.

Teacher characteristics and performance

Westwood (1967) in a survey of the literature on the role of the teacher concluded that there was a need for more detailed research into the dynamics of the teacher's performance — how it is formed, modified and reformulated in interaction over the course of time. One study by Jackson (1968) involving two years' observation of classes in a Chicago elementary school throws some light on teachers' characteristics which have implications for curriculum development. Interviews with 'top' teachers, selected by their administrative superiors, were aimed at finding out how teachers knew when they were doing a good job and what pleasures, if any, life in the classroom held for them.

Four themes emerged. First, immediacy, indicated that teachers believed that the results of their teaching were quite visible, using fleeting behavioural cues to assess how well they were performing. Testing was treated as being of minor importance in helping to understand pupils' achievement. Informality in the classroom was desirable, but not to the extent of interfering with institutional definitions of responsibility, authority and tradition. Autonomy was important: concern was expressed at possible interference by superiors for evaluative purposes.

There was agreement that the teacher should decide the curriculum to be followed, whilst being willing to accept guide lines from curriculum projects. They were also concerned with the well-being of individual members of the class; one of the major satisfactions of the work was to be remembered with affection by former students. Jackson (1968) also noted that teacher talk, unlike that of other professionals, showed a marked absence of technical vocabulary and a tendency to avoid not only elaborate words but elaborate ideas.

If the teacher emerges as a fairly conservative creature, Jackson argues, then it is because his characteristics fit in well with his task of managing a succession of classes and changing events over the course of a school year:

If teachers sought a more thorough understanding of their world, insisted on greater rationality in their actions, were completely open-minded in their consideration of pedagogical choices, they might well receive greater applause from intellectuals, but it is doubtful if they would perform with greater efficiency in the classroom.

Influences on the teacher's role

Of course, we cannot realistically isolate the teacher from other strong influences in the school which reinforce this pragmatic approach. In England, Taylor's (1974) small-scale survey showed that what was taught in the school was influenced by the head and almost as importantly, by fellow teachers, with parents well down the list. Various studies have shown that the characteristic most admired by colleagues in the 'best' teachers is their ability to maintain control. Because of this, the teacher tends to promote certain types of acceptable social behaviour on the part of the pupil, pressures and procedures which have come to be known as the 'hidden curriculum'.

From the individual teacher's point of view, as distinct from the institutional, the greatest influence on his teaching styles and procedures is the pupils. He may prescribe the roles of children in the classroom through the language used in the course of his teaching (Barnes, 1971). He controls the flow of information and can direct pupils towards a pre-ordained answer, as Jules Henry (1955) has amusingly shown. There seems to be plenty of evidence that the style of the teacher affects not only the performance but even the personality of children (Lippitt and White, 1965).

On the other side of the equation is the way in which pupils influence teachers. Students at all levels continually evaluate the performance of their teachers. Sometimes there is a discrepancy between the perceived and actual needs of pupils in the curriculum offered. *Enquiry No. 1* (1968) indicated that fifteen-year-old school leavers wanted their teachers to give them the necessary skills for future employment and placed little premium on character training and behaviour. Teachers, on the other hand, gave low priority to vocational preparation and high priority to moral education. This finding, if correct, has interesting implications for the way in which we view the curriculum.

Negatively, pupils socialize teachers by a number of strategies which frustrate learning, such as looking attentive rather than actually attending, acting docile and if necessary, acting stupid (Holt, 1968).

This process of negotiation between teacher and pupil can be regarded from the former's point of view as indoctrination which is necessary to control children. Another viewpoint is that pupils, if they are to learn, must be the subordinate party, whether faced with teachers, parents or employers. A recent survey (Paisey, 1975) of British and American secondary schools, using pupil assessment of teachers' behaviour as the basis of its findings about the nature and effectiveness of different teaching strategies, painted a gloomy picture. It found that teachers were unable to adopt a strategy which successfully combined a concern with work and with the individual.

Teachers and curriculum development

A third and perhaps more helpful and creative approach is implicit (and in some cases explicit) in many curriculum projects and their material. In the tables in Appendix 2 of the Schools Council Research Study *Pattern and Variation in Curriculum Development Projects* (1973), only three of the projects listed were not concerned to influence both teaching/learning methods and teacher/pupil attitudes.

Some projects generate inquiries into the teacher's role. This can be seen in connection with the development of the Humanities Curriculum Project. The project's evaluation unit concluded, after examining the evidence, that teachers who had undergone training in the use of materials tended to achieve results of a different order from 'non-trained' teachers: the former used strategies which gave pupils more autonomy over their learning and at the same time they were able to reflect more systematically on their own actions.

As a result of these findings, a further project, the Ford Teaching Project, which is described more fully in chapter 22, was instituted. It included amongst its aims the fostering of an action-research orientation towards classroom problems; the monitoring of pupils' accounts of teaching; and identifying problems and strategies among teachers which may be generalizable. (Elliott and Adelman, 1975.)

The British tradition of respect for the autonomy of the teacher in curriculum matters was regarded by some other countries at a recent conference as something of an obsession (Maclure, 1972). Experience of curriculum dissemination and evaluation in England has demonstrated the different perceptions of the project team, local advisers, headteachers and teachers. Shipman (1972, 1973) in an account of the history of the Keele Integrated Studies Project, pointed out that success in planning and implementing curriculum change depends on identifying teachers who are both knowledgeable and enthusiastic rather than on getting schools to accept purchased materials.

In-service training and the teacher

Curriculum development has highlighted the need to encourage teachers who have the necessary skills and expertise to be employed in the way Shipman suggests. The problem is also linked with that of the most efficient way of equipping them for the many new professional demands which are being made. The rapid dissemination of a large body of educational information, the impact of educational technology in its wider sense are rapidly changing curricula, schools and the role of the teacher. Although there is generous provision of post-initial training courses, there has been little systematic analysis of teachers' needs.

Broadly, there are two main aspects involved: personal and professional education. Personal refers to a range of activities, from the retraining of returning teachers to those wishing to pursue academic courses to obtain qualifications. Professional education is more concerned with the needs related to changes in schools, such as the introduction of new forms of organization and new teaching methods in different subject areas.

A number of issues concerning the teacher arise out of this:

1 There is a need to strike a balance between personal and professional education and the employers' concern for the

current needs of schools and pupils. The picture obviously varies over the country. In a different dimension there are short-term needs for a section of teachers, e.g. limited preparation for reorganization into a middle schools system and long-term needs concerning all teachers, e.g. implementation of Bullock (1975) proposals.

2 Who is to identify these needs? The situation is possibly easier in the large secondary school than in a primary setting: help may be needed from advisers and teachers' centres. A start might be made by local education authorities attempting to define and establish clearly the functions of headmaster, deputies and heads of departments in post-initial training.

3 About one-third of the teaching profession has not attended any further courses since initial training. Can this policy of self-selection continue, or might it be necessary, as in other countries, to build obligations into contracts of employment?

4 Following from this, is there a need for a more systematic approach to post-initial training? At the moment, courses are arranged on an *ad hoc* basis from which teachers choose during a professional career. A more carefully structured scheme, taking into account the teacher's different needs at different stages of his service, could be devised possibly using a unit basis.

5 Much of the innovation in English education arises from the schools themselves. It is being increasingly argued therefore that most post-initial training should take place within schools, where training would be most appropriate. It is often difficult for teachers to implement ideas and practices recommended at courses because they are inappropriate or unrealistic in their particular school situations; much of the value of attending the course is therefore dissipated.

6 Little attention has been directed to the effectiveness and evaluation of courses. Is the criterion to be looked for in the subsequent performance of the teacher or of the children — or both? Will it show, as in advertisements, in a before/after way? Probably in the end such measurement cannot be exact: we have little reliable knowledge at the present time of what makes a 'good' teacher. It seems that, ultimately, much will depend on the professional judgment of the teacher

and his skill in the discipline of assessment of his teaching situation.

This chapter has been concerned in looking at only two aspects of the role of the teacher, that is, in the context of the classroom and attitudes towards the curriculum. No discussion of this role is realistic without placing it in a wider context, namely, the changing relationships between teachers and headmasters and the changing expectations of society which are reflected in schools. We now turn to a consideration of these issues.

Further reading

Two general introductions to the topic are Hoyle (1969) and Banks (1968) chapters 7, 8 and 9. One of the most perceptive studies, written as long ago as 1932 but reprinted since, is highly recommended – Waller (1965).

For ease of reference, the books and articles mentioned appear below in the same order as in the chapter. They are Wilson (1962) pp. 15–32; Purvis (1973); Westwood (1967); Jackson (1968); Taylor *et al.* (1974); Barnes (1971); Henry (1955); Lippitt and White (1965); *Enquiry No. 1* (1968); Holt (1968); *Pattern and Variation in Curriculum Development Projects* (Schools Council, 1973); Elliott and Adelman (1975); Maclure (1972); and Shipman (1972, 1973).

Chapter 21

Changing Role of the Teacher

Peter Gordon

If we examine the changing role of the teacher we must look at changes which have been taking place in society and which are reflected in schools. Bernstein (1967) put forward the hypothesis that, in Durkheim's terms, we are moving from a position of 'mechanical' to 'organic' solidarity. 'Mechanical' here refers to a type of society in which individuals share a common belief system and where roles are ascribed. Organic solidarity on the other hand, is based on differences between individuals and where roles are achieved rather than ascribed. This shift can be seen in secondary schools where there has been a move away from a ritual order based on status, to a more personalized one where teachers and pupils confront each other as individuals. The pupil's position is less likely to be fixed in terms of sex, age or intelligence; teaching groups are more flexible, with the class or form weakened as a basis for relationships. Subjects are no longer clearly defined units of the curriculum and are replaced by ideas or themes to be followed e.g. topic-centred and interdisciplinary inquiry work. This latter point has important consequences for the teacher. If there is a move from pupils learning standard operations tied to specific contexts to a pedagogy which emphasizes the exploration of principles, the teacher's role will change from that of providing answers to one of posing problems. The subsequent autonomy of pupils will change the authority relationship between teachers and pupils.

In a later work, Bernstein (1971) develops further the consequences of these changes for teachers. A more closed system encourages a vertical structure of allegiances: staff members work within subject departments, competing with others for resources and promotion, and looking to heads of department and headmasters in these matters. It is argued that with an open system, teachers will no longer be divided by allegiances to subject hierarchies. With their weakening, the centre of gravity of relationships will undergo a radical change; they are likely to be united through a common work situation and this new situation may alter the structure and distribution of power within schools. Of course, Bernstein is careful to stress that he is talking about 'ideal type' organizational structures and that in fact pure examples of either type do not exist.

An alternative view

Although we may agree that Bernstein's analysis is perceptive, there is a gap at present between what may be desirable and what is considered practicable. Experience in some of the larger schools has pointed to the need for a closer definition of the teacher's role rather than a more diffuse one. Elizabeth Richardson (1973) acted as consultant to a grammar school which was about to become comprehensive. Her task was to help staff clarify their problems, such as what happened when an integrated course was introduced, how to resolve conflicts when specialists found themselves in an unspecialized world, when new methods of consulting teachers were devised and the head started to interpret his job differently:

> The fear of structures and hierarchies springs from a distrust of authority; yet it is only within a firm management structure, in which leadership roles can be defined, that individuals are free to work with their own conflicting feelings about their leaders. . . . It is only by coming to terms with the authority that is outside ourselves that we can discover the authority that is inside.

One important distinction made by Richardson (1973) is what she calls the demanding and the caring aspects of the teacher's role: both aspects are loosely defined throughout the hierarchy. This fragmentation of tasks weakens the authority of all members of staff because it leaves everybody unclear about where the boundaries around different areas of responsibility are being drawn. The message seems to be that the teacher will be happier if there is a more closely defined job definition for all working in the school.

Some examples of changes in management structure which were effected are of interest. The school abandoned the network of open working parties and study groups, creating instead a small standing committee corresponding to a cabinet as well as a larger senior staff group and a full staff meeting. The committees did not take decisions; these were left to the head. Monthly staff meetings focused on a single topic, based on discussion papers previously scrutinized at departmental meetings. Roles were defined not simply in terms of titles, such as deputy head, senior mistress, head of upper school and so on; functions were also allocated, in the form of professional tutors, directors of curriculum, resources, careers and so on. Staff and governors were brought into closer contact, but not by having a teacher on the governing body – this would be a confusion of role. Instead, teachers took turns to present a report on their work to governors and a staff governor conference was held each term so that each side could be kept mutually informed.

No system, however logically attractive it may seem, is without its complications. Richardson noted in a later study (1975) that the welfare/curricular split is reflected in another division: that arts and humanities teachers tended to be more concerned about personal development than science and mathematics teachers, who were more concerned about examination achievements.

Headmasters and teachers

Musgrove (1971) looks more closely at the teacher–headmaster relationship and its effect on curriculum:

> Headmasters who wish to reduce their subordinates' power and increase their own will be wise to abolish subjects and integrate the curriculum. For subjects are centres of power. They are also centres of authority. They help to

make up the pluralism of power which is a crucial check on the power of headmasters, principals and vice-chancellors.

In England, the power given to the headmaster in running his school is not matched in some European countries, where curricula, appointment and disposition of staff and resources are largely centrally decided. The English tradition has been that he may cast himself in several roles: as leader within the school, as a representative of the school in the community, as an administrator, as a teacher or as an innovator. Bernbaum (1976) in a survey of headmasters' attitudes found that heads saw themselves as least effective in the roles that are traditionally theirs. Of the 315 replies, 57 per cent rated themselves lowly at getting teachers to introduce new perspectives into their work, and only 14 per cent thought themselves good at helping staff with disciplinary problems.

Looking now at both headmaster and teacher together, we can see that on the one hand, the head has a high degree of authority — positively or negatively — in curriculum innovation. On the other hand, the teacher has considerable classroom autonomy and privacy, which gives him the opportunity to resist innovation or transform it. Therefore the question of authority is less important than that of negotiation, the head having to elicit teacher support for policy-making in which the latter may have had limited involvement.

For a number of reasons, the headmaster's role is changing. Not many would echo the words of the headmaster of Eton at a recent conference: 'I don't very much like the word "leader", I prefer to see myself as a creative minority'; but a growing public interest in the government of schools as witnessed in the activities of the Taylor Committee (1977), is questioning the head's position in curriculum decision-making. In further and higher education, teachers govern their affairs by internal democratic procedures; as school teachers become less isolated and more professionalized, it may be envisaged that there will be a move away from the present position of the traditional authority of the head to one of collegial authority. Noble and Pym (1970) have shown that in industry the 'rounding Cape Horn' approach of the master-manager making his lonely decisions is a myth:

most of the decision-making in fact takes place in committees.

Participation also has its difficulties. Parkes' (1973) study of decision-making in higher education indicates that since the implementation of the Weaver Report and DES Circular 7/70 (1970), power resides with those who sit on a number of committees which link information and function in the institution. These form the new oligarchy of the college.

A document issued by the Headmasters' Association *The Government of Schools* (1972) argued, by using a medical analogy, against staff councils with powers to overrule headmasters by majority vote:

> A crucial choice at the bedside of a sick man is not made through a ballot of junior doctors; the experience, knowledge, skill and judgment of the consultant is recognised and the responsibility of deciding how best to treat the patient is placed firmly upon his shoulders. We believe that many decisions in schools require a corresponding, though more diffuse, expertise.

The effectiveness of teacher participation in decision-making will depend to the extent they are concerned in the problems of innovation, the curriculum and the use of resources. As Taylor (1974) concluded:

> When aims are more precise, when the teacher's power to influence is regularised in terms consistent with the power of the head, and when he can influence policy and not merely be influenced by it, the teacher will in many ways be less personally autonomous but more potent professionally.

Pupils

In the last chapter, we discussed aspects of teacher-pupil relationship in the learning process. Referring back to Bernstein's model, it is clear that as pupils become less separated into streams, bands and sets, the horizontal relationship will increase: as this may correspond with the breaking down of departmental barriers between teachers, we can expect a weakening of the boundary between staff, especially junior staff and pupils.

Some signs of student involvement in aspects of school policy are the growing number of pupil governors and staff-student councils in one form or another. In this sphere, we are a long way behind Scandinavian countries where, since before the last war, pupils' councils, actively supported by national unions of pupils and receiving grants from public funds, have been in existence.

A more crucial dimension is that concerning how teachers perceive pupils according to their political and educational philosophies. Hargreaves (1976) has shown how their conceptions of deviant pupils vary. A 'traditional' teacher will define a pupil's conduct as cheeky whereas a young 'progressive' leader may define it as friendly and open.

The effect is to undermine the traditional consensus on which teacher-teacher relations, and much of teacher-pupil relations, has rested. The battles are not just between teacher and pupil, which has a long-standing tradition, but between teacher and teacher.

Hargreaves' suggested solution is interesting. There is a need to organize large comprehensive schools on different lines. They might be divided into smaller units and along the lines of the philosophies believed in by the staff, parents and children. This would introduce the novel aspect of teacher-matching of schools and presumably a corresponding public pronouncement on their aims and philosophies.

Other trends

Teacher as a professional

The induction year and the changing pattern of teacher-training is likely to throw a greater responsibility on teachers for the professionalization of new entrants. They will need to be more familiar with methods conducive to 'effectiveness' in teaching as well as research techniques, a problem considered in the following chapter. This presupposes an awareness of more objective approaches to practical teaching, such as micro-teaching, interaction analysis and an understanding

231

of group methods. The teacher ought to be acquainted with, for example, performance-based teacher education programmes, and be able to found his judgment on knowledge and not merely hearsay. Studies such as Bennett (1976) in teaching methods should be analysable by teachers rather than left to 'experts' to interpret the findings. The teacher ought to be more than a passive recipient of curriculum development projects and a filler-up of researchers' questionnaires.

It is fairly self-evident that the increasingly sophisticated methods of examining call for a greater understanding of measurement. Plans for a common examination at 16+ would involve a substantially larger number of teachers than at present. But in the Schools Council's proposals (1975, p. 48) for the examination, a chief education officer is quoted as saying that 'there is a real need for teachers to receive specific training and guidance as to what is involved in assessment procedures and techniques'. How far this work should be accommodated in initial- or in-service training is a matter for debate.

Teacher as innovator

An allied point is the likelihood of growing teacher involvement in curriculum development projects at various levels. So far, this has taken the form of testing, evaluating and making choices between different materials. The difficulties encountered by Schools Council at the diffusion stage together with a change of policy from mounting large-scale projects to encouraging innovation within local areas may lead to more projects being based in schools.

The teacher and the community

Even before the Plowden Report (1967) was published, there was evidence of a growing involvement of the teacher in the community: besides well-publicized suggestions for school–home links, there was the growth of community schools, catering for a wide age range of students, the emergence of counsellors and the closer involvement of teachers with the social services. A blue-print for a comprehensive community policy was outlined by the Inner London Education Authority (1973); it was based on a double strategy of encouraging institutions – schools, further and adult education – to work closely together and responding promptly to local demand by mounting community education projects. In areas containing children with special difficulties, projects bring together inspectors, teachers, social workers and administrators.

The relationship between parent and teacher is a delicate one on both sides. It would seem from a study by Lynch and Pimlott (1976) of parents living in an inner-city area of Southampton that there is still a gap to be bridged. There were significant reported differences between what parents thought the school was doing and what teachers thought the parents thought. Whilst appreciating the importance of the child's home in the education process, three-quarters of the teachers said they could teach children without their parents' help.

The school board system in the USA, where locally elected school committees consisting entirely of laymen control school finance, curricula, personnel and salaries (Baron and Tropp, 1961), involves the community much more directly than in England. Miriam David (1973) has argued that the American system makes teachers more readily accountable for their actions, expressing local rather than national views and providing a real link with the community.

The teacher as manager

At governmental level there is discussion on the most economic use of education resources and how schools can be made accountable for the money spent. Jones (1973), among others, has suggested it might be accomplished by setting specific objectives in terms of certain stipulated goals to be achieved by a given time. Allocation of resources would be reviewed for each educational programme to ensure that expenditure was suitably related to the educational and social objectives of the school. In return, schools should be allowed greater discretion in their deployment of resources and perhaps ultimately be given control over their total budget.

Other writers have claimed that schools are underpowered in relation to the goals they try to attain. Teachers, including heads, do not make managerial decisions. Would such powers of decision-making attract more powerful people into the teaching profession? The analogy with business management breaks down when we consider the difficulty of letting less successful schools go out of business: and the unreliability of fixing easily measurable targets, even if this were considered desirable. On the other hand, it is likely that the demand for some form of control over the ways schools operate will continue to grow.

A contrasting view was put forward by the Taylor Committee (1977): 'We believed that the principle of partnership should apply to everything that happened in schools, including the curriculum.' It recommends that governors should establish a school's objectives, keep its work under constant review and have access to professional guidance. Some of these issues are pursued further by Richard Pring in chapter 24.

In conclusion, it can be said that the move towards an all-graduate teaching profession with a more scientific approach to pedagogy is likely to enhance the status of the teacher. There are also factors which are more problematical – for example, the opening up of new avenues of entry into the profession, the still wide divergencies of views and interests among teachers working with different age groups, and the effects of recent demographic trends. Perhaps the key question which will require answering is the extent to which teachers should be expected to cope with the multifarious and often contradictory demands made upon them in present day society.

Further reading

The best general references are Bernstein (1967, 1971) and Richardson (1973, 1975).

On headmasters, see Musgrove (1971) and Bernbaum (1976).

Aspects of participation are dealt with in Noble and Pym (1970), Parkes (1973) and Taylor (1974).

Hargreaves (1976) examines teacher/pupil relationships. For teaching effectiveness see Bennett (1976). New examining techniques are discussed in Schools Council (1975) and Mathews and Leece (1976).

Two contrasting philosophies of community education are provided in ILEA (1973) and Merson and Campbell (1974).

The parent-teacher reference is Lynch and Pimlott (1976). The book by Musgrove and Taylor (1969) has a useful section on this topic.

American and English teachers are compared in Baron and Tropp (1961) and David (1973).

Accountability of schools is explored in Jones (1973).

Chapter 22

Teacher as Researcher

Richard Pring

Introduction

Despite Terry Moore's argument in chapter 1, I believe that educational theory is not theory in any grand sense — a unified explanatory system of propositions analogous to a lot of theory in the sciences. Rather, it should be seen as a critical and systematic reflection upon practice, drawing upon, certainly, theories that have been developed elsewhere, especially in the social sciences but not itself producing theories in that way. Similarly when I talk about the teacher as researcher I do not have in mind someone who conducts complex experiments with control and experimental groups and with sophisticated techniques for testing evidence and measuring results. Rather have I in mind the person who takes seriously the injunction to theorize about practice or to think systematically and critically about what he is doing. It is part of the extended professionalism that Hoyle (1976) talked about and that Peter Gordon refers to in chapter 21.

One might have a view of the teacher as a kind of technician — someone who has mastered certain skills of classroom control and who has learnt certain techniques for transmitting knowledge, skills, or habits, but who in the main is simply putting into practice ideas that have been developed elsewhere. In many respects a lot of early curriculum development was rather like that. Teams of experts formulated aims and ideas, developed material through which those ideas might be expressed and transmitted, put them to the test, adapted them in the light of results, and then handed them over to schools. The teacher was regarded as little more than a technician – the necessary intermediary between the expert team and the ultimate recipient.

Such a view of curriculum development was found from experience to be defective in many respects. The chief defect, however, was the inadequate role assigned to the teacher. Firstly, the teacher is rarely the passive recipient of someone else's ideas. The ideas are transformed, for good or ill, by his handling of them. Secondly, no two classrooms are alike. There are too many variables – not only the personality of the teacher, but the motivation and ability of the children, the organizational structure of the school, even the physical shape of the room. The only person who can tailor the curriculum to the children is the teacher, and there is a limit to the value of research or development conducted by other people elsewhere. If the teacher is to be intelligent about what he is doing then he must rely on research – careful and systematic observation guided by tentative hypothesis and inspired by some vision of what it should all add up to. But that research must be his because he alone has access to the appropriate information and data. What others say in the light of their experience is frequently helpful, but it always needs to be put to the test by oneself in one's own situation. What works for one person may not work for another.

There are, however, clearly problems apart from the sheer practical ones of time (or lack of it) for doing this sort of systematic reflection. I want very briefly to indicate what those are and then to suggest possible ways in which the teacher might adopt a more research-type role.

Objectivity

Central to research is an attempt to provide a more objective basis for one's judgments, and thereby to overcome the rather impressionistic, untested, sometimes almost whimsical way, in which so often one makes practical decisions and judgments. But objectivity in research is usually achieved through experiments which can be carefully observed and noted and which can be repeated by fellow researchers in order to check the experimenter's claims. Surely the privacy of the classroom and the transience of classroom events prevents anything but personal, impressionistic assessments of what has happened and quick, intuitive judgments about how one ought to respond. The teacher, it would seem, is more like the artist making quick intuitive judgments on the basis of past ill-defined experience than the systematic experimenter and researcher.

One way of achieving objectivity, of course, would seem to be the adoption of an objectives model of curriculum planning. On this view one carefully and narrowly defines one's objectives so that one might test the pupils' performances to see if those objectives have been achieved. The objectivity would lie in the test procedures whereby the achievements can be tested, measured, and shown to others for confirmation.

The difficulties in the objectives model were pointed out in chapter 16. One relevant criticism for my present purposes is that whether or not the objectives are achieved is by no means the only relevant curriculum consideration. A student of biology might attain all the objectives set (the assessment would show the 100 per cent success of the teacher's efforts) but he might in the process have been so bored with biology as to resolve never to engage in its study again. Any account or evaluation of the teaching that omitted such information would be far from adequate. Hence, I am reluctant to limit objectivity in research to measuring one's performance against preconceived objectives.

Being objective is contrasted not with being incorrect. One can be objective but wrong, just as one can be true but subjective. Rather is it concerned with taking steps to overcome the arbitrariness or whimsy or prejudice or strong feelings that often colour the judgments one makes. Being objective is to open to public scrutiny the basis upon which one's judgments are made — so that counter evidence and contrary arguments might, if they exist, be levelled against what one says. I may be correct in declaring at the end of a lesson that things went well, but my judgment is subjective in so far as there is no evidence against which another might test the truth of what I say. A school or a teacher to be objective would need to give an account of what happens in such a way that

1 one would know what would count as a critical test of one's account;

2 one takes steps to see if one's account can withstand the critical test.

Being objective about one's teaching performance requires, therefore, two things:

1 the development of habits of self-criticism which for many are acquired very painfully (we spend more time defending what we are doing than criticizing it or looking for shortcomings); and

2 the adoption of particular techniques for identifying the problems, putting tentative solutions to the test, and exposing to the criticism of others the conclusions that one has reached.

Habits of self criticism

Such habits are difficult to acquire because our natural tendency is to defend and to promote what we are doing rather than to find faults in it. One reason for this, of course, is lack of personal confidence, even security. It is not easy to be exposed to the critical gaze of one's colleagues, especially if one has one eye on promotion. It is the good side of oneself that one wants to show off, not the blemishes and the failings. Hence, a usual condition for greater objectivity is the establishment of a supportive framework within the school for self-criticism. Secondly, since objectivity lies in the exposure to public scrutiny and confirmation of what otherwise would be but a private unsubstantiated judgment, it would be necessary to create a framework for interpersonal criticism. The lone researcher is a contradiction. Rather should the school or college be a research community in which inter-subjective criticism and constant adaptation in the light of such criticism are encouraged and provided for.

Practical steps

1 Framework for joint self-examination and criticism:

(a) If a school or college is to be seen as a research community then the framework for this in regular meetings needs to be formalized. There ought to be time set aside on a regular basis in which problems are identified, tentative solutions are suggested, ways of putting them to the test are developed, and the resulting evidence scrutinized.

(b) One obstacle for shared examination of a problem is the lack of shared understandings reflected in the different ways in which teachers understand particular educational labels. In the Ford Teaching Project, some teachers saw themselves to be mainly formal in the methods they adopted, others informal. Upon investigation and discussion some formal teachers found that they were less formal than the so-called 'informal' ones, and vice versa. School-based research would require the gradual development through regular meetings and discussion of an agreed way of giving an account of classroom activity.

2 Action research:

The chief problem is how to get the information or data upon which the teachers can systematically work. Rather crudely, one might say that what one observes will depend very largely on what one is looking for, and this in turn will depend on the 'theory' one takes into the classroom and the 'instruments' through which the information is obtained. Hence, there are two important aspects of classroom research. Firstly, careful formulation of hypotheses can be put to the test. Secondly, there are the test procedures themselves.

(a) Hypothesis: Since one's observations are 'theory laden' it is important to formulate more explicitly the hunches or hypotheses that one is putting to the test. Thus one might be concerned about the problem of initiating classroom discussion and one might hypothesize that a different way of organizing the classroom will encourage wider participation. Remember, however, that hypotheses need to be sufficiently clear and precise that they can be tested, even if (because of the complexity of teaching — there are so many variables) either holding them or rejecting them is rather provisional and tentative. An example of such a research approach is taken from the Ford Teaching Project (1975a, pp. 10–12):

'In order to cut out "the guessing game" and move from a formal to an informal pattern teachers may have to refrain from the following acts:

(i) *Changing Topic*

Hypothesis: When teachers change the topic under discussion they may prevent pupils from expressing and developing their own ideas, since pupils tend to interpret such interventions as attempts to get conformity to a particular line of reasoning.

(ii) *Positive reinforcers*

Hypothesis: Utterances like 'good', 'interesting', 'right' in response to ideas expressed can prevent the expression and discussion of alternative ideas, since pupils tend to interpret them as attempts to legitimate the development of some ideas rather than others.'

(b) Test Procedures: There are so many different ways in which one might make one's observations and put the hypothesis to the test. Here are but a few suggestions. Remember, however, that we are talking about test procedures in a much looser sense than would be accepted in the physical sciences. There can be only so much precision as the subject of study permits.

(i) *Interactive analysis schedule.* There are schedules for putting into specific categories the teacher/pupil interactions that occur. There are limitations to the value of these (they may omit important interactions of the non-verbal kind) but they do at least provide evidence of such things as the amount the teacher talks as opposed to the pupil and such self-knowledge might easily surprise, leading to a change in teaching style.

(ii) *Participant observer.* Our problem is of course that of being more or less objective rather than being either objective or not. Simply having someone else in the room to observe, make notes, and report back on what he has seen makes the situation more objective than otherwise for there is now another person who, on the basis of the same evidence, is able to challenge the teacher's interpretation of events. If you like, team teaching provides greater opportunity for being objective than does class teaching.

(iii) *Recording.* The tape recorder, again, has its limitations but it provides evidence against which one might test out one's interpretation of what happened. Video-tapes would be even better, but generally speaking these are impractical. Good examples of how tape recordings of lessons might be used are to be found in Barnes, Britton and Rosen (1969).

(iv) *First hand reports.* Although there are limitations to one's own reports on what one does, it would be very silly to discount these. But memory often does not serve one well, and certainly it becomes clouded and distorted by subsequent events. I have now started to keep a daily record of my teaching experience so that there is more detailed information than there otherwise would be when, in future, decisions are being made about course improvement.

(v) *Others' perceptions.* Often one believes that a lesson has been well prepared and presented, that the materials are interesting, and that it has been well received. But the truth of such beliefs depends on how the learner sees one's lesson, and the test of the value of one's lesson therefore must lie partly in the reported perceptions of the learners. Hence, a teacher researcher would seek out the learner's perceptions of the teaching. (One should, of course, extend this to other teachers' perceptions of those changes in school organization and policy that affect teaching: for example, unstreaming; and often a school or departmental head might think what he is doing is for the good but has not found out how the teachers perceive it, even though their perceptions must affect the changes.) One way of finding this out is to ask them, possibly via a third person, possibly via questionnaire, possibly on tape. This can be revealing, as the following extract from the Ford Teaching Project (1975a) shows.

Interviewer: There was a time when he said he was making a guess and he asked you if you agreed whether it was a reasonable guess. I don't know if you remember that?
Pupils: Yes.
Interviewer: And one person said yes and everybody else kept quiet. Now what I want to know is whether the person said yes really did agree with him or just said yes because they thought he wanted them to say yes, and why everybody else kept quiet?

Pupil: Well he would have liked us to say yes, really, 'cause I mean you could see it.

Pupil: If you'd said no you'd waste time arguing wouldn't you.

Pupil: Yeh, if you ever say no he'll stand there and just keep on and on.

Pupil: He'll keep on till you come to his way of thinking.

Pupil: So it's best to say yes to start with.

Interviewer: So even if you did disagree when he said 'Do you all agree' you wouldn't.

Pupil: If you said no he'd keep on to you until you said yes.

It is important to remember that such reports are not sacrosanct. The learner might have a chip on his shoulder or might be in a bad mood, and such factors, about which the teacher can do nothing, would colour how he perceives things. Such reports are but further evidence to be taken into account.

(vi) *Triangulation.* The Ford Teaching Project developed what they called the triangulation technique. Roughly, this involved three accounts of a tape-recorded lesson – the teacher's, the pupils', and the independent observer. Each account was tested out against (1) the tape recorded evidence, and (2) the others' accounts. The result was that each account was modified in the process. It would, of course, be quite easy to try this out in seminars (for example, the seminar on the teacher as researcher) before one implements it in the more difficult territory of the classroom.

Educational theory

The relation between theory and practice, as described by Terry Moore in chapter 1, on the whole commends itself to 'theorists' rather than to 'practitioners'. Somehow the theory rarely generates the practical prescriptions that it would if it were a genuinely 'practical theory'. And this should make us question this particular 'theory' of theory and practice.

Firstly, how specific do conclusions of the theory have to be before they qualify as a practical prescription? To someone practising, a practical prescription would be of the kind 'in class x at time y you should do z if you want to achieve w'. But so called practical theories in education never entail that kind of proposition. Hence, in what sense are they practical? Simply to advocate (as a result of the theory) 'discovery methods' or a combination of 'traditional' or 'progressive' styles, is not being practical — it is much too vague for that. Hence, the disillusion that teachers feel about theory as described by Terry Moore. Secondly, there are good reasons why such theory cannot produce the practical prescriptions that a practical theory would need. Practical situations have too many variable, if not unique, features thereby avoiding capture within an all-embracing theory. No theory can be a substitute for the teacher doing his own theorizing — a distinction I shall explain below. Thirdly, a theory whether scientific or practical would have to be sufficiently 'controversial' for it to exclude certain beliefs or practices and sufficiently precise for one to know what these excluded beliefs or practices are. A theory that accommodates almost anything isn't at all helpful; nor is one that is so vaguely expressed that one cannot tell when it is falsified. Terry Moore's general theories aren't, then, genuine theories — especially when we are told that they can both co-exist in practice. By reason of their all-embracing nature, their blurred theoretical edges, and their mutual compatibility, nothing is excluded and hence they can offer no practical prescriptions.

Does this mean that there is no place for educational theory? Far from it. But one needs to distinguish between theory and theorizing. Theorizing can (and in my opinion should) be seen as the systematic and critical reflection upon practice. As Terry Moore rightly points out, theoretical considerations are embedded in practice — beliefs about the physical and social world, about the value of what one is doing, about one's own teaching skills and capacity. Such beliefs and assumptions are not part of *a* theory, but they are all open to analysis, scrutiny, and criticism. Such systematic and critical examination will involve philosophizing, appealing to evidence, reference to (non-educational) theories. But there is no reason for saying that it will all add up to *a theory*. Educational studies, therefore, should be concerned with helping the practitioner to theorize (think more systematically, critically, and intelligently) about his or her practice.

This will involve being more philosophical, psychological, and sociological in one's approach than hitherto. But it will not involve having *an* educational theory.

In a nutshell, there are two contrasting approaches to educational studies: one goes from theory to practice; the other goes from practice to theory — thereby altering the practice that embodies theory. In the first case, there is a mistaken tendency to seek a coherent and unified view — such unification being the chief function of theory. In the second case, there are many different kinds of theoretical questions that can be asked about practice without the need to construct from them *an* educational theory.

Further reading

Eric Hoyle (1976) explains his notion of 'extended professionalism'. Stenhouse (1975, chapter 10) concerns itself with the teacher as researcher, and my paper is very much indebted to that.

A very good, but very difficult, philosophical account of objectivity is by Hamlyn (1970, pp. 136–47, 1972).

I have frequently referred to the Ford Teaching Project, whose director is John Elliott. An account of the project and of action-research techniques can be found in Elliott and Adelman (1973, 1976) and Elliott (1976). Useful articles by teachers engaged in research into their own teaching are: Cooper and Ebbutt (1974) and Bowen and others (1975). An account and examples of interaction analysis schedules are to be found in Stenhouse (1975, chapter 10). A brief interesting account of classroom research is Hamilton and Delamont (1974). But I am a little sceptical about the value of such research when it is conducted by professional researchers rather than by the teachers it is meant to serve — hence, the importance I have attached to the teacher as researcher. Barnes, Britton, and Rosen (1969) gives examples of tape recordings of teaching which help change the teachers' views of what they are doing and achieving.

Chapter 23

Control of the Curriculum

Peter Gordon

One of the difficulties in arriving at agreement on the ideal content of a school curriculum in England is the autonomy given to schools in deciding what shall be taught. The relationship between the content and control of curriculum is being increasingly discussed in a variety of forums at the present time, for example wherever the question of 'standards' in schools is raised.

John White (1975) has shown how, until 1926, curricula were centrally laid down and that the change to an autonomous system took place without a public debate. An increasingly mobile population requires some uniformity and continuity in curriculum from area to area. There are many outside pressures – from examination boards, publishers and new curriculum projects – which may influence individual schools. The last decade has witnessed the reorganization of education on a new basis – first, middle, comprehensive and sixth form colleges which have needed to rethink their curricula without much specific guidance on content.

We also know that there is a range of curricula offered to different children within the same school. Shipman (1973) mentions that in comprehensive schools, the 'more able' receive a traditional academic diet whilst the 'less able' are given alternative subjects, experimental courses (e.g. Raising of the School Leaving Age (ROSLA)) and integrated studies. A commonly decided curriculum would eliminate this particular aspect of unfairness in schools.

White (1969) advocates a public body to protect schools

from too narrow an education. There is a need for someone
to ensure that all children have a broad education in different
forms of thought. If the State were to promote a compulsory
core and then allow pupils to pursue their learning on a
voluntary basis, as in Eastern Europe, this would remove un-
justified constraints on children's liberty.

Of course, such a system presupposes that the central body
would examine the curriculum as a whole. As the recent
Green Paper *Education in Schools* (1977) mentions, 'it would
not be compatible with the duties of the Secretaries of State
. . . to abdicate from leadership on educational issues which
have become of lively public concern'. It proposes an investigation into the possibilities of a core curriculum and a review
of local arrangements for the co-ordination of the curriculum.
In the long term, it might be possible to work towards the
enunciation of fundamental objectives and the specification
of desirable curriculum content. This would then allow for
better co-ordination of teacher training programmes with
school requirements. It would also be possible to fix terminal,
and perhaps intermediate, standards to be achieved in schools
in the five to sixteen range.

This links closely with growing demands for accountability
in education: but how far can schools achieve targets if there
is uncertainty about the indices of achievement? A recent
Labour Party programme (1976), in stressing the need for
standards, mentions that where a school falls short of the
normal attainments of their age group, the local authority
should be required to co-operate with the school to 'remedy
whatever deficiency exists'.

Centrally, the DES has been monitoring 'standards' since
1948, for example, in its reading surveys. The Department's
Assessment of Performance Unit has recently been set up to
monitor performance across the curriculum. Kay (1975),
then a member of the Unit, has identified six areas of pupil
performance — verbal, mathematical, scientific, ethical,
aesthetic and physical. The recognition of a small number
of what are called 'key forms' has, he claims, two advantages:

the profile of assessment might prove to be reasonably
comprehensive without being impossibly complex: second,
this unity of approach to assessment could coexist with

247

the wide diversity with which these central principles are embodied in school subjects: such an assessment process would impose the minimum of constraints upon the school's organisation and design of its curriculum.

Some problems

It is obvious that the centralizing of control of curriculum content raises a number of problems. A fundamental one is the basic assumption that there is some agreement in society on what curriculum content should be. In fact most issues are viewed through a spectrum of political, ideological and moral standpoints and there is a lack of specific value consensus. How can schools reflect this diversity except by diversity?

It might be thought that too great a stress in an agreed curriculum is laid on pedagogy, and leaves out of account the affective aspect of a teacher's performance. In urban schools especially, teachers are as much concerned with providing a framework of security as the content of the curriculum. Teaching methods too are increasingly looking at problems of *how* to learn as well as *what* to learn. If we consider curriculum mainly in terms of the structure of knowledge, then we should also note that Illich (1971) and others have expressed the need to look also at the structure of schooling. There is a distinction between the explicit and the 'hidden curriculum', i.e. the link between the organization of the school and what is taught: the hierarchies of staff especially the headmaster's role and the division into departments or faculties; and the decision to set, stream, unstream, or band as a basis for teaching. Illich challenges the notion that learning is a result of teaching, that schooling and education are the same thing, and that knowledge can be divided into packages, not necessarily related to each other, called a curriculum.

Difficulties arise when we consider the fixing of standards. The previous history of such attempts is not a happy one. 'Payment by results' in the last century led to low teacher status and over-pressure on pupils to pass the appropriate standards. It also made for opposing interests between parents and schools. Would standards be fixed by achievement rather than age (and could they be repeated)? The basis of our present system, the 1944 Education Act, which looked to the 3 As — age, ability and aptitude — would have to be re-examined. Little has been said on who would fix standards, i.e. inspectors and/or local authority advisers; and would the system be acceptable if teachers were not involved? There are few examples of a fully centralized system which point in a hopeful direction. The Scandinavian model is not helpful as this assumes political stability which is not the case in the UK. At the present time, it is difficult to discern the nature of the body who could control the curriculum: neither the DES nor Schools Council seems appropriate bodies for such a task.

Another criticism of central control is that the size of the undertaking might make for difficulties in allowing for changes to take place. So far, most curriculum innovation has come from schools. Problems of encouraging experimentation and diffusion of new ideas would have to be tackled. In the 1880s, the initial teaching alphabet was introduced into London schools, but failed to gain recognition as it did not come within the Code requirements for reading in Standard I.

The autonomy of pupils and teachers, it could be argued, may not be enhanced by a different system. There are dangers that a compulsory curriculum could be regarded as élitist and that not all children do need to go through the same experiences. It is not easy to see how far students would be consulted in deciding on the content of their courses. There is a similar problem relating to teachers. As new curricula have been developed in recent years, there has been increasing teacher participation in making decisions on their implementation. There is an argument for attracting more powerful teachers to the profession: if teachers were to become mere agents rather than activists in curriculum matters, this would not provide a strong incentive.

In any consideration of the problem of the control of curriculum content, there seem to be at least three questions worth asking:

1 How far is such control feasible and desirable?

2 What would a compulsory core look like?

3 What are the implications for teacher autonomy, i.e. is the business of curriculum decision-making a professional one?

Further reading

For an account of the beginnings of autonomy in curriculum see White (1975). A brief introduction to White's argument is outlined in *New Society*, 6 March 1969 and 4 December 1969; and at length, White (1973). An alternative view is stated in Holly (1973).

Concern for national standards in schools is expressed in the document issued by the Department of Education and Science (1976) as the background paper to the national debate. The reference to the DES Assessment of Performance Unit is Kay (1975, pp. 11–18).

On methods of school organization and curriculum see Shipman (1973, pp. 101–6). The 'liberation' argument and aspects of the hidden curriculum are dealt with in Illich (1971) and Reimer (1971).

Chapter 24

Accountability

Richard Pring

Introduction

Many now argue that schools should be more accountable for what they do. Schools, and teachers, claim a degree of autonomy over what is taught and the methods employed which others — the government, parents, industrialists — may well question. The questioning of this autonomy is often equated with a demand for more accountability. But I believe that there are no such simple equations. I intend in this brief paper to raise what I think are central issues of accountability that need to be explored further.

First, however, by way of introduction, I want to illustrate the apparent move towards greater accountability. This seems to be of a twofold character. There is, on the one hand, a concern about standards — the extent to which they have risen or fallen and the extent to which the school system (for example, the change to a comprehensive system), the curriculum content (for example, new mathematics as opposed to old), and teaching methods (for example, formal or informal) might be held responsible for this rise or fall. On the other hand, there is, at a time when money is short and when teacher redundancies and school closures are on the horizon, a cost-efficiency approach to education. What value for money spent?

I do not think that I need to illustrate these points in detail. The public debate arising out of the inquiry into William Tyndale (Auld, 1976), the various pronouncements by politicians on making public the assessible performance of schools, teachers, and pupils, the pressures upon the Assessment of Performance Unit to devise ways of monitoring pupil performance across the curriculum, the exploration of the voucher system for school place distribution, all seem part of a general demand for school accountability. And this and cost-effectiveness.

Are we, however, including too much within this term accountability, thereby fudging over important distinctions? And are we in danger of overlooking the difficulties of giving an adequate account — part of what is meant by accountability?

Meaning

We could enter the question of meaning by examining typical and central cases. Let us take, for example, the case of a private company. The directors are accountable to the shareholders. By this is meant the following:

1 the directors owe an account of the company's performance to the shareholders;

2 the directors are in some way responsible for the performance of the company;

3 the shareholders, in the light of that account and recognizing the degree of director responsibility, have a right to intervene — change policy, impose conditions, or even dismiss the directors.

Note here the interconnection of these features. One cannot ascribe responsibility without an adequate account. Furthermore, the shareholders would be unwise to intervene, whatever their rights, unless an adequate account had been given and unless responsibility had been properly ascribed. The exercise of a right here would presuppose the possibility of having an adequate account of what is happening.

It is of course possible to see analogies between running a company and running a school. The school receives certain resources to do a certain task. The school is either successful or not — it either produces the required performances or not. One could argue, as indeed it ever more frequently is, that the school should be held to account for the resources spent. That is, the schools should be obliged

1 to give an account to the providers (let us say the local authority) of its performance;

2 to distinguish the performances that lie within its power or responsibility from those that are not, and

3 thus to expose itself to intervention on the basis that it has not used these resources properly or responsibly.

Of course this would seem to apply equally to teachers as to schools. One can talk of the accountability of individual teachers to the local authority through the headmaster — obliged to give an account of performance, to show the limits of their responsibility, and to be exposed, if they have not succeeded, to intervention. (The distinction however between teacher accountability and school accountability is an important one, since the teacher's sphere of responsibility is limited by the system in which he is working, the system to a large extent being outside his control. A doctor could be excellent and yet fail hopelessly if he is given no instruments or medicines.)

An excellent example of accountability where the analogy with public companies seems most appropriate would be that of the Michigan State Accountability System. In this, common goals are defined and translated into specific objectives. Schools are assessed on their ability to meet these objectives. Different teaching 'systems' are put to the test and some are advocated. Then, through a specially constructed system of assessment, results are published. 'The teacher is contracted to perform a service, according to agreed upon terms, within an established time-period and with a stipulated use of resources and performance standards' (Sockett, 1976b).

The focus you might say, is upon results obtained for resources used. If the teacher fails (if the pupils do not perform) he has broken his contract and thus the resource providers can intervene — change the policy, insist on replacement, etc.

The criticisms that might be levelled against the Michigan State System pin-point the weaknesses in the analogy with the accountability of a company to shareholders. Firstly, it is disputable whether one is able — right across the curriculum

– to identify sufficiently precise objectives for there to be accountability in terms of easily measurable performances. (Pupil achievement is something very different from good or bad cash accounts.) Secondly, responsibility for pupil achievement is not easy to ascribe. (I was told by an eleven-year-old how he had purposely put down wrong answers in his entry examination to the X public school because he did not want to be seen as a swot, and he wanted to go with his friends to Y comprehensive school. Should the teacher be held responsible in any way for his failure?) Thirdly, it is not as clear as in the case of a public company, who, in the light of an adverse account, has the right to interfere. There is a tradition of teacher autonomy in schools (and academic freedom in universities) which limits (if not denies) the right of the provider of resources to intervene (to hold one to account) even if one's performance (by all accounts) is poor. Certainly teachers are not under contract to get results – although they may be under contract to teach. But the word 'teach' is sufficiently elastic that the obligations under one's contract are slight indeed. Do they go much further than having to turn up in the morning?

Giving an account

All these points indicating the weakness of the analogy might be met as follows – and each reply needs to be the focus of analysis and argument. Firstly, just as the public company owes an account of its activities, so does the school. But in the case of the school, such an account need not be tied to listing the performances or outcomes. Thus the analogy works so long as one does not limit the giving of an objective account to reporting the achievement of preconceived objectives. Hence, the first major question of school or teacher accountability is: How can one give an adequate account of (i.e. be objective and comprehensive in describing) what happens in a school?

Ascription of responsibility

Secondly, the ascription of responsibility might be much

more difficult in schools, but I see no reason why it should be of a different order from the ascription of responsibility in companies. For example, a company's profits might have gone down, but this might also have happened in every similar company because, say, the price of raw materials has risen sharply and this, you might say, was totally outside the power of the directors. They did their best in the circumstances, just as a teacher might have done his best, but (due to circumstances beyond his control, such as an inefficient school or a particularly difficult bunch of children) simply failed.

None the less there do seem to be difficulties in the analogy here. In the case of the public company, the unexpected and uncontrollable circumstances prevented the company achieving the results that otherwise it would have achieved. In teaching it is rarely possible to point to specific circumstances and to say that it was these that made one's teaching ineffective. Especially is this the case where desired results or performances are hard to specify. However, the analogy may still work a little bit. Just as the directors of the company acted according to certain practical principles which, *in normal circumstances*, would have led to successful company results (and thus acted responsibly and could not be held responsible for the company's failure), so the teacher acted according to certain agreed principles of teaching which not always achieve learning in pupils but which *normally* would do. Of course, such agreed principles would not arise simply from their likelihood of achieving results. They would include moral principles about the rightness of proceeding in a certain way irrespective of the results to be achieved. The ascription of responsibility therefore would be partly in the extent to which teachers, whatever their failures, acted in accordance with certain general principles of procedure which together ensured efficient practice in normal circumstances and morally acceptable practice in all circumstances. Such principles might include systematic preparation of work, regular assessment of pupils' performance and learning difficulties, punctuality and regularity in attendance, and so on. Hence, the second major question is: What sort of action are we going to hold a teacher responsible for?

Right of Intervention

On the third point, however, the analogy between schools and companies seems to break down. There is a contract, or something equivalent, between shareholders and directors which gives the former the right to intervene. It is not clear to what extent the providers of resources have such a right in the running of schools. Maybe governing bodies have; maybe the local authority has; in some circumstances (such as serious teacher misconduct) the Department of Education and Science has. But except in exceptional circumstances, these bodies do seem fairly powerless to intervene. The area of accountability, where this implies the right of intervention by the person to whom the school is allegedly accountable, seems very small indeed — either as a matter of fact or within the law — certainly much smaller than the advocates of accountability would like to see. The autonomy of the school over curriculum and teaching methods does seem incompatible with the accountability of the school in these matters.

Here, however, we need to make a distinction in coming to understand the current debate. As a matter of fact schools are not accountable to parents, say, in that they are under no contract to parents to achieve certain things and in that, whatever the parents feel about schools, they have no right to intervene in the curriculum or teaching methods. This is a professional matter and, as in the profession of medicine and law, the teacher is not accountable to his client. But, one might argue, the teacher *ought* to be accountable, meaning that in future he ought to be held to account by the parent. That is, the parent ought to be given rights, like the shareholder, viz.

1 to be given an adequate account of what happens;
2 to question the principles by which responsibility might be ascribed for what happens (a code of conduct as it were, given the difficulties in ascribing responsibility on the basis of results); and
3 the right to intervene either to make certain curriculum stipulations or, as a last resort, to dismiss the teachers as either incompetent or immoral.

Hence, the third question to be considered is: To whom ought schools and teachers to be held accountable? To the local authority, to the taxpayer in general, to parents, to industry, to the children, to professional colleagues?

In answering this third question, I think it is necessary (on the basis of what I have said) to distinguish between accountability and owing an account. The fact that shareholders can hold the directors to account implies that they have rights of intervention. This requires, as a necessary condition, information – i.e. an account of what is happening. But one cannot argue the other way around. One cannot argue that because A is owed an account by B, B is accountable to A in the normal sense that A has power to interfere when B's performance doesn't come up to scratch. It is necessary to decide, in other words, whether one is demanding an extension of the powers of intervention to various groups of people when school or teacher performance doesn't come up to scratch.

Giving an account – a second look

What then is the major question to be answered? It is: How to give an objective account that is not tied to the pre-specification of objectives? Very briefly this is how I see the problem. To be objective in one's judgments is to put them on a firmer footing than a *personal* opinion or impression. Judgments are influenced by past experiences, by dominant beliefs, by strong feelings. There is a sense in which one can never completely trust one's own judgment or that of any single person. To be objective then is to recognize the possibility of error, due to all manner of personal limitations, in one's judgments, and in consequence to take steps to place one's judgments in an inter-subjective framework. This would seem to involve two things viz. 1. to employ a shared language that is conceptually adequate for the purpose, and 2. to clarify what would count as evidence against the judgment that one holds.

Let me briefly take each of these in turn. Very frequently we describe situations, in and out of schools, in a language that is not shared exactly by those we are speaking with. The Ford Teaching Project gives excellent examples of this. Teachers described their teaching styles as formal or informal.

257

But it quickly became apparent that the criteria for applying these concepts were themselves unclear. Different teachers meant different things by the same words.

Even where, however, we remain within a language that is less ambiguous, it is not clear what would be an adequate account for particular purposes. Let us take each of the following propositions about a school incident.

His hand rose.
He raised his hand.
He waved.
He signalled.
He started the riot.

Each statement could be true, in that the truth of any one statement contains the truth of the preceding ones. Thus he started the riot by signalling. He signalled by waving. He waved by raising his hand, etc. Each is true of the same event, and yet each says something completely different. Clearly the last statement not only *describes* the incident but *ascribes* responsibility and also indicates the interconnection of events. How far is it possible to give an account where responsibility is not ascribed or where interpretations and explanations are not incorporated?

A third problem with language is the generality of it very often. One can pitch one's account at such a level of blandness that either it must be true or, if it is not true, it is not clear what would count as evidence against the account. Most educational books are of this nature.

This leads on to the second aspect of being within an intersubjective framework. It presupposes an account of what happens such that

1 one knows what would count as a critical test of one's account, and
2 one takes steps to see if it can withstand the critical test.

Thus to be objective is to present the data on the basis of which one has reached certain conclusions and on the basis of which others might disagree with one's conclusion. Objectivity here makes demands upon an openness to the critical scrutiny of others, and thus to the possibility of others questioning both the conclusion reached and the data on the basis of which those conclusions have been reached. Thus one gives an account of what happens in one's classroom. What makes it an objective account is:

1 that one describes what happens with sufficient clarity and precision that someone else would know what would count against one's description,

2 that one has opened up that classroom sufficiently to enable others, in the light of what they hear and see, to dispute that judgment.

Conclusion

I have looked at three aspects of the current interest in accountability, viz.

1 the need to give an account;

2 the ascription of responsibility for what happens;

3 the right of those, to whom an account is given, to intervene.

With reference to 1. there are problems in attempting to give an adequate and objective account to an outsider of what happens in a school or classroom — partly because of the loose language we use, partly because of what we say cannot be independently verified.

With reference to 2., there are difficulties in putting blame or responsibility for what happens on any one person or any part of the system — the student must be held in some way responsible for what he does. On the other hand, one might hold a teacher responsible for not acting according to certain principles which in normal circumstances are principles of efficient teaching or which are part of an agreed ethical code.

With reference to 3., it is not clear to whom schools or teachers owe an account, or who (on the basis of that account) should have the right to intervene.

Further reading

For an interesting philosophical analysis of the problem of accountability see Sockett (1976b). McIntryre (1977) explores the different criteria in terms of which teachers might accept responsibility for their teaching. House (1975) raises provocative questions about the dangers of accountability in the light of the American experience. Kay (1975) sets out the main purpose and principles of the Assessment of Performance Unit. Other useful publications are Kogan (1975) and Elliott (1976b).

Chapter 25

Authority and Participation

Terry Moore and Denis Lawton

Talk about authority and participation might be regarded as setting out exclusive alternatives with the implication that we have to choose either the one or the other, that educational practices must be based either on the pronouncements of authority or on some shared participatory activity. Such a view would seem to be oversimplified if not incorrect. In this chapter it will be argued that we are not presented simply with a polarity of incompatibles, but with two concepts, both of which have a proper application in an educational context, although in different ways.

To develop the thesis we may begin with the notion of 'pupil-participation'. It is possible to distinguish between two separate senses in which this term may be used in connection with education:

1 Pupil-participation in education in the sense of participation in the business of *being educated*, participation in what is going on in an educative experience.

2 Pupil-participation in education in the sense of participation in decision-making *about what goes on* in an educational situation, about procedures and arrangements in schools and elsewhere.

It will be argued that pupil-participation in sense 1 is justified by logic, in that this sort of participation is necessarily involved in education. Participation in sense 2 is justified, where it is so, by moral rather than by logical considerations. It will be maintained that in both cases there is a connection

261

with *authority*, but that only in sense 2 may the pupil be said to have a justified claim to exercise authority, and even then only in a limited way.

Education, in any normative sense of the term involves initiating pupils into various aspects of knowledge, understanding and skill. This must involve the pupil in *learning* something, coming to understand what he is taught. Now, no one can be *initiated* into anything unless he actively takes part in the initiating proceedings. This is participation in the business of being educated. Participation involves a sharing in an enterprise, with others, taking one's part and knowing that one is doing so. So participation in the business of learning, trying to come to understand, is a necessary condition of being educated. Pupils *must* participate in this sense or education isn't taking place at all. This is the point made in 1 above, participation by the pupil is what is going on, is required by the logic of the term 'education'.

But there is another side to this. In this business of initiation there are *teachers*, who are supposed to be in possession of the knowledge and skills being passed on. Pupils are not in possession, not fully so. It is because they are not fully in possession that they are pupils. This means that initiation involves a transfer, from the teacher to the pupil, the initiation of one by the other, into a public tradition. Thus the enterprise rests on the prerequisite that teachers are, to some extent, *authorities* on what they teach, that they have a right to be listened to. They don't have to be absolute authorities, nor infallible, but they must be authorities relative to those they are trying to educate. Pupils are not authorities in this sphere, since if they were they would not be pupils. There is thus a conceptual connection between *educating* someone and being *an authority*. It simply would not make sense to say the teacher was *educating* his pupil unless he knew what he was talking about, and moreover, knew more about the subject than his pupil. Therefore, in so far as there is an *educational* situation both participation *and* authority are conceptually involved; participation by the pupil in what is going on, the exercise of authority by the teacher. These are conceptual points, matters of logic not matters of empirical fact.

Now let us turn to the other aspect, i.e. participation in decision-making *about* what goes on, *about* educational arrangements. An institution, a school for example, has, as a condition of being an institution, a rule-structure to organize its efforts. The rules have to be made, interpreted and maintained, if the institution is to continue as such. Those who have the right to make, interpret and enforce the rules are *in* authority, authority *de jure*. Those who are in such authority in schools are so, in the vast majority of cases, because they are older, more mature, more experienced than their pupils. They are adults whereas, in most cases, the pupils are children. But, those who are in actual authority *de jure* in schools are not in the logically, superior position *vis-à-vis* those they govern, that the teacher, as *educator* must be *vis-à-vis* his pupils in an educational situation.

Before a teacher can *educate* his pupils he must be an authority i.e. know more than his pupils know about the matter in hand. He must exercise academic authority, which his pupils, as pupils, can't do. But he doesn't have to be wiser, more tactful, more sympathetic, than his pupils to be in authority in the rule-making and rule-enforcing sense. It is just a matter of fact that he usually is so, a contingent matter, not a matter of logic. There is nothing logically sacrosanct in the notion of the teacher alone being in authority, and nothing in logic which keeps the pupil out of this position.

Now, the decisions that people in authority make and the rules they enforce have an impact on the lives of those affected by them and this is particularly the case in schools. In respect of this impact pupils will have as much knowledge and awareness as anyone else. They will know how rules, decisions, even teaching methods affect the quality of their lives. So, it can be argued, there is a moral case for saying that pupils should have some say in the decision-making that affects them, through consultation, representation or whatever other means are appropriate. In other words they should be allowed to participate in the exercise of regulatory authority, so far as they are able, according to their age, intelligence and degree of maturity. For in *this* sphere they too can be authorities, in that they have appropriate knowledge, and so can have the right to be heard. Whilst there would be something logically odd in thinking of the pupil as *an* authority on what he goes to school to learn, there is nothing odd in seeing him as an authority on the impact, consequences, justice and advisability of the rules, conventions and methods employed in educating him. In this sphere he may participate in decision-making and be qualified to do so.

But a note of caution is needed here. To say that participation is appropriate is not to say that all children are capable, ready or willing to share in policy decisions. Age, maturity, a sense of responsibility are also relevant considerations. What is being said is that there is a moral case against any *a priori* attempt to rule out pupil participation merely on the grounds that they are pupils. There is also an educational case, namely that it is through such participation that pupils may come to acquire virtues like tolerance and rationality in decision-making, virtues essential to a democratic society.

The argument of this chapter may be put in summary form:

1 So far as school decisions concern *what is taught*, the decisions must be the teacher's decisions. For teachers alone are authorities in *this* sphere. They alone have the right to be heard, whereas pupils, as a condition of being pupils, have not. The argument here rests on a conceptual point. If a pupil *were* an authority on these matters it is difficult to see how, in any significant sense, he could *be* a pupil.

2 In so far as school decisions affect pupils solely in respect of their membership of the school i.e. in respect of their comfort, dignity, sense of justice, even their effectiveness as learners, here they may have a right to be heard, since in these matters, they too can be authorities, without ceasing to be pupils. Being a pupil doesn't, as such, prevent anyone from the exercise of authority in this sphere. Thus pupil-participation in decision-making is appropriate in this area, although not logically necessary. It is contingent on such factors as age, intelligence, sense of responsibility and general maturity, but in so far as it is a claim it is a moral claim.

What would be wrong would be to permit pupil-participation in decision-making where, since they are pupils, they have no right to be heard or consulted. Teachers would throw up their essential authority if they asked pupils what they thought they should be taught. For here, academic authority is crucial, and pupils, as pupils, do not have this authority. What would be equally wrong would be to deny pupil participation where pupils *do* have a right to be heard, i.e. in cases where, with reservations, they too can be said to be authorities on what goes on. Here they do have a claim, a moral claim, to participation, and it is as well to recognize this claim for what it is.

This point has a bearing on the case for democracy in schools. Democracy, in the liberal, political sense necessarily involves deference to the *opinions* of the governed. In a limited sense there can be such democracy in a school. Teachers can, and generally should, consult pupils' opinions and invite their participation in decisions, in those areas where pupils can be authorities. But in those areas where they are not authorities, and as pupils can't be, their opinions are of no consequence and their participation in decision-making inappropriate. Here the teachers must consult the pupils' interests, not their opinions, and there is no place for democracy or participation in this sphere.

The nature of authority

Max Weber (like many other sociologists) was interested in the question of *social action* (how individuals react towards each other in a relationship), and one aspect of this question of social action is 'why do some people do what others tell them?' One answer would be *power*, and in this section we are concerned with that kind of power regarded by the recipients as *legitimate* i.e. authority. Weber defined power as 'the possibility of imposing one's will on the behaviour of others'. In those social relations where power is *recognized* as 'legitimate' this may be described as *authority*. This distinction between 'power' and 'authority' is a useful and important one.

Weber wrote a great deal about authority and domination and used a typology of three kinds of authority: 1 traditional authority, 2 legal-rational authority, 3 'charismatic' authority.

Traditional authority

This mode of legitimation of a power relationship consists of

265

an acceptance of authority of 'masters'. The legitimation is based on custom. The authority has been acceptable or valid for a long time. 'We have always obeyed this kind of person' (maybe a king or chief). This is an unthinking, non-controversial acceptance of authority: it would be considered wrong even to question the basis of that authority. In our own history the medieval king could exercise arbitrary authority, limited only by the framework of *custom*. For example the arguments in the sixteenth and seventeenth centuries about the right of the king to impose certain kinds of taxes were not questions about whether it was fair or reasonable, but whether it was *customary*.

It may also be important to stress here that none of the three types of authority exist in a pure form; the arguments about divine rights of kings was partly a question of charismatic authority also. Most forms of traditional authority require some kind of myth about the natural superiority of the leader. The three kinds of authority are examples of Weber's use of 'ideal types', i.e. 'pure' examples which do not really exist in a pure form but which are helpful in clarifying our thinking.

Legal-rational authority

This mode of legitimation of power depends on the existence of good reasons for accepting the authority. The authority is part of an institution which is beneficial in some way to those obeying the authority. It is in accord with more general rules such as fairness or justice, or the need for order.

Charismatic authority

This kind of authority is 'legitimated' (if that is the right word) by the special gifts and purpose of the individuals possessing charisma. Such individuals might include such diverse personalities as Christ and Hitler. The authority depends on a belief that the wielder of authority has sacred or super-human qualities. His followers are disciples. Charisma can, however, be transmitted institutionally: for example the ordination of Roman Catholic priests. In this case the principle might be that the office is more important than the individual (there may be elements of this in the role of the teacher — the idea of wearing a gown, cultivating superior manners and aloof and haughty behaviour). This kind of charisma can be taught, though not to everyone, candidates for charismatic authority training having to be selected very carefully and their success depending less on knowledge than on demeanour.

Weber's typology is very elegant and useful, but at least two kinds of warning are necessary:

1 People tend to misuse the classification and talk of 'charismatic personality', sometimes of teachers, but this is a corrupt non-Weberian usage of charisma.

2 The Weberian view is not completely acceptable by all sociologists. (See Bierstedt, 1967.)

Bierstedt (1967), writing about the connection between social control and authority, maintains that the *order* essential in social life is maintained by various expressions of institutionalized authority. But authority is not the same as *competence* (which is closer to R. S. Peters' distinction of *'an* authority' which is different from being *in* authority), and it is not the same as *leadership*. Bierstedt's definition is 'Authority pertains to the exercise of social control through clearly defined status arrangements between those in superordinant positions and those in positions below.' This underlines the important distinction between *authority* which is the legitimate institutionalized exercise of *power*, and *leadership* which is about *influence* (or persuasion). This would imply that Weber's category of charismatic authority was not really authority at all but a kind of leadership. It might be a kind of leadership which would overthrow existing authority and even become legitimated but would not in fact be authority. (This controversy cannot be settled here but you may have noticed that it pushes the argument about authority in a functionalist direction.) There are also interesting questions about how long a charismatic leader can carry on without institutionalizing the authority (e.g. Fidel Castro?). Weber was well aware of the unstable characteristics of charismatic authority.

Both views (i.e. Weber's and Bierstedt's) would agree on the distinction between legitimate authority and coercive control. Power is regarded as coercive control rather than legitimate authority when it acts contrary to the rules established for its legitimation. Thus authority can lose its legitimation *either* by failure to behave justly (i.e. according to the rules) *or* failure to do what it is there for: e.g. if it fails to maintain order.

We should also make a distinction between the basis of authority which is in terms of an institution, and what one has to do as an individual to *maintain* a position of authority: this may involve questions of competence and leadership (and there is some psychological evidence about this – what it is and how to get it). A headmaster or a teacher is presumably a legitimate authority figure because he is part of an institution – the education system. He is entrusted by society to transmit certain kinds of knowledge. What he has to do to exercise authority, to get respect etc., is another question.

The rationalization of authority

One important aspect of the history of this country in the last three or four hundred years has been a gradual growth of rationality in society generally, and in education there has been a move away from traditional authority towards rational-legal authority (without necessarily getting all the way there). In society as a whole there has been a general growth in the feeling that traditional authority is not inevitable and might be replaced by more rational institutions: for example parliamentary democracy, the emancipation of women, and the legal rights of workers. But the process of moving from traditional to rational authority is incomplete: note the continued existence of the monarchy etc.; we live in a 'mixed economy' of rational and traditional (and charismatic if you accept Weber rather than Bierstedt).

This kind of social change has had all sorts of consequences in society e.g. examinations for the Civil Service etc. – people get jobs on the more 'rational' ground of ability rather than the traditional grounds of being a member of a certain kind of family. This was connected with the growth of what Weber called *bureaucracy*.

Authority and education

Superficially there is a similarity between the liberal humanitarian kind of rational movement against injustice and the demand for participation by pupils or students (but see R. S. Peters' opposing point of view in Hirst and Peters (1970)). There may be arguments against some kinds of participation, but in a non-traditional kind of organization based on legal-rational bureaucratic criteria it is inevitable that questions of authority will be mixed up with questions of competence. Pupils are encouraged to ask *why*, and teachers must not only know the answers but be prepared to discuss them.

I have already said that authority is different from competence, and one view of authority is that the person in authority does not have to possess competence (i.e. to be *an* authority). The authority figure is simply given a certain status in order to preserve order: e.g. a policeman does not have to be particularly good at directing the traffic, but he has authority to do so which motorists do not; the treasurer of a society does not have to be better at signing cheques than the other members but he has the authority to do so etc. But there is a weakness in this argument (especially when applied to education): authority of some kinds does depend *to some extent* on competence: e.g. a football referee needs to know the rules otherwise bottles will begin to fly; teachers must have something worthwhile to teach and be able to communicate otherwise their authority may be questioned.

Another difficulty is that education is compulsory. Sociologists are fond of making distinctions between voluntary associations and involuntary associations. In a voluntary association authority tends to rest upon consent (in a club or a debating society a member accepts the authority of the chairman even if he thinks he is a fool; he can leave if he wants to). But in an involuntary association, e.g. the army or a prison, there is no question of consent. Schools are *in fact* involuntary associations but we often act as though they were not. We value liberty so highly that we pretend it exists even when it does not. There is a difficult borderline between manipulation of the pupils and genuine participation, i.e. ultimately we may decide that pupils have to do certain things whether they want to or not, but we will begin by trying to persuade them that they have some choice. (This is of particular relevance, of course, to the current debate on a 'compulsory' core curriculum.)

Yet another problem is that teachers may regard it as part of their job to make themselves and their authority redundant. The authority of a judge or an army officer is static, but the authority of the teacher has to be gradually reduced: part of a teacher's job is gradually to reduce the competence gap between himself and his students. The more he succeeds the less justification for the continued existence of his authority.

Summary

So far we have outlined some of the reasons which might explain both confusion about the nature of authority and the uneasiness many now have in exercising authority.

Authority is often treated as a dirty word in education and is not distinguished from being authoritarian. Our long explanation of the change from traditional to rational authority was intended to indicate that there is nothing wrong with authority as such although there may be much wrong with the way it is still exercised in some schools.

The relation between authority and competence is also important for teachers. Any teaching-learning situation involves authority in terms of the competence gaps: but this is likely to be fairly specific and should not be confused with general superiority-inferiority of a social or moral kind. If I go to a doctor for medical advice I am implicitly accepting his authority (on certain matters), but I would object if he started giving me advice about moral behaviour, and I would also object if he treated me as an inferior human being. Furthermore my initial acceptance of his authority is limited: if I went to him because I had a sore throat and he suggested amputating my leg I would ask for a second opinion.

In teaching, authority tends to be much more complicated.

So much so that many young teachers are unhappy about the question of exercising authority in any way (see Hannam, Smyth and Stephenson (1971) for an account of this problem).

Most organizations have to have rules. It would be strange if schools, at which attendance is compulsory, could do without rules altogether. Most private clubs have the ultimate sanction of expulsion; this is a luxury which private schools retain, but which is much more difficult to operate in state schools. But unless you think that children are saints then we have to have ways of dealing with them when they break rules. The authority should be rational rather than traditional and it should be exercised in a humane way, but it will need to exist.

Finally, although a teacher is inevitably in an authority position he still has to persuade his students to behave accordingly. He has to negotiate with them. He must have something worthwhile to offer but they must also see it as worthwhile — they must participate in some way. To be a teacher in the days of traditional authority was much easier; to be entirely rational is extremely difficult; many schools seem to have settled for an intermediate position — manipulation.

Further reading

The philosophical question of authority and education is a complicated one. It has been discussed in a general way by Peters (1966), Hirst and Peters (1970). For a more detailed examination of authority see Peters (1959). All of these establish the case that education without authority is impossible, but it is important to know what is meant by authority.

On the sociological question of types of authority, and the relation between the form of an organization and the implications for human beings within it, you may like to read Weber (1947), but it is fairly heavy going and you have to make most of the educational implications for yourself. The Bierstedt paper is easier to read and may be found in Rose (1972).

Conclusion

Why Change the Curriculum?

Denis Lawton

It may seem strange to ask this question at the end, when the question has been posed implicitly or explicitly throughout the book. There are many answers to the question which can be found in the previous chapters, and the main purpose of this chapter is to summarize what has come before, and in doing this to raise a few more issues which may not yet have been dealt with. It might be useful to remind you at this stage that one of the basic purposes of this book was to treat the curriculum as 'problematical' rather than something which can safely be taken for granted. I will be looking at the problem of the curriculum and of the question 'Why Change the Curriculum?' under four headings: historical, sociological, philosophical and psychological.

Historical reasons for changing the curriculum

In so far as it is possible to talk sensibly about '*the* curriculum' — and usually it is not — it seems very unlikely that if we were able to start curriculum planning from first principles that our planned curriculum would look much like the typical school programme as exemplified by the time-table on the staffroom wall. *To some extent* we have to admit that most curricula are historical accidents; they have developed in various ways, partly as a result of events long forgotten by the teachers who now find themselves taking the curriculum for granted. Curriculum change has generally been a very untidy business: at one point a new subject being pushed in, at another point an old one being squeezed — but probably not pushed out altogether. It could hardly have been otherwise, but there are times when it is healthy to stand away from an established institution and look critically at it. So the first historical point to be made about the curriculum is that it has developed in an unsystematic, sometimes almost chaotic, way, generally growing in range of content covered. One of the reasons for the current debate on the curriculum is the familiar argument that the time-table is over-crowded and that the basics (whatever they may be) are being neglected. Certainly once a subject is accepted into the curriculum it tends to stay there — this is what some have referred to as 'curriculum inertia'. Perhaps the best example of this is Latin: once a necessary part of any educated European's education, necessary because most books were written in Latin, it survived long after Latin had ceased to serve this purpose and became a badge of rank for the children of the social élite or socially aspiring. It survived even longer as an additional hurdle for those wanting to do certain courses in certain universities. A word of caution is needed here, however: because it can be shown that Latin survived for very strange reasons it does not necessarily follow that it has no place in the curriculum. If a number of schools are now incorporating classical studies into humanities programmes we cannot be sure that we will be right in assuming that the only reason for this is the presence of displaced Latin teachers. There may be good reasons for preserving some kind of classical heritage in the consciousness of all our pupils.

The second historical problem can be dealt with fairly quickly since we devoted the whole of an earlier chapter to this argument, but it is a very important area which you may want to reflect on again. It is possible — without too much over-simplification — to talk of the two (and possibly more) separate curricular traditions in England. In the nineteenth century, schools for the rich and schools for the poor were not simply different in quality, they were different in their curricular aims. The kinds of persons they were trying to produce were quite different. Public schools for the rich were trying to produce leaders — Christian gentlemen who would be the managers in industry at home or district officers in the colonies abroad; for the poor, or the lower orders, elementary schools were designed to produce a labour force able to understand simple written instructions and good enough at arithmetic to make calculations such as sorting things out into dozens. But it was not intended that they would be too educated. It was important that they would be sufficiently obedient to have respect for the property of their betters, but not so well educated that they would develop ideas above their station. These two different sets of schools needed to have different kinds of curriculum. And they did. The importance of all this is that to some extent these two traditions are still with us. One common method today of organizing comprehensive schools is to have two bands divided at an arbitrary point on an unreliable ability scale. The children on the two bands often have strangely different curricula: political history in the upper band, social and economic history for the less able children etc. On a recent visit to one so-called comprehensive school as an external examiner for a student teacher doing her teaching practice, the headteacher apologized to me because the lesson I saw happened to be in a lower band class. He clearly felt that I had not seen the school doing its real work and that I had only seen the fag-end of education. The two traditions still survive in our schools dominating many teachers' thinking about education and in many cases distorting the curriculum planning.

Sociological reasons for changing the curriculum

Sociologists are fond of telling us that schools have many functions in our society apart from (or instead of) the clearly educational ones. In particular, schools in the UK socialize the young for their social roles when they leave schools and act as selecting agencies for the labour market. Some may feel that there is nothing particularly wrong with either of these two functions; others will be horrified at the suggestion that they are partners to such uneducational processes. We should at least ask the question 'to what extent?' and not merely take it for granted one way or the other. Certainly one of the motives for providing elementary education in the nineteenth century was to 'gentle the masses'. Most histories of education provide plenty of examples of this process, but see particularly Mary Sturt (1967, chapter 1). But the idea did not end with the close of the nineteenth century: in 1929 Sir Cyril .Norwood was arguing that elementary education had saved the nation from bolshevism. He felt that this was some compensation for the scarcity of domestic servants caused by compulsory schooling. (See David Glass's essay 'Education and Social Change in Modern England', Halsey, Floud and Anderson, 1961.) But whether schools still have this narrow view of socializing for conformity as a major aim is another question. It does not necessarily follow that because that was one important reason for the establishment of some elementary schools that it is still an important feature of schools today. Opinions differ. Bowles and Gintis (1976), for example, suggest that schools provide a major prop for the capitalist system: pupils are trained to perform for extrinsic rewards rather than out of interest in the subject matter, and they are prepared by the grading system for the inequalities of the capitalist work situation. For a British view which is critical of, but not unsympathetic to, the Marxist approach you should read Brian Davies' recent book *Social Control and Education* (1976).

On the related question of the extent to which schools (especially secondary schools) exist to service the labour market, opinions are again divided. The phrase is itself somewhat emotionally toned, of course, and if we discussed instead the desirability of schools helping the young to earn their own livings the question becomes rather more acceptable. Work is an important aspect of most people's lives, and schools would be foolish to ignore this part of the transition from childhood to adulthood. But it is also true that British and American sociology of education in the 1950s and early 1960s seemed to have sailed a little close to the wind of 'capitalist' economics: for example probably the most important sociology of education text of that time was *Education, Economy and Society*, edited by Halsey, Floud and Anderson (1961). It begins with this sentence: 'Education is a crucial type of investment for the exploitation of modern technology. This fact underlies recent educational development in all the major industrial societies.' As the title of the book suggests much of it was concerned with education and economic efficiency; inequalities of educational opportunity were often seen as 'wasting talent' rather than lack of social justice. But it is easy now to exaggerate: by no means all of the book was of this kind, and it is certainly unfair to label all the authors as functionalists bolstering up the existing economic system. Many of them were also concerned with questions of social justice and still are.

The relationship between education and work is a very complex one. I would be tempted to say that schools in fact pay too little attention to the world of work but too much attention to preparation for jobs in a narrow sense. Partly for historical reasons, teachers in schools are hostile to the notion of vocational training, but this does not stop them acting in all sorts of ways as selectors, sorters and classifiers for the job market. At the same time schools may have very little in the curriculum to help them to prepare the young for a complex, industrial society; the vast majority of boys and girls leave school politically, economically, socially and technologically illiterate. This is the real gap in the curriculum. Raymond Williams made a similar point in *The Long Revolution* (1961). For socio-historical reasons science and technology have been neglected in the mainstream of curriculum development. It was too practical to be high status knowledge for the élite and it thus became associated with low level vocational training for those who worked with their hands. This has had disastrous effects on the curriculum – and maybe on the economy.

Thus I would agree with those sociologists who want to make the curriculum into a problem and question the whole of the content of what is taught in schools. I would not, however, accept the extreme views of those such as M. F. D. Young (1971) who appear to suggest that all knowledge is socially constructed, and therefore arbitrary. These are dangerous prophets, encouraging the young to enjoy their ignorance. As Brian Davies (1976, p. 66) puts it in the book already quoted:

Every generation is required to rewrite its history but not to lose it. The wilful cutting adrift from historical reason by self-styled radicals believing that sound social analysis was born yesterday out of their discovery that education is a massive empire of interest groups doling out and receiving the possession of knowledge unequally, misses the point that having the knowledge is good, lacking it troublesome. They have it and would withhold it only from others, and in the name of populism. More precisely, in many cases they would have their late-arrived version universalised and others made subservient to it.

Thus although agreeing with sociologists who want to look critically at the existing curriculum, I believe that we must preserve the necessary historical methods of distinguishing one kind of knowledge from another and to build our curriculum upon that. The reasons for changing the curriculum are twofold: first, that all children in a democratic society need access to the same kinds of knowledge although they will not reach the same levels of attainment. Second, we need to make sure that the curriculum is relevant to modern society but not necessarily subservient to undesirable aspects of it.

Philosophical arguments for changing the curriculum

One of the criticisms levelled against those sociologists who adopt an extreme relativist position on knowledge is that they have ignored two thousand years of epistemology. (See, for example, Alan Harris' (1975) letter to *The Times Educational Supplement*.) Philosophical studies of knowledge have attempted to distinguish different kinds of knowledge and also to establish certain criteria for saying that some kinds of knowledge and experience are more worthwhile than others. Both these issues are difficult and complex and I will not try to summarize them here. It seems to me, however, that most philosophers are in agreement on the idea that knowledge can be divided into different kinds, although they are likely to argue for ever about how many kinds there are. Maybe it all depends whether you want a delicate, fine classification or just a crude system marking out the major forms. But all seem to be agreed that mathematics is different from history, for example, or that scientific understanding is different from aesthetic appreciation. Whether you want to distinguish anthropology from sociology (and if so where) is a question at a different level of classification. If there are different kinds of knowledge this should be borne in mind when curricula are planned, although there is no need to go as far as making the time-table reflect a philosophical view of the structure of knowledge. Some schools have decided to model the curriculum on Hirst's forms of knowledge, but this begs a number of questions (including some about Hirst's seven forms). But teachers and others involved in curriculum planning need to have examined the philosophical views on knowledge in order to achieve anything like a balanced curriculum. Even that metaphor of 'balance' carries with it assumptions which might need to be analysed further: given that there are different kinds of knowledge or understanding does an educated person need to be initiated into all of them? Even if the answer is 'No', should not the pupil at least be *introduced* to all the important areas even if he does not decide to continue with all of them?

Probably the most difficult aspect of curriculum planning is concerned with deciding what needs to be in the compulsory core curriculum and what can be left as an optional extra. John White has made a valiant attempt in his *Towards a Compulsory Curriculum* (1973). This book is one which you ought to read: even if you do not finally agree with White his argument is worth following and his distinction between the essential core and the less important kinds of knowledge is surely required reading for all concerned with curriculum planning. Before reading White's book you might also re-read R. S. Peters' *Ethics and Education*, especially the section dealing with worthwhile activities. These are all difficult questions in philosophy but it is important to get to grips with the arguments, not only in order to be able to plan a worthwhile curriculum but also to be able to *justify* the curriculum to those outside the profession who have a legitimate interest in the curriculum. This kind of accountability is one which can no longer be avoided.

On the other hand there are some philosophers who argue that a curriculum should be based on children's interests. I have never been able to accept this idea: there seems to be a concealed view of the perfectly good child behind this kind of argument (for example Wilson's (1971) book on interests and education). Unless you accept the naive Rousseau idea that the child is perfect but spoiled by an imperfect society it is difficult to see how a child can be left to choose for himself when it comes to curricular activities. My own view is that children develop by interacting in a very complex way with their environment both physical and social. In a society as complicated as ours there is much to learn — too much to be left to chance. Education must therefore be concerned with those aspects of our culture which are too important to be left to chance. Back to the criteria for worthwhile knowledge and experience again: we have to decide what teachers need to push hard for and what they need not bother about, on the basis that what children are most interested in is not always in their interest. Others, including Richard Pring, are more sympathetic to this interest-based curriculum idea. My basic point, however, is that there are philosophical arguments for changing the curriculum on the grounds that schools ignore important areas of wothwhile and relevant knowledge and pay too much attention to the trivial, often failing to achieve a reasonable balance between the essential core of knowledge and options. Most option schemes are very poor substitutes for curriculum planning.

Psychological reasons for changing the curriculum

Psychologists are of course concerned with what children learn as well as how. They are, for example, also interested in the question of whether children would choose a balanced curriculum for themselves if given the choice. This is an empirical question as well as a logical one. Unfortunately good empirical evidence on this is hard to come by — for obvious reasons — but what there is (for example on progressive schools and free schools etc.) does not convince me that children are the best people to do the curriculum planning.

To what extent are schools already paying attention to psychology in the way that they plan their courses? Very little according to Philip Taylor (1970). Sometimes Piaget's work on stages of development is applied, but often in a very negative way — teachers are discouraged from including something in the curriculum at too early a stage in children's development rather than being encouraged to introduce an important part of the curriculum at the most appropriate stage. Piaget has sometimes been oversimplified on the concept of 'readiness' which Bruner has rightly criticized as 'a dangerous half truth'. Curriculum projects such as Science 5 to 13 involving Piagetian stages have not been welcomed by many teachers. Maybe this has something to do with the way that psychology is taught in initial training courses. Whatever the reason, psychology is largely neglected in curriculum planning at classroom level. It seems to be regarded as something very remote and academic. Another reason may be that attempting to apply psychology to thirty or forty children in a class is inevitably doomed to failure if we assume that the children are all more or less the same and progressing at more or less the same rate. Perhaps we must begin again with the teacher as professional using psychological theories of learning, development, instruction and ideas about sequence and organization to plan learning on an individual or small group basis. Attempts to move towards small group and individual learning by developing programmes based on worksheets are laudable but most have a very long way to go.

So the basic psychological argument for changing the curriculum is simply that the average curriculum ignores psychological principles almost entirely. Attempts have been made in the past with large-scale centre-periphery models of curriculum development to encourage teachers to make use of psychological devices but the answer is probably that teachers must begin in a much more local way.

Conclusion

It may be misleading to deal with the need for curriculum change under the four headings which I have used above. One of the important features of this book has been to stress the overlap between the traditional disciplines. Nevertheless it is sometimes useful to use headings in this way — so long as we do not take the categories and the boundaries too seriously. Where sociology ends and history begins is not really very significant. More important is the fact that if we try to operate with only one discipline we run the risk of

making elementary mistakes — as for example in the sociology of knowledge which if studied without asking any philosophical questions about the nature of knowledge results in
very naive thinking about the curriculum. Curriculum studies
is an essentially inter-disciplinary activity and that is one of
the reasons why it is so difficult both at the theoretical level
and perhaps even more difficult at the practical level. Perhaps
what all of this amounts to is that teacher education needs to
concentrate much more on this kind of inter-disciplinary
work on the content of education. It may be true to say that
anyone can teach — most people do — but that the professional teacher's contribution is to be able to plan a good
curriculum.

Bibliography

Adelman, C., Jenkins, D., and Kemmis, S. (1976), 'Rethinking Case Study: Notes from the Second Cambridge Conference', *Cambridge Journal of Education*, vol. 6, no. 3.

Archambault, R. D. (1956), 'The Philosophical Basis of the Experience Curriculum', *Harvard Educational Review*, vol. 26, no. 3.

Atkinson, J. W. (1964), *Introduction to Motivation*, Van Nostrand.

Auld, R. (1976), *William Tyndale Junior and Infant Schools: Public Enquiry*, ILEA.

Ausubel, D. P. (1968), *Educational Psychology, A Cognitive View*, Holt, Rinehart & Winston.

Ayer, A. J. (1946), *Language, Truth and Logic*, Gollancz.

Bamford, T. W. (1967), *The Rise of the Public Schools*, Nelson.

Banks, O. (1955), *Parity and Prestige in English Secondary Education*, Routledge & Kegan Paul.

Banks, O. (1968), *The Sociology of Education*, Routledge & Kegan Paul.

Bantock, G. H. (1968), *Culture, Industrialisation and Education*, Routledge & Kegan Paul.

Barker Lunn, J. C. (1970), *Streaming in the Primary School*, NFER.

Barnard, H. C. (1971), *History of English Education from 1760*, University of London Press.

Barnes, D. (1971), 'Classroom Context for Language and Learning', *Educational Review*, vol. 23, no. 3.

Barnes, D. (1976), *From Communication to Curriculum*, Penguin.

Barnes, D., Britton, J. and Rosen, H. (1969), *Language, the Learner and the School*, Penguin.

Baron, G. and Tropp, A. (1961), 'Teachers in England and America' in A. H. Halsey, J. Floud and C. A. Anderson (eds), *Education, Economy and Society*, Free Press.

Beard, R. (1969), *An Outline of Piaget's Developmental Psychology for Students and Teachers*, Routledge & Kegan Paul.

Bennett, N. (1976), *Teaching Styles and Pupil Progress*, Open Books.

Berger, P. and Luckmann, T. (1966), *The Social Construction of Reality*, Allen Lane.

Bernbaum, G. (1976), 'The Role of the Head' in R. S. Peters (ed.), *The Role of the Head*, Routledge & Kegan Paul.

Bernstein, B. (1967), 'Open School, Open Society', *New Society*, 14 September.

Bernstein, B. (1971), 'On the Classification and Framing of Educational Knowledge' in M. F. D. Young (ed.), *Knowledge and Control: New Directions for the Sociology of Education*, Collier-Macmillan.

Bernstein, B. (1973), *Class, Codes and Control*, vol. 1, Routledge & Kegan Paul.

Bierstedt, R. (1967), 'The Problem of Authority' in P. Rose (ed.), *The Study of Society*, Random House.

Bloom, B. S., Krathwohl, D. R. *et al.* (1956), *Taxonomy of Educational Objectives*, Handbooks 1 and 2, Longman.

Blumer, H. (1965), 'Sociological implications of the thought of George Herbert Mead', *American Journal of Sociology*, vol. 71, pp. 535-44. Reprinted in B. R. Cosin *et al.* (1971), *School and Society*, Routledge & Kegan Paul.

Board of Education (1911), *Report of the Consultative Committee on Examinations in Secondary Schools*, HMSO.

Board of Education (1926), *Report of the Consultative Committee on the Education of the Adolescent* (Hadow Report), HMSO.

Board of Education (1938), *Report of the Consultative Committee on Secondary Education with Special Reference to Grammar Schools and Technical High Schools* (Spens Report), HMSO.

Board of Education (1943), *Report of the Secondary School Examination Council on Curricula and Examinations in Secondary Schools* (Norwood Report), HMSO.

Bottomore, T. B. and Reubel, M. (1963), *Karl Marx: Selected Writings in Sociology and Philosophy*, Penguin.

Bowen, R. B. *et al.* (1975), 'Teacher as Researcher', *Journal of Inservice Education*, vol. 2, no. 1.

Bowles, S. and Gintis, H. (1976), *Schooling in Capitalist America: Educational Reform and the Contradictions of Economic Life*, Routledge & Kegan Paul.

Boyle, D. G. (1969), *A Student's Guide to Piaget*, Pergamon Press.

Brereton, J. L. (1944), *The Case for Examinations*, Cambridge University Press.

Broudy, H. S. (1962), 'To regain educational leadership', *Studies in Philosophy of Education*, no. 11, Spring.

Brown, M. and Precious, N. (1968), *The Integrated Day in the Primary School*, Ward Lock.

Bruner, J. S. (1960), *The Process of Education*, Harvard University Press.

Bruner, J. S. (1965), *Studies in Cognitive Growth*, Wiley.

Bruner, J. S. (1966), *Towards a Theory of Instruction*, Harvard University Press.

Bruner, J. S. (1972), *The Relevance of Education*, Allen & Unwin.

Bryant, P. (1974), *Perception and Understanding in Young Children*, Methuen.

Butcher, H. J. *et al.* (1968, 1973), *Educational Research in Britain*, vols 1 and 3, University of London Press.

Child, D. (1973), *Psychology and the Teacher*, Holt, Rinehart & Winston.

Collings, E. (1923), *An Experiment with a Project Curriculum*, Macmillan, New York.

Cooper, D. and Ebbutt, D. (1974), 'Participation in action research as an inservice experience', *Cambridge Journal of Education*, vol. 4.

Cosin, B. R. *et al.* (1971), *School and Society*, Routledge & Kegan Paul.

Costanzo, P. R. (1973), *Child Development*, no. 44.

Cronbach, L. J. (1963), 'Evaluation for Course Improvement' in R. Heath (ed.), *New Curricula*, Harper & Row.

David, M. (1973), 'The Citizen's Voice in Education', *New Society*, 30 August.

Davies, B. (1976), *Social Control and Education*, Methuen.

Department of Education and Science (1959), *15–18* (Crowther Report), HMSO.

Department of Education and Science, Committee of Higher Education (1963), *Higher Education* (Robbins Report), HMSO.

Department of Education and Science (1966), *The Government of Colleges of Education*, HMSO.

Department of Education and Science (1967), *Children and their Primary Schools* (Plowden Report), HMSO.

Department of Education and Science (1970), *Government and Conduct of Establishments of Further Education*, Circular 7/70, April.

Department of Education and Science (1976), *Educating our Children: Four Subjects for Debate*, HMSO.

Department of Education and Science (1977), *Education in Schools: A Consultative Document*, HMSO.

Department of Education and Science (1977), *A New Partnership for our Schools* (Taylor Report), HMSO.

Dewey, J. (1916), *Democracy and Education*, Macmillan.

Dewey, J. (1933), *How We Think*, Heath.

Dewey, J. (1938), *Experience and Education*, Collier-Macmillan.

Duska, R. and Whelan, M. (1977), *Moral Development: A Guide to Piaget and Kohlberg*, Gill & Macmillan.

Edwards, A. D. (1976), *Language in Culture and Class*, Heinemann.

Eggleston, J. F. and Kerr, J. F. (eds) (1969), *Studies in Assessment*, English University Press.

Eggleston, S. J. (1973), 'Definitions of Knowledge and the School Curriculum', *Education for Teaching*, Autumn.

Eisner, E. W. *et al.* (1969), *Area Monography Services on Curriculum Evaluation*, vol. 3, Rand McNally.

Elliott, J. (1976a), 'Developing hypothesis about classroom from teachers' practical constructs', *Interchange* (obtainable from Cambridge Institute of Education).

Elliott, J. (1976b), 'Preparing Teachers for Classroom Accountability', *Education for Teaching*, no. 100.

Elliott, J. and Adelman, C. (1973), 'Reflecting where the action is: the design of the Ford Teaching Project', *Education for Teaching*, Autumn.

Elliott, J. and Adelman, C. (1975), 'Teacher Education for Curriculum Reform', *British Journal for Teacher Education*, vol. 1, no. 1.

Elliott, J. and Adelman, C. (1976), 'Innovation at the Classroom Level' in *Curriculum Design and Development*, unit 28, Open University Press.

Entwistle, N. J. and Nisbet, J. D. (1972), *Educational Research in Action*, University of London Press.

Flavell, J. H. (1963), *The Developmental Psychology of Jean Piaget*, Van Nostrand.

Floud, J., Halsey, A. M., and Martin, F. M. (1956), *Social Class and Educational Opportunity*, Heinemann.

Flude, M. and Ahier, J. (1974), *Educability, Schools and Ideology*, Croom Helm.

Ford, J. (1969), *Social Class and the Comprehensive School*, Routledge & Kegan Paul.

Ford Teaching Project (1975a), *Three Points of View in the Classroom*, unit 2, Centre for Applied Research in Education.

Ford Teaching Project (1975b), *The Innovation Process in the Classroom*, unit 3, Centre for Applied Research in Education.

Froebel, F. (1826), *The Education of Man*.

Gagné, R. M. (1970), *The Conditions of Learning*, Holt, Rinehart & Winston.

Gagné, R. M. (1974), *Essentials of Learning for Instruction*, The Dryden Press, Holt, Rinehart & Winston.

Glass, D. (1961), 'Education and Social Change in Modern England' in

A. H. Halsey, J. Floud and C. A. Anderson (eds), *Education, Economy and Society*, Free Press.

Golby, M., Greenwald, J. and West, R. (eds) (1975), *Curriculum Design*, Croom Helm.

Gorbutt, D. (1972), 'The New Sociology of Education', *Education for Teaching*, Autumn.

Gosden, P. H. J. H. (1969), *How They Were Taught 1800-1950*, Blackwell.

Gray, J. L. and Moshinsky, P. (1938), 'Ability and Opportunity in English Education' in L. Hogben (ed.), *Political Arithmetic*, Allen & Unwin.

Halford, G. (1972), 'The Impact of Piaget on Psychology in the Seventies' in P. C. Dodwell (ed.), *New Horizons in Psychology 2*, Penguin.

Halsey, A. H. (1972), *Educational Priority*, vol. 1, HMSO.

Halsey, A. H., Floud, J. and Anderson, C. A. (eds) (1961), *Education, Economy and Society*, Free Press.

Hamilton, D. and Delamont, S. (1974), 'Classroom research: a cautionary tale', *Research in Education*, no. 11.

Hamlyn, D. (1970), *The Theory of Knowledge*, Macmillan.

Hamlyn, D. (1972), 'Objectivity' in R. Dearden, P. H. Hirst and R. S. Peters (eds), *Education and the Development of Research*, Routledge & Kegan Paul.

Hannam, C., Smyth, P. and Stephenson, N. (1971), *Young Teachers and Reluctant Learners*, Penguin.

Hargreaves, D. (1967), *Social Relations in a Secondary School*, Routledge & Kegan Paul.

Hargreaves, D. (1976), *Deviance in Classrooms*, Routledge & Kegan Paul.

Harris, A. (1975), Letter to *The Times Educational Supplement*, 23 May, reprinted in *The Child, the School and Society*, unit 5, Open University Press.

Hartog, P. and Rhodes, E. C. (1935), *An Examination of Examinations*, Macmillan.

Henry, J. (1955), 'Docility, or Giving Teacher What She Wants', *Journal of Social Issues*, vol. 9.

Heren, J. (1971), 'Karl Mannheim and the Intellectual Elite', *British Journal of Sociology*, vol. 22, no. 1.

Hill, W. F. (1964), *Learning: A Survey of Psychological Interpretations*, Methuen.

Hirst, P. H. (1965), 'Liberal Education and the Nature of Knowledge' reprinted in P. H. Hirst, *Knowledge and Curriculum*, Routledge & Kegan Paul, 1975.

Hirst, P. H. (1972), 'The Nature of Education Theory', *Proceedings of* the *Philosophy of Education Society of Great Britain*, vol. 6.

Hirst, P. H. (1975), *Knowledge and Curriculum*, Routledge & Kegan Paul.

Hirst, P. H. and Peters, R. S. (1970), *The Logic of Education*, Routledge & Kegan Paul.

Holly, D. (1973), *Beyond Curriculum*, Paladin.

Holt, J. (1968), *How Children Fail*, Penguin.

House, E. (1975), 'Accountability in the USA', *Cambridge Journal of Education*, vol. 5, no. 2.

Hoyle, E. (1969), *The Role of the Teacher*, Routledge & Kegan Paul.

Hoyle, E. (1976), 'Innovation, the School and the Teacher (II)' in *Curriculum Design and Development*, units 29 and 30, Open University Press.

Hudson, L. (1972), *Contrary Imaginations*, Penguin.

Humanities Curriculum Project (1970), *The Humanities Project: An Introduction*, Heinemann Educational.

Illich, I. D. (1971), *Deschooling Society*, Penguin.

Inner London Education Authority (1973), *An Education Service for the Whole Community*, ILEA.

Jackson, P. A. (1973), *A Teacher's Guide to Tests and Testing*, Longman.

Jackson, P. W. (1968), *Life in Classrooms*, Holt, Rinehart & Winston.

Jenkins, D. (1976), 'Curriculum Evaluation' in *Curriculum Design and Development*, units 19 and 20, Open University Press.

Jones, G. (1973), 'Balancing the Books', *The Times Educational Supplement*, 7 December.

Jones, R. M. (1972), *Fantasy and Feeling in Education*, Penguin.

Jones, T. P. (1972), *Creative Learning in Perspective*, University of London Press.

Kay, B. W. (1975), 'Monitoring Pupils', *Trends 2*, DES.

Kelly, A. V. (1977), *The Curriculum Theory and Practice*, Harper & Row.

Kerr, J. (1968), *Changing the Curriculum*, University of London Press.

Kilpatrick, W. H. (1934), 'The Activity Movement' in National Society for the Study of Education, 33rd Year Book, *The Activity Movement*, Public Schools, Illinois.

Kogan, M. (1975), 'Institutional Autonomy and Public Accountability' in M. Hughes and J. Richards (eds), *Autonomy and Accountability in Educational Administration*, Proceedings of the Fourth Annual Conference of the British Educational Administration Society.

Kohlberg, L. (1963), 'Development of Moral Character and Moral

Ideology' in H. Stevenson (ed.), *Child Psychology 62nd Year Book, National Society for the Study of Education*, University of Chicago Press. Also in M. L. Hoffman and L. W. Hoffman (eds) (1964), *Review of Child Development Research*, vol. 1, Russell Sage Foundation.

Kohlberg, L. (1976), 'Moral Stages and Moralization: the Cognitive-Developmental Approach' in T. Lickona (ed.), *Moral Development and Behaviour*, Holt, Rinehart & Winston.

Labour Party (1976), 'Labour's Programme for Britain', *Labour Weekly*, 28 May.

Lacey, C. (1970), *Hightown Grammar*, Manchester University Press.

Lawson, J. and Silver, H. (1973), *A Social History of Education in England*, Methuen.

Lawton, D. (1968), *Social Class, Language and Education*, Routledge & Kegan Paul.

Lawton, D. (1973), *Social Change, Educational Theory and Curriculum Planning*, University of London Press/Hodder & Stoughton.

Lawton, D. (1975), *Class, Culture and the Curriculum*, Routledge & Kegan Paul.

Lewis, D. G. (1974), *Assessment in Education*, University of London Press.

Lindsay, K. (1926), *Social Progress and Educational Waste*, Routledge & Kegan Paul.

Lippitt, R. and White, R. H. (1965), 'An Experimental Study of Leadership and Group Life' in H. P. Proshansky and B. Seidenberg (eds), *Basic Studies in Social Psychology*, Holt, Rinehart & Winston.

Lowe, R. (1867), *Primary and Classical Education*, Edinburgh.

Lunzer, E. A. and Morris, J. F. (1968), *Development in Learning I: The Regulation of Behaviour*, Staples Press.

Luria, A. R. (1959), *Speech and Development of Mental Processes in the Child*, Staples Press.

Luria, A. R. (1961), *The Role of Speech in the Regulation of Normal and Abnormal Behaviour*, Pergamon Press.

Lynch, J. and Pimlott, J. (1976), *Parents and Teachers*, NFER.

Lyon, H. C. (1971), *Learning to Feel – Feeling to Learn*, Merrill.

Lytton, H. (1971), *Creativity and Education*, Routledge & Kegan Paul.

MacDonald, B. (1973), 'Briefing Decision-Makers', reprinted in Schools Council, 1974.

MacDonald, B. and Parlett, M. (1973), 'Rethinking Evaluation: Notes from the Cambridge Conference', *Cambridge Journal of Education*, vol. 3.

MacIntosh, H. G. (ed.) (1974), *Techniques and Problems of Assessment*, Arnold.

MacIntosh, H. G. (1976), *Assessing Attainment in the Classroom*, Hodder & Stoughton.

McIntyre, D. (1977), 'What responsibilities should a teacher accept?', Department of Education, University of Stirling.

McLellan, D. (1975), *Marx*, Blackwell.

Maclure, S. (1968), *Educational Documents 1816-1968*, Methuen.

Maclure, S. (1972), *Styles of Curriculum Development*, Organization for Economic Co-operation and Development.

McPhail, P. *et al.* (1972), *Moral Education in the Secondary School*, Longman.

Mannheim, K. (1936), *Ideology and Utopia: An Introduction to the Sociology of Knowledge*, Routledge & Kegan Paul.

Mannheim, K. (1956), 'The Problem of Intelligentsia' in K. Mannheim (ed.), *Essays on the Sociology of Culture*, Routledge & Kegan Paul.

Maslow, A. H. (1943), 'A Theory of Human Motivation', *Psychological Review*, vol. 50, pp. 370-96.

Maslow, A. H. (1954), *Motivation and Personality*, Harper & Row.

Maslow, A. H. (1968), 'Some Educational Implications of the Humanistic Psychologies', *Harvard Educational Review*, vol. 38, no. 4, Fall.

Mathews, J. C. and Leece, J. R. (1976), *Examinations: Their Use in Curriculum Evaluation and Development*, Methuen Educational.

Merson, M. W. and Campbell, R. J. (1974), 'Community Education: Instruction for Inequality', *Education for Teaching*, Spring.

Mill, J. S. (1861), *Utilitarianism*, Fontana, 1962.

Montgomery, R. J. (1965), *Examinations*, Longman.

Moore, T. W. (1974), *Educational Theory: An Introduction*, Routledge & Kegan Paul.

Munro, R. (1977), *Innovation, Success or Failure*, Hodder & Stoughton.

Musgrave, P. (1965), *The Sociology of Education*, Methuen.

Musgrove, F. (1964), *Youth and the Social Order*, Routledge & Kegan Paul.

Musgrove, F. (1971), *Patterns of Power and Authority in English Education*, Methuen.

Musgrove, F. and Taylor, P. H. (1969), *Society and the Teacher's Role*, Routledge & Kegan Paul.

National Foundation for Educational Research (1976), *Catalogue of Psychological Tests and Clinical Procedures*, NFER.

National Foundation for Educational Research (1977), *Catalogue of Tests for Educational Guidance and Assessment*, NFER.

Nisbet, R. A. (1967), *The Sociological Tradition*, Heinemann.

Noble, T. and Pym, B. (1970), 'Collegial Authority and the Receding Focus of Power', *British Journal of Sociology*, vol. 2, no. 4.

Norwood, C. (1929), *The English Tradition of Education*, Murray.

O'Connor, D. J. (1972), 'The Nature of Education Theory', *Proceedings of the Philosophy of Education Society of Great Britain*, vol. 6.

Bibliography

O'Connor, D. J. (1957), *An Introduction to the Philosophy of Education*, Routledge & Kegan Paul.

Paisey, H. A. (1975), *The Behavioural Strategies of Teachers*, NFER.

Parkes, D. (1973), 'Circular 7/70 and the Government of Schools', *Educational Administration Bulletin*, vol. 1, no. 2.

Parlett, M. and Hamilton, D. (1976), 'Evaluation as Illumination' in D. Tawney, *Curriculum Evaluation Today: Trends and Implications*, Schools Council/Macmillan.

Parsons, C. (1976), 'The new evaluation: a cautionary note', *Journal of Curriculum Studies*, vol. 8, no. 2.

Pearce, J. (1972), *Schools Examinations*, Collier-Macmillan.

Peters, R. S. (1958), *The Concept of Motivation*, Routledge & Kegan Paul.

Peters, R. S. (1959), *Authority, Responsibility and Education*, Routledge & Kegan Paul.

Peters, R. S. (1966), *Ethics and Education*, Allen & Unwin.

Peters, R. S. (1967), 'In defence of Bingo: a rejoinder', *British Journal of Educational Studies*, June.

Peters, R. S. (1973), *Reason and Compassion*, Routledge & Kegan Paul.

Peters, R. S. (1975), 'Aims of Education: A Conceptual Enquiry' in R. S. Peters (ed.), *Philosophy of Education*, Oxford University Press.

Peters, R. S. (1977), *Education and the Education of Teachers*, Routledge & Kegan Paul.

Phenix, P. H. (1964), *The Realms of Meaning*, McGraw-Hill.

Piaget, J. (1932), *The Moral Judgment of the Child*, Routledge & Kegan Paul.

Piaget, J. (1971), *The Science of Education and the Psychology of the Child*, Longman.

Piaget, J. and Inhelder, B. (1958), *The Growth of Logical Thinking from Childhood to Adolescence*, Routledge & Kegan Paul.

Pidgeon, D. and Allen, D. (eds) (1974), *Measurement in Education*, BBC Publications.

Pilliner, A. E. G. (1968), 'Examinations' in H. J. Butcher (ed.), *Educational Research in Britain*, University of London Press.

Popper, K. R. (1952), *The Open Society and its Enemies*, vol. II, Routledge & Kegan Paul.

Pring, R. A. (1972), 'Knowledge out of Control', *Education for Teaching*, Autumn.

Pring, R. A. (1975), 'The Language of Curriculum Analysis', *The Curriculum: Studies in Education – 2*, University of London Institute of Education.

Pring, R. A. (1976), *Knowledge and Schooling*, Open Books.

Pring, R. A. (1977), 'Common sense', *Proceedings of the Philosophy of Education Society of Great Britain*, vol. XI.

Purvis, J. (1973), 'Schoolteaching as a career', *British Journal of Sociology*, vol. 24, no. 1.

Radford, J. and Burton, A. (1974), *Thinking: Its Nature and Development*, Wiley.

Reimer, E. (1971), *School is Dead*, Penguin.

Richardson, E. (1973), *The Teacher, the School and the Task of Management*, Heinemann Educational.

Richardson, E. (1975), *Authority and Organisation in the Secondary School*, Macmillan Educational.

Richmond, W. K. (1971), *The School Curriculum*, Methuen.

Roach, J. (1971), *Public Examinations in England 1850–1900*, Cambridge University Press.

Roberts, T. B. (1975), *Four Psychologies Applied to Education*, Halstead Press.

Rogers, C. R. (1961), *On Becoming a Person*, Houghton Mifflin.

Rogers, C. R. (1969), *Freedom to Learn*, Merrill.

Rose, P. I. (1967), *The Study of Society*, Random House.

Rose, P. I. (1972), *See Ourselves*, Knopf.

Rousseau, J.-J. (1762), *Emile*, Everyman, 1911.

Rowntree, B. S. (1901), *Poverty: A Study of Town Life*, Macmillan.

Rowntree, D. (1977), *Assessing Students – How Shall We Know Them?*, Harper & Row.

Rubinstein, B. and Simon, B. (1969), *Evolution of the Comprehensive School (1926–72)*, Routledge & Kegan Paul.

Ryle, G. (1949), *The Concept of Mind*, Hutchinson.

Scheffler, I. (1965), *Conditions of Knowledge*, Scott Foresman.

Schofield, H. (1972), *Assessment and Testing: An Introduction*, Allen & Unwin.

Schools Council (1963–77), *Examination Bulletins 1–37*, Schools Council and Evans/Methuen Educational.

Schools Council (1963–77), *Working Papers*, Schools Council.

Schools Council (1968), *Enquiry No. 1*, HMSO.

Schools Council (1972), *16–19: Growth and Response 1. Curricula Bases*, Working Paper no. 45, Evans/Methuen Educational.

Schools Council (1973), *16–19: Growth and Response 2. Examination Structure*, Working Paper no. 46, Evans/Methuen Educational.

Schools Council (1975), *Examinations at 16+: Proposals for the Future*, Schools Council.

Schools Council (1972), *Science 5–13 Curriculum Project: With Objectives in Mind*, Macdonald.

Schools Council (1973), *Evaluation in Curriculum Development: Twelve Case Studies*, Macmillan.

Schools Council (1977), *Profiles*, Schools Council.

Schutz, A. (1972), *The Phenomenology of the Social World*, Heinemann.

Schwab, J. J. (1962), 'Discipline and Schools', *The Scholars Look at the Schools*, National Educational Association, Washington DC.

Schwab, J. J. (1964), 'Structure of the Discipline: Meaning and Significance' in G. W. Ford and L. Pugno (eds), *The Structure of Knowledge and the Curriculum*, Rand McNally.

Scottish Council for Research in Education (1977), *Pupils in Profile*, Hodder & Stoughton.

Scriven, M. *et al.* (1967), *Area Monograph Services on Curriculum Evaluation*, vol. 1, Rand McNally.

Shipman, M. (1972), 'Contrasting Views of a Curriculum Project', *Journal of Curriculum Studies*, vol. 4, no. 2.

Shipman, M. (1973), 'Curriculum for Inequality' in R. Hooper (ed.), *The Curriculum Context, Design and Development*, Oliver & Boyd.

Shipman, M. (1973), 'The Impact of a Curriculum Project', *Journal of Curriculum Studies*, vol. 5, no. 1.

Shipman, M. (1974), *Inside a Curriculum Project*, Methuen.

Simon, A. and Ward, L. O. (1973), *Journal of Moral Education*, no. 2.

Skinner, B. F. (1957), *Verbal Behaviour*, Appleton Century-Crofts.

Sockett, H. (1976a), *Designing the Curriculum*, Open Books.

Sockett, H. (1976b), 'Teacher Accountability', *Proceedings of the Philosophy of Education Society of Great Britain*, vol. X.

Stake, R. (1974), *Program Evaluation Particularly Responsive Education*, Centre for Instructional Research and Curriculum Evaluation, University of Illinois.

Stark, W. (1958), *The Sociology of Knowledge*, Routledge & Kegan Paul.

Stenhouse, L. (1975), *An Introduction to Curriculum Research and Development*, Heinemann.

Stewart, W. A. C. and McCann, W. P. (1967–8), *The Educational Innovators* (vols 1 and 2), Macmillan.

Stones, E. (1966), *An Introduction to Educational Psychology*, Methuen.

Stones, E. (1968), *Learning and Teaching: A Programmed Introduction*, Wiley.

Stones, E. (ed.) (1970), *Readings in Educational Psychology*, Methuen.

Sturt, M. (1967), *The Education of the People*, Routledge & Kegan Paul.

Sumner, R. and Robertson, T. S. (1977), *Criterion-referenced Measurement and Criterion-referenced Tests: Some Published Work Reviewed*, NFER.

Tawney, D. (1976), *Curriculum Evaluation Today: Trends and Implications*, Schools Council/Macmillan.

Taylor, P. H. (1970), *How Teachers Plan their Courses*, NFER.

Taylor, P. H. *et al.* (1974), *Purpose, Power and Constraint in the Primary School Curriculum*, Schools Council/Macmillan.

Thompson, K. and Tunstall, J. (eds) (1971), *Sociological Perspective*, Penguin.

Thyne, J. M. (1974), *Principles of Examining*, University of London Press.

Turiel, C. (1974), *Child Development*, no. 45.

Turner, J. (1975), *Cognitive Development*, Methuen.

Tyler, R. (1949), *Basic Principles in Curriculum Instruction*, University of Chicago Press.

Vernon, M. D. (1969), *Human Motivation*, Cambridge University Press.

Vernon, P. E. (ed.) (1957), *Secondary School Selection*, Methuen.

Vernon, P. E. (ed.) (1970), *Creativity*, Penguin.

Vincent, D. and Cresswell, M. (1976), *Reading Tests in the Classroom*, NFER.

Waller, W. (1965), *The Sociology of Teaching*, Wiley.

Warnock, G. (1967), *Contemporary Moral Philosophy*, Macmillan.

Warnock, M. (1977), *Schools of Thought*, Faber.

Weber, M. (1947), *The Theory of Social and Economic Organisation*, ed. T. Parsons, Oxford University Press.

Westwood, L. J. (1967), 'The Role of the Teacher', *Educational Research*, vol. 9, no. 2; vol. 10, no. 1.

White, A. R. (1967), *The Philosophy of Mind*, Random House.

White, J. P. (1969), 'The Curriculum Mongers: education in reverse', *New Society*, 6 March.

White, J. P. (1971), 'The Concept of Curriculum Evaluation', *Journal of Curriculum Studies*, vol. 3, no. 2.

White, J. P. (1973), *Towards a Compulsory Curriculum*, Routledge & Kegan Paul.

White, J. P. (1975), 'The End of the Compulsory Curriculum', *The Curriculum: Studies in Education – 2*, University of London Institute of Education.

Wilkinson, R. H. (1964), 'The Gentleman Ideal and the Maintenance of a Political Elite', reprinted in P. W. Musgrave (ed.), *Sociology, History and Education*, Methuen, 1970.

Williams, J. (1977), *Learning to Write or Writing to Learn?*, NFER.

Williams, R. (1965a), *Culture and Society*, Penguin.

Williams, R. (1965b), *The Long Revolution*, Penguin.

Wilson, B. (1962), 'The teacher's role', *British Journal of Sociology*, vol. 13, no. 1.

Wilson, J., Williams, N., and Sugarman, B. (1967), *An Introduction to Moral Development*, Penguin.

Bibliography

Wilson, P. S. (1967), 'In defence of Bingo', *British Journal of Educational Studies*, vol. 15, no. 1.

Wilson, P. S. (1971), *Interest and Discipline in Education*, Routledge & Kegan Paul.

Wilson, P. S. (1974), 'Interests and Educational Values', *Proceedings of the Philosophy of Education Society of Great Britain*, vol. 8, no. 2.

Wiseman, S. and Pigeon, D. (1970), *Curriculum Evaluation*, NFER.

Wiseman, S. (ed.) (1973), *Intelligence and Ability*, Penguin.

Young, M. F. D. (ed.) (1971), *Knowledge and Control*, Collier-Macmillan.

Index